The Transformation of University Institutional and Organizational Boundaries

Higher Education Research in the 21st Century Series

Volume 8

Series Editors:
Barbara M. Kehm, INCHER, Kassel University (Germany)
Christine Musselin, CNRS and Science Po Paris (France)

This new series provides overviews about state of the art research in the field of higher education studies. It documents a selection of papers from the annual conferences of the Consortium of Higher Education Researchers (CHER), the world organisation of researchers in the field of higher education. This object and problem related field of studies is by nature interdisciplinary and theoretically as well as methodologically informed by disciplines such as sociology, political science, economics, history, philosophy, law and education. Each book includes an introduction by the editors explaining the thematic approach and criteria for selection as well as how the book can be used by its possible audience which might include graduate students, policy makers, researchers in the field, and practitioners in higher education administration, leadership and management.

Please email queries to kehm@incher.uni-kassel.de

International Editorial Advisory Board:

Patrick Clancy, University College Dublin (Ireland)
Creso Sà, University of Toronto (Canada)
Pedro Teixeira, Centre for Research in Higher Education Policies, University of Porto (Portugal)
Jussi Välimaa, University of Jyväskylä (Finland)
Don F. Westerheijden, Centre for Higher Education Policy Studies, University of Twente (The Netherlands)

The Transformation of University Institutional and Organizational Boundaries

Edited by

Emanuela Reale and Emilia Primeri
*IRCrES, Research Institute on Sustainable Economic Growth of
National Research Council, Rome, Italy*

SENSE PUBLISHERS
ROTTERDAM/BOSTON/TAIPEI

A C.I.P. record for this book is available from the Library of Congress.

ISBN: 978-94-6300-176-2 (paperback)
ISBN: 978-94-6300-177-9 (hardback)
ISBN: 978-94-6300-178-6 (e-book)

Published by: Sense Publishers,
P.O. Box 21858,
3001 AW Rotterdam,
The Netherlands
https://www.sensepublishers.com/

Printed on acid-free paper

TABLE OF CONTENTS

Section 3: Blurring Boundaries in Academic Professions

ACKNOWLEDGEMENT

The book "The transformation of University institutional and organizational boundaries" represents the joint efforts of scientists who joined the 27th Annual Conference of the Consortium of Higher Education Researchers (CHER) in Rome on September 2014. The Conference witnessed that the interest of Higher Education studies community is broadening, crossing geographical boundaries. In fact more than 20 countries were represented at the Conference with their speakers and guests from Europe, United States, Russia, Canada, Africa, Australia and Asia.

Speakers brought at the Conference and into this book different perspectives and approaches related to the topic of institutional and organizational boundaries.

We thank colleagues who contributed to this joint effort and we thank the CHER Consortium for having provided us the opportunity to host this Conference and to welcome participants from around the world.

EMANUELA REALE AND EMILIA PRIMERI

INTRODUCTION

UNIVERSITIES IN TRANSITION: SHIFTING INSTITUTIONAL AND ORGANIZATIONAL BOUNDARIES: INTRODUCTIVE REMARKS

An emerging issue in higher education studies is the extent to which the transformations affecting the organizations, the institutions and the academic profession produce effects on the institutional and organizational boundaries. Several signals of shifting boundaries can be envisaged in higher education and research institutions, such as the replacement of permanent positions for researchers by temporary contracts, the involvement of firms with research groups and university boards, new alliances, collaborations and networking with non-academic organizations (e.g., public or private research organizations, firms), as well as universities participating in private companies or agencies.

The analysis of boundaries also supplies interpretative frameworks for the interactions between the development of professions and disciplines, as well as the relationships of the science with various parts of society such as state, professionals and the market. So it is useful for fuelling further discussion to point out some characteristics of boundaries and their relevance in higher education.

Conceptualizing Organizational and Institutional Boundaries

Institutional and organizational boundaries represent an interesting and fruitful approach to monitor and to interpret the dynamics of change. Lamont and Molnar (2002) explored the concept of boundaries in social sciences, putting into evidence the distinction between symbolic boundaries and social boundaries. The former are conceptual distinctions made by social actors to categorize objects, people, practices, time and space. They allow to capturing the dynamic dimensions of social relations, and to separate people into groups and generate feelings of similarity and group membership.

Social boundaries allow "researchers to develop a relational and systemic perspective on knowledge production sensitive to historical processes and symbolic strategies in defining the content and institutional contours of professional and scientific activity". Thus boundaries are helpful to map how models of knowledge are diffused across countries and impact local institutions and identities.

The authors highlight that studying the interplay between symbolic and social boundaries highlight the dynamic of social processes. Different approaches can be used, such as studying the properties of the boundaries (permeability, salience, durability, visibility) and why boundaries assume certain characteristics – e.g. salience and demarcation function (Bourdieu, 1984) *vs* tolerance and inclusiveness (Lamont, 1992).

Boundaries do not only serve as markers of differences, they are also interfaces facilitating knowledge production; they not only put an emphasis on some characters, silencing others, but also enable communications across communities (using standardization as one example). The concept of "boundary object" (that are material objects, organizational forms, conceptual spaces or procedures) indicates the interface allowing to develop and to maintain coherence across social worlds. Furthermore the concept of boundary object acknowledges boundaries as conditions not only for separation and exclusion but also for inclusion, exchange and bridging. In this respect, Guston (2001) pointed out the concept of boundary organization, which provides opportunities for the creation and use of boundary objects (and standardized packages). Boundary organizations involve the participation of the actors from both the sides of the boundaries (politics and scientist in the Guston's discussion), and they exist "at the frontiers of the two relatively different social worlds".

Santos and Eisenhardt (2005) provide a deeper understanding of organizational boundaries by developing four conception of boundaries, conceiving them as "demarcation between the organization and its environment. Thus, they "reflect the essence of organization", since "they speak why organization are unique and advantaged, and why they fail", addressing what is outside and what is inside the organization. The four conceptions of boundaries Santos and Eisenhardt elaborated have some distinctive features that ground on the conception of organizations and elements to be considered for the demarcation of the organization; boundary of efficiency, of power, of competence, and of identity points different situations where respectively advantages of fiat, monitoring and incentive alignment, reducing the dependence and exercise the power, delimitate the resources owned by the organization and delineate the dominant mind-set of 'who we are', are the salient organizational boundaries.

Scott (2004) recalled the importance in organizational sociology of theoretical developments related to understanding how and in what way the boundaries of organizations have become more open and flexible. Boundaries are legal, normative and cultural-cognitive; changing boundaries affect how institutions relate to their environment, such as processes eventually linked to strategies for absorbing external elements (workers, technologies, technical and organizational expertise) or using external units to perform activities that are not the core competence of the organizations. Beside the mentioned events, organizations are not necessarily boundary-less despite the fact that significant changes occurred in the "scope, position, duration and enforcement mechanisms" (Scott, 2004).

Other approaches focus on mechanisms associated with the production of boundaries in science -the credibility contexts outlined by Gieryn, or focus on the problem of cultural membership, how social actors build groups as similar and different and how the notion of boundaries shapes their understanding of the responsibilities toward such groups. Saying differently, boundaries reveals how individuals think of themselves as equivalent and similar to, or compatible with, others (Lamont, 2001), and how they perform their differences and similarities.

Changing Functions, Objectives, and Scope of Higher Education Institutions

A number of theoretical approaches look at shifting boundaries from the perspective of institutional change (Hackett, 2005), which modifies the old academic logic in to a new entrepreneurial one; government policies and policy instruments, such as funding schemes and performance assessment, can support the mentioned shift. Another element contributing to overcome the institutional boundaries is collaborative research, which involves also the overcoming of geographical boundaries, asking for a specific strategy to manage institutional constraints that can hamper the possibility to have an effective inter-institutional knowledge flow.

Laudel and Glaser (1998) investigating the institutional boundaries and the way to overcome them, pointed out that institutions as systems of social rules have some features that characterize them, namely they govern the actions of individual, corporate or collective actors, they link attributes to an actor's situation with forms of expected behaviour, and sanction deviant behaviour.

The authors show that scientific community is governed by the institutions of two social systems, namely the scientific community they belong to, which define research problems, provide knowledge and collaboration, evaluate the results, and the formal organization, which provide resources for research and links the research to that of other scientists working in the organization. Institutions of both social systems caused collaborations and institutional prerequisites for collaboration exist. The prerequisites observed as necessary conditions to realize collaboration are:

- The provision of resources from research organization to cover the costs (financial resources and time) needed to build a collaborative effort;
- The coherence of research processes in the scientific community -perceptions of cognitive links, development of a shared language, development of trust in potential collaborations' skills,
- The institutionalization of communications between institutions and communities;
- Framing good rules of collaboration within research organizations (e.g., joint use of equipment and supply of services)
- The presence of diffuse reciprocity between the scientific communities
- A set of shared rules for distributing the outcome of collaboration within the scientific community as well as rules for rewarding the collaboration.

The authors also depict a hierarchy of collaboration difficulties, with increasing difficulty for boundary-spanning collaboration:

1. Collaboration from the same community working in the same institute;
2. Collaboration from the same community working in different institutes;
3. Collaboration from different communities working in the same institute;
4. Collaboration from the different communities working in different institutes.

The possibility to overcome growing difficulties of institutional boundaries depend by the presence of the prerequisites; institutional boundaries, although important are "only one factor affecting collaborations and its influence can be changed or even overridden by others." Moreover, once established, boundary-crossing collaborations tend to become permanent, since the hindering conditions tend to hinder mostly the emergence of collaboration.

Collaborations have a cost (money and time) that might impede the scholars to engage in boundary-spanning. Thus policies toward collaboration are useful to overcome institutional boundaries, overlapping the existing the institutional frameworks of both scientific communities and research organizations. The reverse effect is also expected: the emergence of a new institution creates a new set of boundaries between those belonging to those institutions and the outsiders. "Collaboration network seems to be one institutional solution for crossing institutional boundaries. They allow the scientists to retain to their traditional social systems (the research institutes and the scientific community) and simultaneously to establish new links to members of other social systems. The means by which a collaboration network promotes collaboration are the same as the means working in the traditional social systems – scientific communities and research organizations" (Laudel & Glaser, 1988).

Interestingly enough the network's institutional framework of universities and non-university research institutes, which includes rules promoting collaborations, necessarily spanning the original institutional boundaries, also affect the networks between universities and firms (Meissner, 2009).

Moving beyond Sectoral and Disciplinary Boundaries

Heinze and Kuhlman (2008) explored institutional boundaries emerging in highly differentiated research systems such as Germany, and in emerging research domains such as nanotechnology. The exploration allows to deepening constraints to collaboration coming from established cognitive boundaries, which are broken down in nanotech research, and the collaboration across organizational boundaries in different university and non-university research entities. Using three governance dimensions of research collaboration – thematic interdependence, organizational dimensions and resource endowment- they found that organizational dimensions impeding cross boundary collaboration are stereotypes and prejudices based on reputation of scientific communities belonging to different research organizations, incompatible working routines anchored to different organizational missions; lack of interface managements to organize follow up when they results can be of interest for researchers working in other organizations; funding cuts and restrictions, which has the immediate effect of blocking on-going cooperation, a fact that is especially visible in the case of universities, with other emerging effects linked to status hierarchies between the university and the extra-university sector.

One interesting result of the quoted investigation is that cross-boundary collaboration emerging from the observation of the co-authorships are less pronounced than those emerging in research contracts and cooperative relationships, often informal relationships. Rationales for collaborations at individual level are expanding and improving the research capacity, benefit from institutional complementarities, and enhancing visibility in the research field, which goes beyond the curiosity intellectual companionship and sharing the research area with other colleagues, which emerged in the literature (Beaver, 2001). Thus institutional conditions are conducive to inter-institutional research collaborations, which move beyond institutional boundaries.

In the same line, Cummings and Kiesler (2005) focused on scientific collaboration across disciplines and university boundaries, and show some constraints that are related to the management of communication between different partners belonging to diverse organizations even when these organizations are all universities. Collaborations in large cross-institutional networks have some costs that are not actually faced by funding agencies and require a dedicated strategy. Coordination mechanisms can reduce the negative impact of putting together researchers that are physically distant.

Moreover, shifting boundaries are also investigated as changing relationships between academic scientists and the marketplace, putting into evidence the contamination between science and business as to the norms and practice of the academic work (Owen-Smith & Powell, 2001). The mentioned transformation can be positively commented as an evolution suitable to follow the intrinsic changes in the modes of knowledge production (Gibbons et al., 1994; Nowotny et al., 2005); by contrast, they can be judged as a risk for the role traditionally played by the institutions and the scientists, for their autonomy and identity.

Blurring Boundaries in Academic Professions

One important issue is defining and institutionalize boundaries of profession against outsider and also struggling of professionals among themselves. Scientists as other professionals want to distinguish themselves from outsiders thus building the boundary of what can be considered as 'science' (Gieryn, 1983). The concept of "boundary-work" describes the "discursive practices by which scientists attempt to attribute selected qualities to scientists, scientific methods, and scientific claims" in order to delimitate their own domain from those of other non-scientists professionals (Lamont & Molnar, 2002).

The quoted authors pointed that boundary-work can be articulated into different type of processes, namely expulsion, expansion and protection of autonomy. The former occurs where there are rival authorities each claiming to be scientific, thus boundary-work is a mean of social control "sanctioning the transgression of symbolic boundaries of legitimacy." Expansion describes the case when one rival epistemic authority tries to monopolize the control over a disputed ontological domain. Protection of autonomy against outside powers is another aim of boundary-work toward legislators or corporate managers: different conceptualizations of "sociological ambivalence" (Merton, 1976) and "boundary work" (Gieryn, 1983) have been developed to analyse how scientists act in order to defend their autonomy and to secure resources despite the on-going transformations (using the power of interpretative strategies to build a space for science in pursuit of authority within the epistemic community, thus contributing to the institutionalization of disciplines, and theoretical orientations within science, Gieryn, 1999).

Several empirical investigations of boundaries in academic profession have been developed. For instance, Whitchurch (2008a) build a categorization of professional staff identities as having bounded, cross-bounded, and unbounded characteristics. The former is composed by those that locate themselves "within the boundaries of a function or organizational location", and that are governed by 'rules and resources'; the second are those that "recognize and use boundaries to build strategic and institutional capacity"; the latter are those that disregard boundaries, taking an "exploratory approach to the broadly based projects" where they are involved. Starting from this categorization the same author (2008b) describes a further category of blended professionals "who here mixed backgrounds and portfolios, comprising elements of both professional and academic activity"; in this way blended professionals occupy a third space between academic and professional domains.

Lam (2010) explored the different work orientation of academic scientists in the relationships with the business sector, and the different ways of shaping boundaries within the academic work. Four orientations emerge from her investigation, namely the traditional scientists, characterized by boundary separation and expulsion, traditional hybrids, which share some characteristics of the traditionalists (maintaining boundaries between academia and industry) but are prepared to explore the emerging opportunities of relationships, and are wiling to accommodate their research agenda when they perceive possible benefits. A third group includes the entrepreneurial hybrids, which combine an orientation toward entrepreneurial behaviour with the core values and norms of academia. The possibility of crossing science and business boundaries is open because industrial links are perceive as very useful for their research activity. The entrepreneurial scientists, characterized by boundary inclusion and fusion, compose the fourth group.

In sum, different facets of the transformation of University institutional and organizational boundaries can be observed: changes in the function, objectives and scope of higher education and research institutions, the move beyond sectoral and disciplinary boundaries and increasingly blurred boundaries of academic professions and of scientific work. Public policies and HE reforms can push or impede the mentioned transformations, but they can also derive from individual likelihood of moving in blurring spaces or from the transformations of the epistemic communities and the emergence of new fields and sectors.

The chapters that follow contribute to highlight the complexity and heterogeneity, which characterizes scientific knowledge today and underline as boundaries crossing represents a key issue when looking at University transformations across contexts and policies, instruments and practices.

The book begins with two contributions from the keynote speakers at the CHER Conference in Rome (2014) aimed at provides examples of universities transformation and the crossing of institutional and organizational boundaries. *Alice Lam* discusses the rise of the entrepreneurial university and its consequences on the norms and practices of academic scientific work. The chapter deals with the responses of scientists to the shifting institutional environment. Lam argues as most of the discussions about the 'new knowledge regime' introduced by the increasing shifting boundary between academia and private business is mostly based on a macro-level perspective which does not draw attention to the internal diversity in academic scientific work, and to the complex and often contradictory dynamics and institutional logics behind changes. Lam proposes to adopt a micro-level perspective, deepening the analysis of the strategic role of actors, namely scientists themselves, and the way they interpret and shape changes and the shifting boundary between university and industry. The main assumption is that scientists are active agents seeking to shape the boundary between science and business developing different modes of engagement with the emerging knowledge regimes. Between the two extreme positions of those sticking to the 'traditional' norms of basic science and the others exhibiting an 'entrepreneurial' orientation, a third major group of scientists display an 'hybrid' orientation. This group of scientists put in place negotiation strategies to protect their autonomy and role, getting by the fuzzy boundaries between science and business. Lam argues then as the move from the 'traditional' to the 'entrepreneurial' mode is not necessarily eroding the norms and values of academic science neither it emerges as a linear process of change, rather it is likely to display the existence "of continued diversity" that can be "halted, or even reverted" by scientists. The chapter by *John Aubrey Douglass* introduces the concept of world-class universities with the attempt to advocate the notion of Flagship University as a more relevant ideal for both public and private universities and as more desirable achievement for national ministries and governments. Some key requisites Flagship universities should address are introduced providing a tentative profile of how this should be: an academic institution ranked top beyond its research results, rooted in national and regional ethos, accountable towards society at large and engaged to make itself, through internal mechanisms for supporting quality and excellence, improving and getting always better instead of being positioned as the best. It is a much broader charge the one required to be a Flagship University. Finally the question – not directly addressed- is: how could University embrace such status if the WCU rhetoric is the driving force? The move towards a new university model entails then that some universities decide to cross their institutional and organizational boundaries to embrace a new institutional identity, to seek a new internal culture and to adopt different organizational assets.

The book is dived into three main thematic sections. The first section deals with the transformation of Universities institutional and organizational boundaries focusing on the change of functions, objectives and scope this would entail. This section includes four chapters. *Maarja Beerkens* is the author of the first chapter. The chapter deals with the risk of increasing agencification of HE because of the increasing importance of quality assurance and of autonomous agencies, which are presented as one corner of the regulatory triangle, together with policy makers (parliament, government) and universities. So far, quality assurance agencies are likely to impact on universities' organizational boundaries: the regulatory state becoming more and more weak, agencies can improve their role of intermediation between the universities and the state and can assume increasing policy decision making power. Two are the main rationales for creating autonomous regulatory agencies in the public sector: separating politics and administration, because of their autonomy, and improving efficiency, because of greater specialization of agencies. Nonetheless, the increasing agencification still represents a problem. This phenomenon is studied in four countries: The Netherlands, United Kingdom, Norway and Denmark.

Evidences show that quality assurance has become a mature regulatory field in HE and agencies have strengthened their role reinforcing their credibility and legitimacy. However agencies also risk becoming major policy actors in the HE landscape, contributing to increase fragmentation and lack of coordination in the HE landscape.

Tatyana Koryakina Antunes, Cláudia S. Sarrico and Pedro Teixeira discuss the universities' third mission activities and how they represent a challenge to extending boundaries. They focus on universities' organizational transformation with relation to third stream activities. They argue these are gaining increasing importance but little is known about their effects on the institutional setting of HEIs. The chapter presents an explorative study of the impact of income diversification on Portuguese universities' governance and management, and considers third mission activities as diversified income sources. What do university managers perceive as external barriers towards third mission activities? What do university managers identify as internal barriers? What are different and converging elements between different universities? These questions are addressed through a case-study methodology aimed at analyzing the perceptions of two Portuguese universities' top and middle managers on relations with the external environment. The authors argue that a certain degree of differentiation emerges in the way third mission activities are institutionalized within each university studied. This shows as path dependency influences the ways universities, although sharing similar narratives, engage differently in third mission activities. Also third stream activities are described as "scattered across the academic and research units, showing different degrees of involvement", thus highlighting differences across and within the universities analysed. The role of institutional leadership and the way institutional communication is managed are considered as key elements shaping third stream engagement.

Deepening the discussion about changes driven to HEIs by new entrepreneurial logics, *Andrew Kretz and Creso Sá* discuss this with respect to learning practices. They provide an analysis of how entrepreneurship education is shifting institutional boundaries in higher education. The impact of entrepreneurship education on the functions, objectives and scope of HEIs are concerned. Main assumption is that entrepreneurship in higher education has to be considered "*as a broad socio-cultural phenomenon, rather than just a response to market opportunities, commercial logics, and pushes for third stream activity*" which redraws university boundaries in multiple ways. Discussion is based on two research projects on entrepreneurial education at universities and colleges in the United States and Canada and the study is guided by a grounded theory based approach. They use the concept of "Boundary spanners" that is organizations, organizational units and programs, originating inside and outside the university which facilitate the development of university entrepreneurship programs, initiatives, and communities of practice. Authors argue that entrepreneurship education is shifting institutional boundaries in universities, going beyond simple teaching concerning start up activities and creating shared spaces from which academic and entrepreneurial actors may educate students from across academic departments.

To conclude this section dedicated to changes in institutional and organizational boundaries of HEIs the chapter by *Dimitri Gagliardi, Deborah Cox, and Yanchao Li* discusses the increasing complexity in science, focusing the attention on changes to HEIs institutional arrangements driven by the introduction of open science. Changes they consider are: a new way of doing science, the increasing relevance of attention towards science and research output and the multiple actors being involved more and more in scientific deliverables. Drivers and barriers to the adoption of open science are investigated in this exploratory study, focusing on the roles of the research performing stakeholders in the scientific process and their conflicting interests as well as on institutional arrangements, new methods and cultural changes driven by the adoption of open science. Policy implications deriving from the emergence of open science and its adoption within the existing organisational settings are also discussed. Their findings confirm the positive effect of the introduction of open science: however they argue as this is mostly related to researchers personal curiosity and interest of researchers and that there is not a strategy supporting the opening of science and that institutional barriers still play a role in the uptake of open science.

The following section includes two chapters which discuss the shift of university sectoral and disciplinary boundaries: the first considers the developments and organizational changes concerned doctoral training in the social sciences in the UK, while the second chapter considers boundaries changes in university governance focusing on the role of external stakeholder. *Rosemary Deem, Sally Barnes, and Gill Clarke* discuss consequences, both intended and unintended, of policies concerning doctoral training in the Social Sciences in the UK. culminating in the DTCs policy (Doctoral Training Centres) and the early years of its implementation. They consider changes introduced from 1992 to 2014 which concerned mainly the gradual move first to specification of discipline-specific training requirements and department-specific accreditation, then to delegation of the selection of candidates for Economic and Social Research Council (ESRC) doctoral studentships to universities rather than a national competition and finally to institution-wide or inter-institutional arrangements for doctoral education . How universities have responded to these changes, which invested doctoral training in the Social Science? This is the main question addressed in the chapter.

They consider changes and the impact they had on institutions, on university autonomy, leadership and student diversity and inclusion. To discuss changes they use collaborative narratives technique and field notes of the three authors ("tales") providing many interesting hints on changes in doctoral training. Changes in policies and practices concerning doctoral training as well as its reorganization in the years represent the bulk of the narration of the authors. Some important lessons concerning the move towards collaborative training emerge from the narrations.

Differently *Sofia Bruckmann* focuses on the shifts in boundaries between HEIs and the society discussing changes driven by the introduction of NPM logics in university governance, taking institutional reforms, which invested HE system in Portugal, as example. What is the role of university external stakeholders in the changed role of university towards the society and the changes in the state-universities relationships? To answer the question, the roles of stakeholder in the top positions of university governing bodies are analysed for a sample of Portuguese universities.

The final section of the book includes two chapters which move the attention to boundaries changes in the academic professions focusing on two key concepts: that of academic leadership and the one of academic excellence.

Joakim Caspersen and Nicoline Frølich address the theme of leadership in higher education. The general observation introduced by the authors is that leadership in higher education has shifted from *"old modes of leadership based in academic and collegial values to new modes of governance increasingly based in social responsibleness and managerialism."* To explore changes in academic leadership they use the case of qualification frameworks and learning outcomes (HELO-Higher Education Learning Outcomes). The assumption behind the discussion is that HELO should be considered as a governance and management tool beyond a simple device for teaching and learning assessment the extent to which it pushes universities towards more results orientation. They question then how academic conceive these instruments and what the interplay between HELO introduction and different leadership models is likely to be. Their findings show *"old modes of new governance,* played out in relation to new policy initiatives such as HELOs"*: thus authors argue as HELO does not drive changes into leadership models rather is more likely to push academics to put in place different blended and mixed version of leadership models.

Finally, *Marek Kwiek* deals with academic research productivity and the role of top research performers across Europe. The author observes as inequality characterizes the academic knowledge production: the productivity distribution patterns across European systems emerge to be strikingly similar, despite starkly different national academic traditions. Thus about ten percent of academics – which the author label as "research top performers" – are at the echelons of highly productive academics and provide, on average, almost half of all academic knowledge production. The "quality quantity dilemma" of academic productivity is then the central issue of this chapter. Instead of discussing these observations using widely used metrics and bibliometric tools he investigates the "what" of academic knowledge production and the "why" of it (individual and institutional predictors of high research performance). Moreover, how does this relate to different universities profiles? The main assumption concerns the balance between academic productivity and professional recognition, the latter being assumed to be proportional to the former, which give rise to different "academic professions" communities and productivity patterns in European Universities. Policy implications (what if systems are primarily institutionally-based research funding?) and policy dilemma (should highly ranked scientists be supported or highly ranked institutions giving rise to further segmentation with academic landscape?) for academic professions in a changing academic environment more and more focused on academic measurable scientific performance are discussed.

The book brings then together different contributions, which allow capturing the complexity of the debate around the transformation of universities and changes of institutional and organizational boundaries. If several changes have invested HE in the last twenty years, the way these have impacted on universities internal organizational dynamics, institutional settings, governance models, sectoral and scientific fields relationships as well as on the works of academics and the way science is produced are far from being completely drawn. Observing the move of institutional and organizational boundaries of universities represents then a way for tracking changes and for figuring out paths of academic institutions transformation.

REFERENCES

Bourdieu, P. (1984). *Homo academicus*. Stanford, CA: Stanford University Press.

Cummings, J. N., & Kiesler, S. (2005). Collaborative research across disciplinary and organizational boundaries. *Social Studies of Science*, 35(5), 703–722.

Gibbons, M., Limoges, H., Nowotny, H., Schwartzman, S., Scott, P., & Trow, M. (1994). *The social production of knowledge*. Oxford, England: Oxford University Press.

Gieryn, T. F. (1983). Boundary-work and the demarcation of science from non-science: Strains and interests in professional interests of scientists. *American Sociological Review*, 48, 781–795.

Gieryn, T. F. (1999). *Cultural boundaries of science: Credibility on the line*. Chicago, IL: University of Chicago Press.

Guston, D. H. (2001). Boundary organizations in environmental policy and science: An introduction. *Science Technology & Human Values, 26*(4), 399–408.

Hackett, E. J. (2005). Essential tensions: Identity, control, and risk in research. *Social Studies of Science, 35*, 787–825.

Heinze, T., & Kuhlman, S. (2008). Across institutional boundaries? Research collaboration in German public sector nanoscience. *Research Policy, 37*, 888–899.

Lam, A. (2010). From 'ivory tower traditionalists' to 'entrepreneurial scientists'? Academic scientists in fuzzy university-industry boundaries. *Social Studies of Science, 40*(2), 307–340.

Lamont, M. (1992). *Money, morals and manners: The culture of the French and American upper-middle class.* Chicago, IL: University of Chicago Press.

Lamont, M. (2001). Symbolic boundaries. In N. Smelser & P. Baltes (Eds.), *International encyclopedia of social and behavioral sciences.* Oxford, England: Elsevier.

Lamont, M., & Molnar, V. (2002). The study of boundaries in social sciences. *Annual Review of Sociology, 28*, 167–195.

Laudel, G., & Glaser, J. (1998). *What are institutional boundaries and how can they be overcome? Germany's collaborative research centres as boundary-spanning networks* (pp. 98–401), Working Paper WZB N.

Meissner, C. (2009). *Innovation across institutional boundaries: Networks between universities and firms in the UK as source of innovation.* London, UK: City University of London.

Nowotny, H., Scott, P., & Gibbons, M. T. (2001). *Re-thinking science: Knowledge and the public in an age of uncertainty.* Cambridge, UK: Polity Press.

Owen, S. J., & Powell, W. W. (2001). To patent or not: Faculty decisions and institutional success at technology transfer. *The Journal of Technology Transfer, 26*(1–2), 99–114.

Santos, F. M., & Eisenhardt, K. M. (2005). Organizational boundaries and theories of organization. *Organization Science, 16*(5), 491–508.

Whitchurch, C. (2008a). Beyond administration and management: Reconstructing the identities of professional staff in UK higher education. *Journal of Higher Education Policy and Management, 30*(4), 375–386.

Whitchurch, C. (2008b). Shifting identities and blurring boundaries: The emergence of third space professionals in UK higher education. *Higher Education Quarterly, 62*(4), 377–396.

Emanuela Reale
IRCrES CNR
Research Institute on Sustainable Economic Growth of
National Research Council

Emilia Primeri
IRCrES CNR
Research Institute on Sustainable Economic Growth of
National Research Council

ALICE LAM

SHIFTING INSTITUTIONAL BOUNDARIES

'Boundary Work' of Academic Scientists in the Entrepreneurial University

INTRODUCTION

The rise of the entrepreneurial university has aroused intense debates about the changing relationship between academic scientists and the marketplace, and the consequences of the increasingly blurred boundaries between science and business for the norms and practices of academic scientific work (Owen-Smith & Powell, 2001; Vallas & Lee Kleinman, 2008). Some scholars view the institutional transformation in a positive light and stress the growing convergence between academia and industry. They describe the emerging structures as a 'new mode of knowledge production' (Gibbons et al., 1994) or 'triple helix' (Etzkowitz & Leydesdorff, 2000) that links the university, private industry and government together in a productive relationship. Authors in this camp herald the arrival of a new class of 'entrepreneurial scientists' who integrate academic research with its commercial exploitation. By contrast, other researchers are deeply critical of close university-industry ties and warn of the normative and institutional risks associated with academic entrepreneurialism (Beck & Young, 2005; Hackett, 2001). Slaughter and her colleagues use the term 'academic capitalism' to describe the encroachment of a profit motive into academia (Slaughter & Leslie, 1997; Slaughter & Rhoades, 2004). These critics emphasise growing conflict of values and crisis of role identities experienced by academic scientists, and the erosion of academic freedom and autonomy.

Despite the on-going debate, our understanding of the 'new knowledge regime' and its consequences for academic scientific work has been limited by oversimplified theoretical assumptions about the underlying process of change. There is a tendency among many authors to view the shifting boundary between academia and private business as an institutional change that occurs as a linear historical process in which the old institutional logic of academic science is under attack (Beck & Young, 2005; Hackett, 2001) and will be eventually replaced by the new logic of entrepreneurial science (Etzkowitz et al., 2000). Both the 'new knowledge production' and the 'academic capitalism' perspectives are built on the presumed inevitability of the entrepreneurial university. Their analysis takes place at a high-level of aggregation and generalisation. This approach all too easily obscures the internal diversity in academic scientific work, and the complex dynamics of organisational change

E. Reale & E. Primeri (Eds.), The Transformation of University Institutional and Organizational Boundaries, 1–28.

that permit the co-existence of contradictory institutional logics (Murray, 2010; Smith-Doerr, 2005; Vallas & Lee Kleinman, 2008). More importantly, it fails to take account of the strategic role of actors, namely scientists themselves, in interpreting and shaping change.

The analysis presented in this chapter seeks to go beyond these limitations by adopting a micro-level perspective to examine how the shifting boundary between university and industry is experienced and can be shaped by academic scientists themselves. The analytical framework draws on the theoretical insights of the new institutional school of organisational change which highlights actor choice and strategic action in shaping change (Barley & Tolbert, 1997). The sociology of science literature provides the main concepts and micro-theories for interpreting the strategic responses of scientists to the changing work environment. The analysis stresses how scientists exploit the 'sociological ambivalence' (Merton & Barber, 1963) of their 'boundary work' (Gieryn, 1983, 1999) to defend and negotiate their positions, while at the same time seeking to acquire critical resources in pursuit of their career goals. The evidence presented shows that scientists are active agents seeking to shape the boundary between science and business, and have developed different modes of engagement with the emerging knowledge regimes. While some adhere to the 'traditional' norms of basic science and resist the encroachment of commercial practices, others exhibit an 'entrepreneurial' orientation and partake in the realms of both science and business. Between the two polar positions of the 'old' and the 'new', the majority of the scientists display 'hybrid' orientations and are particularly adept at mapping out their own social spaces for strategic manipulation at the fuzzy boundaries between science and business. The analysis challenges the protagonists' views on the emergence of a dominant market norm in academic science and provides evidence of continued diversity.

Scientists as Strategic Actors in Shifting University-Industry Boundaries: 'Sociological Ambivalence' and 'Boundary Work'

Neo-institutional theorists treat the change and reproduction of institutions as a dynamic, ongoing process in which actions and institutions are recursively related (Barley & Tolbert, 1997; Oliver, 1991). Oliver (1991) argues that individuals and organizations do not simply conform to institutional pressures but respond positively to them and in some cases modify them. She proposes five types of strategic responses to institutional process, from passivity to increasingly active resistance: acquiescence, compromise, avoidance, defiance, and manipulation. Institutions may also vary in their normative power and their effect on behaviour, depending on how widely and deeply institutions are accepted by members of a collective (Tolbert & Zucker, 1996). Moreover, actors can take different orientations with regard to the social structures in which they are situated and develop different modes of engagement (Mouzelis, 1989).

It is also possible for an institution seem to change at the formal policy level without concomitant changes in cultural norms at the organisational or individual levels. Aldrich and Fiol (1994) distinguish between socio-political legitimacy where practices or rules are approved or mandated by the state, and cultural-cognitive legitimacy, in which ideas are more subject to actor interpretation. Moreover, these two component parts need not be in congruence as we often assume. A study by Colyva and Powell (2006) on the institutionalisation of academic entrepreneurship in the US shows that new practices can be more or less legitimated, and they may fail to become deeply cognitively embedded despite apparent formal compliance. Moreover, the new practices that are becoming legitimated can also be transformed in the process as actors interpret them and imbue them with new meanings according to the institutional logics of their specific domains or strategic goals. As DiMaggio (1997: 265) notes, institutions or culture are 'complex rule-like structures that constitute resources that can be put to strategic use.' Murray (2010), for instance, examines how geneticists in the US resisted and accommodated 'patenting' and, in the course of doing so, they re-interpreted the meaning of patenting by treating it as an alternative currency for building academic reputation, and also used it as a means to exclude unwanted commercial intrusion. Thus, actors have the leeway and flexibility to use their existing relations and understandings to incorporate, transform, or resist new practices. Hence, our understanding of the dynamics of institutional change will need to recognise the ambivalence inherent in the structural conditions of change as well as the responses of actors.

Early research in the sociology of science highlights the sociological ambivalence of scientists and their active agency role in defending their positions in response to external challenges. Merton's (1957) early formulation of the norms of basic science as characterised by universalism, communism and disinterestedness regulated by a scientific-community has been criticised by some as overly idealised, and ignoring both the practical realities of scientific work and the day-to-day negotiation among scientists to secure resources for their work (Latour & Woolgar, 1979; Mitroff, 1974). His later work (Merton & Barber, 1963; Merton, 1976) on the notion of 'sociological ambivalence', together with Mitroff's (1974) concept of 'counter-norms', suggest that the role of scientists reflects a dynamic interaction between countervailing orientations to dominant norms and subsidiary counter-norms. For example, scientists may portray their research as either basic or applied, and the boundary between production and exploitation of knowledge may be clearly demarcated or blurred depending on the demands of the situation and external challenges encountered. Such 'sociological ambivalence' may generate inner conflicts and tensions among scientists (Hackett, 2005). However, it serves also as a useful social device for scientists to cope with the contingencies that they face in trying to fulfil their functions. Mulkay (1980) argues that sociological ambivalence provides scientists with alternative cultural resources which they may use for legitimating work boundaries and defending their positions in different contexts.

Gieryn (1983, 1999) coined the term 'boundary work' to denote the active agency role of scientists in drawing and redrawing the boundaries of their work to defend their autonomy and secure resources in pursuit of professional goals. He stresses the power of scientists' interpretative strategies in constructing a space for science for 'strategic practical action'. His historical analysis of scientists' efforts to preserve autonomy and enlarge resources for research showed that the boundary between basic and applied research was clearly established when the scientific community wanted to protect their professional autonomy and ensure that basic research was free from government interference. However, it often became obscure, if not dissolved, when scientists sought to secure increased resources and public support for research. Gieryn (1983: 789) refers to 'boundary work' as an ideological style found in scientists' attempt to present their social and collective image to the external world in their struggle for autonomy and public support. This concept has also been widely used to examine the occupational demarcation problems of professionals, and the strategies that they use to defend the content of their work and institutional arrangements that undergird their practice (Lamont & Molnar, 2002: 177–8).

Work boundaries and role identities are intertwined, and challenges to external work boundaries may threaten stable role identities (Ashforth et al., 2000; Kreiner et al., 2006). Beck and Young (2005) argue that the contemporary transformation in the relationship between academia and the marketplace presents a major challenge not only to the external conditions of academic work, but more fundamentally, to the core elements of academic professional identities. The professional role identity of academic scientists has historically been deeply rooted in a distinctive scientific community marked by strong external boundaries and a special relationship to knowledge production (Henkel, 2005; Kogan, 2000). This self-regulative bounded world is associated with the Mertonian norms of disinterestedness and communism, traditionally upheld by the scientific community as the default ideals that promote the free pursuit of knowledge. Although scientists do not always adhere to these ideals in practice, they have great normative significance for the community and serve to underpin its professional autonomy and role identity. The increased penetration of the marketplace into academia and commercialisation of knowledge pose a challenge to this professional ideal. Some authors point out that a scientist's decision to go down the commercialisation path potentially involves a role transition and inner sense-making process akin to managing multiple role identities (George et al., 2005; Pratt & Foreman, 2000). What strategies, then, do scientists employ to negotiate their work boundaries and role identities as they embark on commercial roles? How do they reconcile the tension between the contradictory logics of science and business?

The analysis presented below explores these questions by drawing on prior empirical work by the author.[1] The evidence is based on 36 in-depth individual interviews and a survey sample of 734 academics scientists from five major UK research universities, covering the following disciplines: biological sciences, medicine, physical sciences and, computer science and engineering. Much of the recent debate about research commercialisation has concerned these disciplines.

A Typology of Scientists: 'Old School' Traditionalists vs. 'New School' Entrepreneurial Scientists

In contrast to the protagonists' views on the growing dominance of an entrepreneurial orientation, my study finds a great deal of variation in the scientists' responses to university-industry ties. The analysis develops a typology of scientists to explore their diverse work orientations. It draws on the insights of earlier research on the differentiation of scientists according to their attachment to scientific values and goals (Box & Cotgrove, 1966) and a more recent study by Owen-Smith and Powell (2001) on the attitudes of university scientists to research commercialisation. It places the scientists on a continuum defined by two polar types representing the 'old school' traditionalists vs. the 'new school' entrepreneurial scientists at the opposite ends, with two mixed types, the 'traditional hybrids' and 'entrepreneurial hybrids', situating in between. The five key dimensions differentiating the four categories are summarised in Table 1.

These dimensions were initially derived inductively from the interviews and later cross checked against the survey data. In the interviews, scientists were asked detailed questions about the extent and intensity of their engagement in industrial links, their motivations and incentives for such engagements, their work roles and professional identities, their attitudes towards academic-industry relations and assessment of the influence of industrial engagements on their research and careers. Those who had been actively engaged in industrial activities were asked to elaborate on the ways in which they managed the boundary relationships and, resolved potential tensions and conflicts. At the end of the interviews, the scientists were shown a card with the statements describing the four categories (see, Appendix A) and asked to select one category that best described their orientations. Although not all the scientists saw themselves as falling into 'pure' categories, their dominant orientations could be identified from their responses to the descriptive statements and other questions asked in the interviews. In the data analysis, the scientists' 'self-definitions' were cross checked against their responses to other relevant questions and generally found to be consistent. The classification was subsequently refined and used in the survey where the respondents were asked to select their 'first best' and 'second best' choice of statements that described their professional orientations (see, Appendix A). The distribution of the responses shows that in the great majority of the cases, the second choice was contiguous to the first which illustrates the consistency of the choices. The first choice category was adopted for the quantitative analysis in mapping the scientists' orientations onto other relevant dimensions pertaining to the typology.

The distribution of the interview and survey samples by the four types, and the variation in their engagement in industrial links are shown in Table 2. It should be noted that 22 of the 36 interviewees also responded to the survey which enables cross-checking of the consistency in the classification. Table 3 shows the factors that have motivated them to engage in industrial links

Table 1. A typology of scientists' orientations towards university-industry links

	Beliefs about academia and industry boundary	Extent and modes of engagement with industry	Main motivating factors	Perceived legitimacy of commercialisation	Boundary work strategies and role identities
Type I 'Traditional'	• Believes academia and industry should be distinct and pursue success strictly in academic arena	• some collaborative links but of an intermittent nature	• Mainly to obtain funding and resources for research	Resistance • seen as an assault on academic ethos and autonomy	• Boundary separation and expulsion • Retain extant academic role identity
Type II 'Traditional hybrid'	• Believes academia and industry should be distinct, but also recognises the need to collaborate	• mainly collaborative links with intermittent involvement in some commercial activities	• Funding and resources for research most important amongst other factors	Accommodation • not necessarily desirable but an inevitable development	• Boundary testing and maintenance • Retain and protect dominant academic identity
Type III 'Entrepreneurial hybrid'	• Believes in the fundamental importance of science-business collaboration but recognises the need to maintain boundary	• continuous engagement in a range of collaborative and commercial activities	• Funding and resources for research most important • Application/exploitation of research, knowledge exchange and professional networking also important	Incorporation and co-optation • pursue commercialisation but not all its associated meanings	• Boundary negotiation and expansion • Hybrid roles but retain strong focal academic identity
Type IV 'Entrepreneurial'	• Believes in the fundamental importance of science-business collaboration	• continuous engagement in a range of collaborative and commercial activities • strong commercial ties with firms	• Application/exploitation of research most important • Funding and resources for research, knowledge exchange and professional networking also important • Personal pecuniary gains also relevant	Acceptance and veneration • commercial practices embedded in work routines	• Boundary inclusion and fusion • Fuse dual role identities

Table 2. Distribution of the interview and survey samples by type
and engagement in industrial links

Typology	Interview sample*	Survey sample	Engagement in industrial links (Survey respondents)		
			None	Collaborative**	Commercial***
Type I Traditional	3 (8%)	108 (17%)	57%	30%	13%
Type II Traditional hybrid	8 (22%)	215 (33%)	21%	48%	31%
Type III Entrepreneurial hybrid	16 (44%)	251 (39%)	14%	44%	42%
Type IV Entrepreneurial	9 (25%)	69 (11%)	15%	26%	59%
Total No. of survey respondents/ interviewees (N)	36 (100%)	643 (100%)	24%	41%	35%

*   All the interviewees were engaged in industrial links: 10 had collaborative links only and 26 were involved in both collaborative and commercial links.

**   Collaborative links: including collaborative research, contract research, consultancy, student sponsorship and joint publication.

*** Commercial links: including patenting, licensing, affiliation with start-ups and company formation.

Table 3. Factors motivating industrial links

Q. Which of the following factors have motivated you personally to engage in industrial links activities? (Multiple answers)

% selected the 'important' and 'very important' replies

Motivating factors*	Type I	Type II	Type III	Type IV	All types combined
To increase funding and other research resources	55%	85%	90%	71%	82%
Application & exploitation of research results	32	56	82	84	68
To create opportunities for Knowledge exchange/transfer	40	50	78	73	65
To build personal and professional networks	35	48	68	64	57
To enhance the visibility of your research	26	38	61	50	46
To increase your personal income	14	20	27	51	26

* Variation between types significant p < 0.001

N = 510 (Total no. of those with industrial links responding to the question)

7

In this classification, *Type I 'traditionalists'* are characterised by a strong belief that academia and industry should be distinct and they pursue success primarily in the academic arena. They comprise 17% of the survey sample which may be an underestimate of their importance in the population.[2] Although they may develop some links with industry (e.g., collaborative research, student sponsorships), the main reason for doing so was to acquire financial and other resources to support academic research. Type I scientists typically do not pursue commercial mode of engagement and tend to be suspicious of those who do so.

In contrast, *Type IV 'entrepreneurial scientists'* see the boundary between academia and industry as highly permeable, and they believe in the fundamental importance of science-business collaboration for knowledge application and commercial exploitation. They comprise a much smaller proportion (11%) of the survey sample relative to the other categories. However, the dominant majority of these scientists had involvement in industrial links and 59% were engaged in commercial activities of one kind or another, with 29% being company founders. The importance of knowledge application and exploitation to these scientists is clearly indicated in the survey; 84% agreed that this was an 'important/very important' factor motivating them to engage in industrial links. What also sets this category apart from the other three Types is the relative importance of personal financial gains (Table 3).

Between the two polar types, nearly three-quarters of the scientists surveyed exhibit a 'hybrid' orientation combining elements of both the 'old' and 'new' schools. Hybrids appear to adopt contradictory positions and express paradoxical views about the nature of relationships between science and business. There are two categories of hybrid scientists: *Type II 'traditional hybrids'* [3] share the old school commitment that the boundary between academia and industry should be distinct, while at the same time recognising the need to engage in science-business collaboration for scientific advancement. Over three-quarters of them reported having involvement in industrial links over the last ten years, and just under one-third were engaged in commercial activities. These scientists adopt a pragmatic orientation towards science-business interaction, while maintaining a strong academic identity. Like their Type I colleagues, they pursue industrial links primarily to obtain funding resources to support their research, although knowledge transfer and exploitation was also seen as important by some.

The other hybrid position, described as *Type III 'entrepreneurial hybrids'*, comprises the largest category (39%) of those surveyed. Scientists in this category share the new school belief in the importance and benefits of science-business collaboration, while maintaining the old school commitment to the core scientific values. The majority of the Type III scientists had engagement in industrial links and 42% were involved in commercial mode of activities, with 16% affiliated with start-up companies and another 12% being company founders. While Type II scientists were not entirely at ease with commercial endeavours, scientists holding a Type III position perceived such endeavours as largely legitimate and desirable for their scientific pursuits. Besides obtaining funding for research, Type III scientists were motivated by a range of other knowledge, reputational and network building factors in their pursuit of industrial links.

Universities are complex organisations comprising different academic disciplines and departments, and science itself is a disunified endeavour pursued by groupings of experts who are separated from each other by heterogeneous research approaches (Knorr-Cetina, 1999). The diversity in scientists' orientations toward science-business links reflects, in part, the different disciplinary norms, history of industrial engagement, and the divergent pressures and opportunities for research commercialisation in the different fields. For example, the survey shows that the traditional types (I and II) have a more conspicuous presence in physical sciences (55%) than in the applied subjects such as engineering and computer science (38%); whereas the entrepreneurial types (III and IV) are more prominent in the latter (62%) than in the former (45%). In subject areas where recent scientific advancement has blurred the boundaries between basic and applied research, and opened up new opportunities for commercial exploitation (e.g., biosciences and biomedicine), it is roughly an equal split between the traditional and entrepreneurial types.

However, beyond disciplinary variation, two observations are notable. The first is that all the different types are present within each disciplinary category. This suggests that an academic discipline may influence but does not determine scientists' orientations to industrial engagement. Previous research shows that scientists' early socialisation and work experience can influence their propensity to develop industrial links (Bercovitz & Feldman, 2003; Stuart & Ding, 2006). The second is that 'hybrids' (Types II and III) are the dominant category (70%+) across all the subjects. Their strong presence suggests that the conventional approach of conceptualizing the outcomes of the institutional transformation in terms of a simple dichotomy of the 'new' entrepreneurial scientists vs. the 'old' traditionalists fails to capture the complex variation in scientists' responses to the shifting academic landscape.

Boundary Work, Professional Autonomy and Role Identity

This section examines how scientists characterised by the different orientations use varied strategies of boundary work to defend, maintain or negotiate their positions. The analysis draws heavily on the individual interviews, supplemented by the relevant survey data on the respondents' evaluation of science-business relations (Table 4) and also analysis of the written-in comments provided by 152 respondents, spread widely across the four types.

Type I 'Traditional Scientists': Boundary Separation and Expulsion

For the Type I 'traditionalists', the boundaries between academia and industry are markers of differences between two distinct institutional domains. The distinction between basic and applied research, grounded in different types of organisations,

9

Table 4. Evaluation of industrial links and perceived influence on research and careers

% agree/agree strongly
[% disagree/disagree strongly]

	Type I	Type II	Type III	Type IV
Engagement in commercial activities has the potential to confuse university's central commitment to knowledge production (N = 637)	74 [12]	66 [14]	48 [33]	38 [39]
I am willing to alter my research programme to accommodate industrial demands (N = 475)*	16 [60]	29 [39]	38 [27]	60 [18]
Industrial links have stimulated me to develop new areas of research (N = 475)*	16 [53]	43 [15]	73 [9]	65 [19]
Have positively influenced my academic career and scientific reputation (N = 475)*	22 [54]	30 [27]	60 [12]	54 [26]

Variation between types significant p < 0.001
% of 'neutral' replies not shown
* Only those with industrial links were asked to respond to these questions.

continues to represent a boundary that has meaning and significance for these scientists. The university, according to the Type I scientists, should be the setting for the pursuit of disinterested basic research, while applied work should be done in the commercial setting. A Type I computer science professor interviewed, for example emphasised the importance of differentiating academic research from industrial problem-solving and talked about the need to 'protect' himself and his colleagues from 'the pressure to make a lot of connections with industry'. He believed that 'real academics' should focus mainly on basic research and, those engaged in industrial problem-solving 'are more like scientists in the research and development of big industrial firms', and they 'should not be in the university in the first place.' Another Type I professor, in physics, described one of his colleagues who engaged in applied work as someone who was 'not really an academic' because 'he doesn't write many papers... his aim is to produce instruments...'. These accounts in the interviews were evidently boundary-making in themselves in that the scientists' role identity was intimately associated with the pursuit of basic science in the context of the university. Their definition of who is and who isn't a 'real academic' amounts to a strategy of symbolic expulsion to protect and defend their own academic role identity.

Type I scientists believe that commercialisation of research is harmful to academic science and they see the growing pressures for applicability in research as a threat to scientific autonomy. In the survey, the majority said that they were not prepared 'to alter their research programmes to accommodate industrial demands', indicating their resistance against industrial encroachment. Three-quarters agreed with the statement that 'engagement in commercial activities has the potential to confuse university's central commitment to knowledge production' (Table 4). This sentiment was also vividly expressed by many of those who wrote their remarks on the questionnaires:

> I strongly believe that the commercialisation of research by academia has harmed and has the potential to further harm the role of academia in society... (Professor, bio-engineering)

> Universities are selling their souls to the gods of patents and profits. (Lecturer, physics)

Type I scientists responded to the rising tide of commercialisation by avoidance or contestation. Some dismissed the environmental changes and others actively contested the legitimacy of these activities. They often evoked the traditional ideals of pure, 'disinterested' research to guard the boundary of basic science. Especially among those who did not see the relevance of industrial engagement, their suspicion of industrial links may well reflect their personal desire to maintain an 'ivory towerish' world of academic science. At first sight, it would appear that these Type I traditionalists were using the norms of basic research as a protective resource for self-justification. However, there is also ample evidence to suggest that their resistance against commercial endeavours also reflects a genuine concern that private interests may undermine the objectivity of research and pose moral threats to the enterprise of science:

> ... most commercial companies have little interest in research for its own sake, or even sometimes in the truth, they always had to put the bottom line first. This is probably inevitable, but it means that industry support is not in my view a satisfactory way to support academic activity. Findings unhelpful to a commercial company are suppressed, and favourable findings exaggerated. (Professor, medicine)

> Industrial links are not all the same although they are all more or less problematic. For example, links between basic science and the defence industry are entirely morally wrong, links with commercial drug companies are highly problematic, while other links have their own specific associated questions... (Researcher, mathematics).

The 'boundary work' of Type I scientists seeks to reinforce the institutional logics and integrity of academic science, and maintain their extant role identity. The norms of 'disinterestedness' and 'communalism' were often invoked, in their conversations and written comments, not simply for self-interested protection but also to defend the collective enterprise of academic science against the encroachment of commercial interests.

Type II 'Traditional Hybrids': Boundary Testing and Maintenance

Scientists belonging to this category share the traditionalists' view that engagement in commercial activities can be harmful to academic science and they also believe in the importance of maintaining a boundary between academia and industry. However, they adopt a more accommodating attitude and are prepared to test the boundary relationships to explore the emerging opportunities in anticipation of possible benefits. About one-third of those surveyed said they were 'willing to alter their research programmes to accommodate industrial demands' (31% neutral), indicating a more flexible approach (Table 4). Many also recognise a need to meet the growing expectations for industrial collaboration. Several of those who had been involved in start-up companies talked about their 'social obligations' as scientists and the 'culture' of their departments:

> ... we felt obliged as one is obliged actually, apart from some arty research, to do your best to commercialise the outfits... From my perspective, I feel starting up starter companies is kind of what you are supposed to do. It's kind of what you should try to do, obviously the government gives you money because it's supposed to help the economy and to do research ultimately it should help the economy. (Professor, biosciences)

> ... it was a directive from above, you know, our Head of Department was very keen that we open up... it was the culture of the department at the time... You know if you were going to be a top academic that's one of the things you had to cover... (Professor, biosciences)

Underlying this apparent institutional compliance was a pragmatic personal adaptive strategy that many of the traditional hybrids pursued in the changing research environment. Many believed that demonstrating an entrepreneurial stance in their work would enhance their chance of obtaining the much needed research funding. One young professor in biophysics, who had been successful in obtaining major funding for his lab in the past few years, described in a somewhat cynical manner how he went about this:

> The Government was making it harder and harder to do pure research and so if you could show application in the context of, you know, collaborative work with industry, it was much easier to get funding.... So, for example, I have to write a report for my Wellcome Trust Senior Fellowship, my annual report saying how great I am. And one of the questions there is, you know, what have you done that is impressive outside just running a lab? So you know, I think, oh it would be great if I had some... you know if I showed I'd started a company

or ... Yeah, so I'm going to bullshit about my contacts with company X and you know, and it's all a case of building that up and that is more impressive than saying, "oh well I gave four lectures and three tutorials"...

The 'traditional hybrids' were individualistic and pragmatic in crafting their own versions of 'boundary work.' While retaining many of the characteristic traits of the Type I traditionalists, they sought to test the science-business boundary relationships by experimenting with new practices and trying out new roles. Many recognised that commercial engagement had gained increased institutional legitimacy and it was something that might bring academic credentials and benefit their careers. However, such activities also challenged their focal scientific values and they were only too acutely aware that commercial activities had not gained wide acceptance at a deeper cultural-cognitive level among their colleagues. A Type II bioscientist engaged in a start-up company, for example, expressed his concerns about being seen by his colleagues as having 'crossed over to the dark side.' Another mocked his own activities in seeking company funding by repeatedly saying that he was 'selling his soul...' and thought those who were too deeply involved in commercial activities were 'walking a very narrow line.' These narratives reveal the scientists' deep-seated worries about the potential career and identity risks that commercial activities entail.

The position of the traditional hybrids was somewhat indeterminate and ambiguous. Kosmala and Herrbash (2006: 1399) argue that ambivalence is a strategy of self-protection – it enables individuals to distance themselves from external control, and to create a 'free space' for autonomy. The Type II scientists sought to experiment with new work practices without undermining the established scientific norms and their dominant academic role identity. This ambivalence allows them to create 'provisional selves' (Ibarra, 1999: 765) as temporary solutions to experiment with new roles.

One might even say that these scientists were 'hedging their bets' and they would change directions based on evaluations of the success or failures of the trial efforts. The accounts of the interviews and written comments on the questionnaires show the scientists' meticulous assessment of their experiences. Many of these served as warnings about the risks of over-stepping the science-business boundaries:

Research donations (unencumbered, charitable) from industry are now our preferred option since any explicit "research contract" outlining collaborative or contractual research with funding from industry nowadays brings massive and ill-conceived IP terms and conditions... (Senior lecturer, computer science)

In retrospect, the time I spent on commercial links with industry distracted my concentration on research objectives, and my career might have had more fundamental impact if I had pursued those research objectives single-mindedly. (Professor, biosciences)

Several of the traditional hybrids told negative stories of their own or their colleagues' 'failures' in company ventures. They talked about how their own attitudes and the 'culture' of their Departments had shifted from away from the 'entrepreneurial' pull towards more a basic research orientation as a result of the unsuccessful ventures.

The boundary work of the traditional hybrids is both individually self-serving and organisationally significant in creating opportunities for testing new behaviour. It creates a free space for navigating a transition and experiencing alternative perspectives without posing a major threat to the established norms. Type II scientists seek to 'test' as well as 'maintain' the science and business boundary.

Type III 'Entrepreneurial Hybrids': Boundary Negotiation and Expansion

Type III scientists are also hybrids in that they combine a new school entrepreneurial orientation with an old school commitment to the core values and norms of academic science. For these scientists, the boundary between university and industry is permeable and provides an open space within which knowledge production and application can be effectively combined. They emphasised an interactive relationship between basic and applied research, and appeared to be comfortable and confident in crossing the science-business boundary. Relative to their traditionally-oriented colleagues, a much smaller proportion of the Type III scientists surveyed agreed that 'engagement in commercial activities has the potential to confuse university's central commitment to knowledge production'. Conversely, a higher proportion said that they were 'willing to alter their research programmes to accommodate industrial demands' (Table 4). The majority believed in the positive benefits of industrial engagement:

> Industrial links have been very important with respect to gifts of reagents without which many of my basic scientific research questions could not be addressed. (Reader, medicine)

> The consultancy work is invaluable in turning up ideas for research. (Professor, chemical engineering)

These scientists are experienced and strategic in the way they interface with industry. They will attempt to influence or manipulate the expectations of their industrial partners in order to shape the relationships. As one scientist put it: 'we have very clear ideas of what we want to do and we'll play the company's [game]... you know, we're not going to be pushed around.' For these scientists, the boundary between academia and industry provides an overlapping space where bargaining and negotiation takes place. While recognising the benefits of industrial ties, the entrepreneurial hybrids are also aware of their pitfalls and potential risks. They would seek to protect the hard core of scientific values when they felt that industry had overreached: 'science must come first, no compromise' (interview with a professor). The problems of 'publication restriction', 'control over intellectual property rights' and 'conflicts of interests' were often mentioned in the interviews as threats that could impinge on their academic freedom and autonomy. Many would actively devise strategies to deal with the problems and exert control over the collaborative relationships to ensure that they were conducted on the 'right terms', in the words of one professor. For many of the Type III scientists, as in the case of their more traditionally-oriented colleagues, the norm of communism that supports open dissemination and publication of research results must be protected. They would rigorously safeguard this when entering into collaborative agreements with industry:

> What you need is clear contracts with industry so that if there are people, you know who are doing PhDs or who are doing basic research, you have to have clear clauses to say that, you know... the company for example should be given the results freely but there should be no embargo on publication... the ownership comes into it as well, you know who actually owns the IP and so that needs to be very carefully sorted out before you start, you know who owns what. (Professor, biosciences)

Some scientists would use their specialist expertise and personal scientific eminence to exert control over their industrial partners. One bioscience professor, for example, used non-exclusive licensing deals with companies to ensure that no one single company could have complete control over his work:

> ... when I published a paper on X, which is an enzyme involved in high blood pressure and I suggested this might be used to design anti-hypertensives and a lot of companies wrote to me and so I made a deal with thirty companies...
>
> I sold them the same thing. Polygamy works very well. If you are monogamous in your relationship with a large company then you become completely ruled by your partner. If you have a lot of partners you become very powerful and more effective... I licensed to a lot... *(Laughing)*

Unlike the Type II traditional hybrids, the Type III scientists did not appear to experience cognitive dissonance or role identity tension when they embarked on commercial ventures. They perceived such endeavours as largely legitimate and would use 'old' academic frames to interpret the meaning of commercial engagement to resolve any normative tension. For many of the entrepreneurial hybrids, knowledge application and commercialisation amounts to an extension of their scientific role following long years of fundamental research: '... I like to think our jobs are a mixture of that degree of freedom to operate and to push the boundaries, that may well lead... that boundary may well lead to some commercial thing or a licensing or a spin out...' (Professor, biosciences). For some, forming a spin-off company was a way of asserting control over the knowledge exploitation process so as to exclude unwanted commercial interests from big companies: '... but I suspect at the end of the day, you know to get sort of independence and to be able to do things beyond a certain level, I suspect you really need to have a company ...' (Professor, biosciences; company founder).

Like Type II traditional hybrids, Type III scientists also frequently mentioned how they used industrial links to generate the much needed financial resources for their laboratories (see also, Table 3). The 'resource frame' for some of the entrepreneurial hybrids includes also personal income. This money incentive, however, is not supposed to be a legitimate one for 'truthful' scientists engaging in 'disinterested' research. The scientists reframed what this meant for them to justify their involvement in 'profit making' activities which appear to be at odds with their socialised academic identity. For example, some talked about their 'freedom' and 'right' to engage in such activities to compensate for their low pay:

> ... I think I'm being underpaid and so I've always campaigned for better salaries in the university world but I've also always championed the rights that if we're going to be paid very little we should be able to write books or do consultancies or form companies. (Professor, biosciences)

Beyond this nuanced 'self-interested' economic narrative, the majority of the entrepreneurial hybrids interviewed stressed the wider societal benefits of their commercial ventures. The following comment is illustrative:

> ... even if I get no drugs in the end and we still have a good chance, I've put a lot of money into the local economy, I've given jobs and what I'm absolutely convinced is that the method we've developed is going to be useful in making drugs in the comings years... I think that we as academics have a responsibility, especially in University X, to the nation really, we're in a very privileged position... And our money comes from the State or from charities. (Professor, biosciences)

The entrepreneurial hybrids have been able to expand the boundaries of their work to incorporate commercial practices without sacrificing their focal academic identity. The majority interviewed saw themselves as 'a scientist first and foremost'. They believed that their commitment to academic values, clear research agenda and scientific reputation had enabled them to reap the benefits of commercial endeavours without the attendant negative implications. A professor who had been actively engaged in commercial activities described his scientific reputation as 'a central core' that gave him the freedom to do many other things outside academia: '... my first priority is to be a world leader in my research myself... the only defence of somebody like myself is to do better than anyone else in my academic job...'. These scientists are similar to what Zucker et al. (2002) describe as 'star scientists' who pursue dual knowledge production while remaining firmly rooted in the academic community. They pursue commercialisation of research but not all its related commercial implications. They actively seek to determine the shape and content of their enterprise activities so as to maintain their scientific autonomy.

At the socio-cognitive level, Type III scientists use 'mediating beliefs' (Pratt & Foreman, 2000) to reconcile the internal inconsistencies associated with their simultaneous partake in science and business. Patenting and company formation, for example, are not seen as vehicles for profit making but as mechanisms that enable them to have control over knowledge exploitation and thus to protect the integrity of science. At the more practical level, they are meticulous in maintaining clarity and social order across the academic-business boundary in their daily work. They would ensure that the two domains were kept separate in their laboratories to avoid conflict of interest:

> ... I kept the topics distinct and I kept the equipment distinct, I duplicated things if necessary. I had a yellow line down the middle of the lab, you couldn't see it but nothing crossed it. (Professor, biochemistry)

The boundary work of Type III entrepreneurial hybrids is complex and clever. These scientists actively negotiate the boundaries between science and business, and seek to map out new social spaces for their work while protecting their autonomy and role identity. The way they negotiate the blurred boundaries between the two arenas often involves an apparent paradoxical combinations of contradictory institutional logics and perspectives. Yet, these scientists are adept at resolving normative tension and avoiding conflict of interest. Henkel (2005: 173) argues that scientists in the contemporary environment 'must negotiate between social and institutional pressures and preservation of identity.' The boundary work of the entrepreneurial hybrids does precisely this.

Type IV 'Entrepreneurial Scientists': Boundary Inclusion and Fusion

Type IV 'entrepreneurial scientists' see the boundary between academia and industry as entirely permeable and flexible, and use it as a basis for bridging and inclusion. Like their Type III counterparts, Type IV scientists are also experienced participants in university-industry links. However, they have gone further down the 'entrepreneurial path', with a conviction to linking knowledge production more tightly to its practical use and commercial exploitation. The dominant majority surveyed said they were 'willing to alter their research programmes to accommodate industrial demands' (Table 4).

To the entrepreneurial scientists, science is inherently commercial and the pursuit of commercial science is entirely logical and compatible with their academic role. The traditional ideal of 'disinterested science' seems to bear little significance to the way these scientists approach their research. A Type IV professor in physics, for example, talked about the 'need to be aware of [commercial] opportunities and the need to spot them', and the importance of 'having a perspective on how commercialisation of fundamental research works' so that 'you're not working in areas of science that has absolutely no chance of being kind of exploitable'. Those in the more applied disciplines believed that the worlds of science and commerce were completely merged and it would be difficult to draw a clear boundary between

17

the two: 'The world is more industrial... to talk about science as separate from marketing aims of big corporations is naïve' (interview with a biomedical professor). To these entrepreneurial scientists, the Mertonian ideal of academic science was no more than an imaginary mythical world that only existed for those who believe in '... some Victorian nirvana of ivory towers doing wonderful intellectual research', in the words of a Type IV professor interviewed.

Scientists holding a Type IV orientation are ardent advocates of Burton Clark's (1998) notion of the 'entrepreneurial university' in that they believe in the critical importance for universities and academics to participate in the market and maximise opportunities for commercialisation in order to achieve financial self-reliance. The following remarks by a Type IV professor in bio-medicine sum up this view well:

> ... well the key thing that my message to you is that Universities will not be successful until we understand the value of intellectual property in University and how to exploit that. The Universities in the UK need one thousand Company X (a spin-off) if we're going to have real funding of the University independent of the Government, I believe in that very much...

In contrast to their traditionally-oriented colleagues who often use the ideal of 'disinterested research' to protect and defend the boundary of academic science, Type IV scientists do precisely the opposite. They develop their own distinctive version of boundary work to challenge the institutional rules and values of academic science. They do so by mocking and belittling the role and contribution of basic research as opposed to applied research. One Type IV professor in computer science, for example, pointed out that the 'theoreticians' in his department were 'at least twenty years behind' and that they would need to justify their existence in relation to those who were engaged in applied work. For the most entrepreneurial new school scientists, research without practical relevance or that bears no technological fruits is less valuable.

The boundary work of the entrepreneurial scientists also challenges the norm of communism that gives priority to publication over patenting. To these scientists, patents not only constitute an alternative source of scientific credit but they are also an important economic resource that must be exploited:

> ... if you discover something then I believe you should patent it immediately if you want to patent it which is very cheap and then publish... and also those who say we need open, free dissemination of science, what we need as well is for that science to have an effect on society and the effect on society... I do not believe that patenting and free dissemination are in conflict. (Professor, biomedicine)

At a practical level, the entrepreneurial scientists sought to incorporate their mode of operation into the established academic structure. One professor in computing science talked about how he would 'cheat in every way possible in the system to bring applied people in and make their lives possible' in the department. Another in biosciences actively championed and developed what he described as an 'ideal organizational structure' to 'allow the companies to do their research within the university labs'. Unlike the Type III entrepreneurial hybrids who often draw a clear line between their academic and commercial activities to avoid conflict of interest, the Type IV scientists seek to integrate the two into a single structure.

For these scientists, deep engagement with industry constitutes part of their established work routines and role identities. For example, one Type IV scientist interviewed described 'entrepreneurial engagement' as part of 'the repertoire, base skills' that he should retain as a professional scientist. Others saw their parallel activities in the academic and commercial arenas as an integral part of their work roles: '... it's part of my life, you know. it's not dislocated particularly'. Another Type IV professor pointed out in the interview that technology transfer in his case was his 'academic self' talking to his 'industrial self': 'It all happens together... that's the heart of how it works, no barriers right. You can do the same thing at once...'. This 'talking to himself perspective' reflects the fusion of two different role identities into a hybrid, two-faced one.

While Type III scientists use various legitimating themes and mediating beliefs to accommodate commercial science within their academic frames, Type IV scientists assert the rationality and righteousness of their entrepreneurial convictions. Some openly acknowledged the importance of personal financial gains. The following remarks made by two company founders are illustrative:

> ... you've got to make money, the company is to make money, right, it's not like another item on your frigging CV, it's to make money! That's why you do it! It's not a CV driven thing, it's not like a publication... (Professor, computer science)

> Money. Money, money, money. It is just money. I mean if you think about academic jobs whether perfectly reasonably paid... You are never going to earn the same thing as a banker or you know a lawyer or something. So I think if you can incentivize people – even with a few thousand pounds actually, you know, it is quite helpful. (Professor, biosciences)

It would appear that commercial practices have achieved a deep cultural cognitive legitimacy among the Type IV scientists. However, probing deeper into their work experiences and role identities reveals a much more ambiguous and tension-prone picture. Several of the Type IV scientists interviewed complained about how the 'old norms' and the 'real culture' continued to erect barriers to their boundary bridging activities, and that they would have to 'push back on that' and 'work very hard to manage the considerable suspicion' from their colleagues. Another pointed out that there was 'an institutionalised negativity' towards entrepreneurial activities because they were not seen as 'high grade' and the view that 'industrial stuff is not nice' still 'permeate the entire system'. Besides the subtle cultural sanction, the Type IV scientists were particularly adamant that the system continued to reward predominately scientific achievements in the form of publications and peer recognition, and downplayed their contributions to knowledge exploitation. For the scientists who simultaneously commit themselves to academic and commercial science, a successful career would imply performing well in their dual roles across the science and business realms, and meeting the goals and performance criteria of the two very different systems.

The majority of the Type IV scientists interviewed felt that their decision to go down the entrepreneurial path was a 'risky' endeavour because it could jeopardise their academic careers. Those who were professors described themselves as being 'lucky' and 'managed to get away with it'. For those who had not yet made it to the top of the career hierarchy, the career risk was genuine and there was a constant fear of being de-coupled from the core academic system. One young bio-scientist, who had founded a company, described his position as being like 'a waiter with all those plates' and feared that the 'whole thing could collapse' around him any time. Another who was a Reader in physics, also a company founder, had experienced such difficulties in balancing his dual role that he was making a genuine assessment about whether to remain full time in academia: 'I think I have had to make a careful and studied decision that I want to go down this road in the knowledge that it is almost certainly preventing my promotion within the university...'

Even among the apparently successful entrepreneurial professors, the narratives in the interviews reveal a sense of anxiety in keeping up their academic performance. One professor thought his publication track record was 'a bit thin' for a professor in a top research university of his, and mentioned several times in the interview that he was 'no 400 paper journal man' compared with one of his more eminent colleagues. Another talked about his role conflict in satisfying the different responsibilities and not having time for his own research: 'I have nightmares about the volume of work I have to deal with... I genuinely wake up sweating in the middle of the night... these [industrial] activities take time and they take time away from other things and if you value them more highly you spend more time on them, and the time that's spent on them is time away from teaching, time away from you know, fundamental research and theoretical speculation, time away from scholarship...' Conflict of commitment and role overload appear to be a widespread problem experienced by the Type IV entrepreneurial scientists.

The boundary work undertaken by Type IV scientists is contentious and tension-prone. They attack and dismiss the traditional model of academic science which remains as the default ideal for many. This inevitably breeds tension and risks jeopardizing their acceptance by academic colleagues. The tension inherent in the boundary work of Type IV scientists is also manifest at the individual level in the role identity conflict experienced. For the individual scientists, the decision to pursue commercial activities is akin to managing multiple role identities which can lead to role identity overload and conflict (George et al., 2005). Individuals may adopt different strategies to resolve the conflict. Type III scientists resolve the tension by maintaining one dominant academic identity and creating mediating beliefs to reconcile the internal inconsistencies. Type IV scientists, by contrast, seek to fuse the academic role with the entrepreneurial one to make a two-faced hybrid identity. However, the hybrid identity maintains distinct elements from the pre-existing identities, and thus role tension may occur when any elements from the original identities come into conflict (Pratt & Foreman, 2000: 31–2). The transition from the role of a scientist to that of an entrepreneur, even in the case of the most entrepreneurial Type IV scientists, appears to be partial and fraught with inner tension. This is not only because the gap to be bridged between the identities is considerable, but also forgoing the focal academic identity would mean threatening the very professional self and scientific esteem upon which the entrepreneurial one is built.

Discussion

The increased penetration of the marketplace into the institutional fabric of universities has generated much debate and uncertainty about the shifting nature of academic scientific work. Proponents of academic entrepreneurialism stress the growing prominence of the new school entrepreneurial scientists. Critics, by contrast, paint a dark world of academic capitalism where the norms and values of academic science are gradually being eroded, and the position of traditional scientists is under threat. The analysis presented in this chapter does not lend support to either view. The emerging picture is far more complex and fluid than is presented in these generalized observations.

The typology of scientists based on a continuum defined by two polar sets of values, the 'traditional' vs. 'entrepreneurial', has provided a useful framework for examining the emerging patterns of conflict and agreement in scientists' responses to the changing environment. It avoids the limitations of a dichotomous view which projects a clear divide between the 'old' Mertonian values of basic science and 'new' values of entrepreneurialism, assuming a linear process of change with the new displacing the old. It is important to note that both traditional and entrepreneurial types of academics have always existed in universities, but changes in social conditions may determine which type becomes more dominant and which set of values gains greater legitimacy at any given time. As Hacket (2001: 203) notes, 'historical events that disturb society do not create new values and ethics out of whole cloth, nor do they necessarily pose novel value conflicts, but instead they alter the balance between pre-existing polar opposites'. The two polar positions, I and IV, represent two gravitational fields or latent pairs of principles in academic science which are always in tension. Recent changes in science-business relationships appear to have altered the balance, giving the entrepreneurial type a greater degree of socio-political legitimacy than before. The hybrids, Types II and III, denote the sociological ambivalence of scientists and their attempts to bridge across contradictory positions. Treating hybrids as distinctive types enables us to explore the potential for strategic action and change at the intersection of different institutional spheres.

All the scientists studied have a clear sense of shifting boundaries but they diverge in their adaptive strategies. Type I traditional scientists see the demands of industrial application as constraints to their work and an assault on their professional autonomy. The boundary work of these scientists seeks to maintain the traditional ideals of basic science and protect their academic role identity. Although these scientists may be increasingly constrained by their continued reliance on diminishing public funding, they remain a powerful force especially in the disciplines characterised by a strong basic research orientation. Their determined opposition to the rising tide of commercialisation restrains the move towards entrepreneurialism and keeps the controversy and debate alive. In contrast, Type IV entrepreneurial scientists perceive increased commercialisation as an opportunity to establish an alternative mode of knowledge production. This category may well be gaining greater prominence in the fields with growing market opportunities for research commercialisation. Their attempt to fuse the science-business boundaries and assimilate a strong commercial perspective, however, breeds tension and risks jeopardizing their acceptance by academic colleagues. Type IV scientists comprise a relative small share of the survey sample (11%) and their actual presence in the academic population may well be less significant. Their 'boundary work' may not constitute what Gieryn (1983: 789) refers to as an 'effective ideological style' that could establish entrepreneurial science as a hegemonic model in academia.

The hybrids, Types II and III, comprise the great majority and have been particularly adept at mapping out their own social spaces for navigating a transition. Although the two categories differ in the strength of their gravitation towards entrepreneurialism, they both seek to exploit and manipulate the changing circumstances to their advantage. Oliver (1991) argues that manipulation is the most active response to institutional pressures because actors actively seek to influence, change or co-opt institutional expectations and evaluations. Type II traditional hybrids use the social space at the intersection of science and business for experimentation. Their fluid position enables them incrementally to move towards entrepreneurialism or retreat into the bounded academic arena, depending on changing circumstances or the outcome of their trail- and -error efforts. This indeterminate position may cause cognitive dissonance and psychological discomfort, but it also creates opportunities for evaluation, learning and making sense of the new possibilities (Piderit, 2000). Moreover, it allows them to 'float' at the intersection of different institutional domains, change direction or define a new hybrid domain by mixing elements of the intersecting institutions.

Type III entrepreneurial hybrids are those who have developed a distinctive negotiation zone at the interface between academia and industry. They vigorously seek to mobilise material and knowledge resources across the two arenas to support and expand their research. These scientists have acquired substantial entrepreneurial knowledge through work experience and are particularly skilled at controlling the research agendas in both worlds. This is the category of scientists most likely to report positive influence of industrial links on their research and careers (see, Table 4). While looking towards the industrial world and selectively crossing the boundaries, their values and role identity are firmly embedded in the academic community. The ambivalence of these scientists lies in their apparently paradoxical combination of the logics of science and business in their work, and their use of seemingly conflicting frames to legitimate their boundary crossing activities. However, Type III scientists do not appear to experience psychological discomfort despite their structurally ambivalent position. They actively negotiate their roles and seek to incorporate business practices into their repertoire of behaviour, doing so on their own terms. These tactics neutralize opposition and enhance the legitimacy of their commercial ventures in the academic arena. At the individual cognitive level, they resolve role identity conflict by altering the meaning of commercial practices to better fit with the logic of academic science.

It is clear that scientists do not respond uniformly to the changing institutional environment. There is evidence of open or subtle resistance against the encroachment of a commercial ethos, but also obvious attempts to bridge the contradictory demands of science and business, whether reluctant or positive. Such sociological ambivalence, arguably, is a character of science and scientists have always had to defend their position in response to external challenges. The increasingly blurred boundary between university and industry, and growing pressure on scientists to exploit the commercial opportunities in an expanding array of scientific fields have brought the ambivalence of scientists to the forefront. Gieryn (1999) argues that boundary work is most apparent in situations in which boundaries are contested. The scientists looked at in this study are engaging in collective professional boundary work as well as personal boundary work (Waterton, 2005) as they seek to defend and establish the value of their work in the shifting terrain of academic science. Collectively, scientists are engaging in what Friedson (1994) referred to as the 'maintenance project', searching for a coherent professional identity as they increasingly operate within open and contested terrains. At the individual level, they are crafting their own versions of boundary work to map out social spaces for pursuing their professional and career goals.

Amidst the apparent ambivalence and diversity, the majority of the scientists engaged in industrial links, notably types III and IV, perceived a positive impact of industrial links on their research and careers (see, Table 4). This indicates that they have been able to assert a sufficient degree of control over the science-business relationship to pursue their own objectives. The analysis also reveals strong continuity and stability in the role identity of the majority of the scientists. While it is possible for individuals to hold multiple identities salient to various roles and contexts (Kreiner et al., 2006), some aspects of individuals' identity are 'central' and often remain salient and can be held strongly even in the face of external challenges (Markus & Kunda, 1986). For the majority of academic scientists, their role identity is deeply rooted in a strong scientific ethos that cherishes autonomy and dedication to knowledge. This focal identity is also the result of long years of graduate training and socialisation, and is intimately tied to an institutionalised career reward system based on scientific credibility and peer status and it differs substantially from an entrepreneurial one associated with commercial science. The boundary between science and business is becoming fuzzy, but not dissolved. It continues to have great symbolic significance for the majority of scientists and serves to underpin their role identity.

This continuity has enabled scientists to adapt to the external challenges without undermining the core logic of academic science. It has to be remembered that one of the unique features of universities is the strong influence of academics on defining their missions and goals, and the management of daily routines of work. Radical transformation in academic science is unlikely to take place without widespread acceptance of commercial practices among the majority of scientists at the deeper socio-cognitive level. This does not appear to have occurred. These observations are consistent with the results of several other studies (Enders, 1999; George et al., 2005; Henkel, 2005) which also show a strong continuity in the professional role identity of academic scientists, despite challenges from the environment. Even in the US where the institutional framework for promoting academic entrepreneurialism is much more developed than in the UK, empirical evidence on the effects of these changes on the norms and practices of academic scientific work suggests a picture that is largely mixed and riddled with inconsistencies and anomalies (Owen-Smith & Powell, 2001; Vallas & Lee Kleinman, 2008; Welsh et al., 2008).

Conclusion

The remaking of boundaries between science and business is a contentious and contested process. Science itself is a diverse activity full of anomaly and paradox, and managing ambivalence is part of the daily routine of scientific work which also shapes the social structure that produces it. Neo-institutional theory highlights the agency role of actors in shaping the change and reproduction of institutions. It postulates that actions can either maintain or transform existing institutional structures. This chapter has demonstrated the capacity of scientists to defend and negotiate their positions, and to exercise agency through boundary work.

Those who see the growing power of the marketplace and the ethos of commercial science capturing and corrupting the cognitive norms of scientists will need to take account of how actors can resist change and alter the meanings of new practices to fit with their 'old' norms (McLoughlin et al., 2005; Murray, 2010). Authors who predict a shift in the work orientations of scientists towards the 'new' entrepreneurial mode should bear in mind that this can occur within a strong continuity of the 'old' academic frame as actors mix disparate logics at the blurred boundaries between institutional sectors. DiMaggio (1997: 268) argues that individuals are capable of maintaining inconsistent action frames which can be invoked in particular situational contexts. Hybrids in boundary-spanning positions can bridge contradictory logics and act as powerful agents of change. However, it should be noted that the move from the 'traditional' to the 'entrepreneurial' mode is not necessarily a linear process as it can be halted, or even reverted, as a result of actor learning or contestation. As Coyvas and Powell note (2006: 346), social life is full of situations of partial institutionalisation in which new practices or values can prompt resistance from incumbents.

This chapter highlights the contribution of a micro-level perspective to understand the responses of scientists to the shifting institutional environment. It has looked at the experience of 'elite scientists' in major research universities who have relatively strong bargaining power and varied resource options to exert control over the environment. The situation may be more constraining for scientists in smaller or newer universities with less reputational and institutional resources to defend their positions. Future research could be extended to include different types of institutions to explore the potentially divergent experience of a wider population of academics.

NOTES

[1]   The study was funded by the U.K. Economic and Social Research Council (ESRC Grant No. 160250018), Science in Society Programme. Full details of the findings are reported in Lam (2010, 2011) and Lam and de Campos (2015).

[2]   Scientists who had no engagement and no interest in industrial links would have been less inclined to respond to the survey and especially to the question about their orientations to science – business interface. There were 56 cases of no reply to the question and 77% of them did not have any involvement in industrial links, suggesting that the majority could be Type I scientists. Some wrote at the end of the questionnaire that they did not feel that the question was relevant to them as they did not have any involvement with industry.

[3]   This category was labelled 'Type II pragmatic traditional' in Lam (2011).

REFERENCES

Aldrich, H. E., & Fiol, C. M. (1994). Fools rush in? The institutional context of industry creation. *Academy of Management Review, 19*(4), 645–670.

Ashforth, B. E., Kreiner, G. E., & Fugate, M. (2000). All in a day's work: Boundaries and micro role transitions. *The Academy of Management Review, 25*(3), 472–491.

Barley, S. R., & Tolbert, P. S. (1997). Institutionalization and structuration: Studying the links between action and institution. *Organization Studies, 18*(1), 93–117.

Beck, J., & Young, M. F. D. (2005). The assault on the professions and the restructuring of academic and professional identities: A Bernsteinian analysis. *British Journal of Sociology of Education, 26*(2), 183–97.

Bercovitz, J., & Feldman, M. (2003, June 12–14). *Technology transfer and the academic department: Who participates and why?* Paper presented at the DRUID Summer Conference 2003, Copenhagen, Europe.

Bernstein, B. (1996). *Pedagogy, symbolic control and identity: Theory, research and critique.* London, UK: Taylor and Francis.

Boltanski, L., & Thevenot, L. (1999). The sociology of critical capacity. *European Journal of Social Theory, 2*(3), 359–377.

Box, S., & Cotgrove, S. (1966). Scientific identity, occupational selection, and role strain. *The British Journal of Sociology, 17*(1), 20–28.

Clark, B. R. (1998). *Creating entrepreneurial universities.* Oxford, England: Pergamon Press.

Colyvas, J., & Powell, W. W. (2006). Roads to institutionalization: The remaking of boundaries between public and private science. *Research in Organizational Behavior, 27*, 315–363.

DiMaggio, P. J. (1997). Culture and cognition. *Annual Review of Sociology, 23*, 263–287.

Enders, J. (1999). Crisis? What crisis? The academic professions in the 'knowledge' society. *Higher Education, 38*, 71–81.

Etzkowitz, H., & Leydesdorff, L. (2000). The dynamics of innovation: From national systems and 'mode 2' to a triple helix of university-industry-government relations. *Research Policy, 29*(2), 109–123.

Etzkowitz, H., Webster, A., Gebhardt, C., & Terra, B. (2000). The future of university and the university of the future: Evolution of ivory tower to entrepreneurial paradigm. *Research Policy, 29*(2), 313–330.

Friedson, E. (1994). *Professionalism reborn: Theory, prophecy, and policy.* Chicago, IL: University of Chicago Press.

Galison, P. (1997). *Image and logic: A material culture of microphysics.* Chicago, IL & London, UK: University of Chicago Press.

George, G., Jain, S., & Maltarich, M. A. (2005). *Academics or entrepreneurs? Entrepreneurial identity and invention disclosure behavior of university scientists* [Unpublished paper]. London, UK: London Business School.

Gibbons, M., Limoges, C., Notwotny, H., Schwartzman, S., Scott, P., & Trow, M. (1994). *The new production of knowledge.* London, UK: Sage.

Gieryn, T. (1983). Boundary-work and the demarcation of science from non-science: Strains and interests in professional ideologies of scientists. *American Sociological Review, 48*(6), 781–795.

Gieryn, T. F. (1999). *Cultural boundaries of science: Credibility on the line.* Chicago, IL & London, UK: University of Chicago Press.

Hackett, E. J. (2001). Science as a vocation in the 1990s: The changing organizational culture of academic science. In J. Croissant & S. Restivo (Eds.), *Degree of compromise: Industrial interests and academic values* (pp. 101–138). Albany, NY: Sunny Press.

Hackett, E. J. (2005). Essential tensions: Identity, control, and risk in research. *Social Studies of Science, 35*(5), 787–826.

Henkel, M. (2005). Academic identity and autonomy in a changing policy. *Higher Education, 49*, 155–176.

Henkel, M. (2007). Can academic autonomy survive in the knowledge society? A perspective from Britain. *Higher Education Research & Development, 26*(1), 87–99.

Ibarra, H. (1999). Provisional selves: Experimenting with image and identity in professional adaptation. *Administrative Science Quarterly, 44*, 764–791.

Kenney, M., & Goe, R. W. (2004). The role of social embeddedness in professorial entrepreneuriship: A comparison of electrical engineering and computer science at UC Berkeley and Stanford. *Research Policy, 33*, 691–707.

Knorr-Cetina, K. (1999). *Epistemic cultures: How the sciences make knowledge.* Cambridge, MA: Harvard University Press.

Kogan, M. (2000). Higher education communities and academic identity. *Higher Education Quarterly, 54*(3), 207–216.

Kosmala, K., & Herrbach, O. (2006). The ambivalence of professional identity: On cynicism and jouissance in audit firms. *Human Relations, 59*(10), 1393–1428.

Kreiner, G. E., Hollensbe, E. C., & Sheep, M. L. (2006). On the edge of identity: Boundary dynamics at the interface of individual and organizational identities. *Human Relations, 59*(10), 1315–1341.

Lam, A. (2010). From 'ivory tower traditionalists' to 'entrepreneurial scientists'? Academic scientists in fuzzy university-industry boundaries. *Social Studies of Science, 40*(2), 307–340.

Lam, A. (2011). What motivates academic scientists to engage in research commercialization: 'Gold', 'ribbon' or 'puzzle'? *Research Policy, 40*(10), 1354–1368.

Lam, A., & de Campos, A. (2015). 'Content to be sad' or 'runaway apprentice'? The psychological contract and career agency of young scientists in the entrepreneurial university, *Human Relations, 68*(5), 811–841.

Lamont, M., & Molnar, V. (2002). The study of boundaries in the social sciences. *Annual Review of Sociology, 28*(1), 167–195.

Latour, B., & Woolgar, S. (1979). *Laboratory life: The construction of scientific facts.* Beverly Hills, CA: Sage.

Markus, H., & Kunda, Z. (1986). Stability and malleability of the self-concept. *Journal of Personality and Social Psychology, 51*, 858–866.

McLoughlin, I. P., Badham, R. J., & Palmer, G. (2005). Cultures of ambiguity: Design, emergence and ambivalence in the introduction of normative control. *Work, Employment & Society, 19*(1), 67–89.

Merton, R. K. (1957). Priorities in scientific discovery: A chapter in the sociology of science. *American Sociological Review, 22*(6), 635–659.

Merton, R. K. (1976). *Sociological ambivalence and other essays.* New York, NY: Free Press.

Merton, R. K., & Barber, E. (1963). Sociological ambivalence. In E. A. Tiruakian (Ed.), *Sociological theory, values and sociocultural change.* Glencoe, NY: The Free Press.

Mitroff, I. I., (1974). Norms and counter-norms in a select group of the Apollo moon scientists: A case study of the ambivalence of scientists. *American Sociological Review, 39*, 579–595.

Mouzelis, N. (1989). Restructuring structuration theory. *Sociological Review, 37*, 613–635.

Mulkay, M. J. (1976, January 1). Norms and ideology in science. *Social Science Information, 15*(4–5), 637–656.

Mulkay, M. J. (1980). Sociology of science in the west. *Current Sociology, 28*, 1–184.

Murray, F. (2010). The oncomouse that roared: Hybrid exchange strategies as a source of distinction at the boundary of overlapping institutions. *American Journal of Sociology, 116*(2), 341–388.

Oliver, C. (1991). Strategic responses to institutional processes. *Academy of Management Review, 16*(1), 145–179.

Owen-Smith, J., & Powell, W. (2001). Careers and contradictions: Faculty responses to the transformation of knowledge and its uses in the life sciences. *Research in the Sociology of Work, 10*, 109–140.

Piderit, S. K., (2000). Rethinking resistance and recognizing ambivalence: A multidimensional view of attitudes toward an organizational change. *Academy of Management Review, 25*(4), 783–794.

Pratt, M. G., & Foreman, P. O. (2000). Classifying managerial responses to multiple organizational identities. *Academy of Management Review, 25*(1), 18–42.

Slaughter, S., & Leslie, L. L. (1997). *Academic capitalism: Politics, policies, and the entrepreneurial university.* Baltimore, MD: Johns Hopkins University Press.

Slaughter, S., & Rhoades, G. (2004). *Academic capitalism and the new economy: Markets, state, and higher education.* Baltimore, MD: Johns Hopkins University Press.

Smith-Doerr, L., (2005). Institutionalizing the network form: How life scientists legitimate work in the biotechnology industry. *Sociological Forum, 20*(2), 271–299.

Stuart, T. E., & Ding, W. W. (2006). When do scientists become entrepreneurs? The social structural antecedents of commercial activity in the academic life sciences. *American Journal of Sociology, 112*(1), 97–144.

Tolbert, P. S., & Zucker, L. G. (1996). Institutionalization of institutional theory. In S. Clegg, C. Hardy, & W. Nord (Eds.), *Handbook of organization studies.* London, UK: Sage.

Vallas, S. P., & Kleinman, D. L. (2008). Contradiction, convergence and the knowledge economy: The confluence of academic and commercial biotechnology. *Socio-Economic Review, 6*(2), 283–311.

Waterton, C. (2005). Scientists' conceptions of the boundaries between their own research and policy. *Science and Public Policy, 32*(6), 435–444.

Welsh, R., Glenna, L., Lacy, W., & Biscotti, D. (2008). Close enough but not too far: Assessing the effects of university-industry research relationships and the rise of academic capitalism. *Research Policy, 37*(10), 1854–1864.

Zucker, L., Darby, M., & Torero, M. (2002). Labor mobility from academe to commerce. *Journal of Labor Economics. 20*(3), 629–660.

Alice Lam
School of Management
Royal Holloway University of London

APPENDIX A

Survey Question Used to Categorise Orientations of Scientists

Please indicate which of the following statements best describe your professional orientation (indicate your first best and second best choice if appropriate)

	First best	Second best
1. I believe that academia and industry should be distinct and I pursue success strictly in the academic arena	( )	( )
2. I believe that academia and industry should be distinct but I pursue industrial links activities mainly to acquire resources to support academic research	( )	( )
3. I believe in the fundamental importance of academic-industry collaboration and I pursue industrial links activities for scientific advancement	( )	( )
4. I believe in the fundamental importance of academic-industry collaboration and I pursue industrial links activities for application and commercial exploitation	( )	( )

JOHN AUBREY DOUGLASS

WHAT IT MEANS TO BECOME A FLAGSHIP UNIVERSITY[1]

Seeking a New Paradigm

INTRODUCTION

It's a familiar if not fully explained paradigm. A "World Class University" is supposed to have highly ranked research output, a culture of excellence, great facilities, a brand name that transcends national borders. But perhaps most importantly, the particular institution needs to sit in the upper echelons of one or more world rankings generated each year by non-profit and for-profit entities. That is the ultimate proof for many government ministers and for much of the global higher education community. Or is it?

The relatively recent phenomena of international university rankings are fixated on a narrow ban of data and prestige scores. Citation indexes are biased toward the sciences and engineering, biased in which peer reviewed journals are included – (largely US and European, and the English language), and tilted to a select group of brand name universities who always rank high in surveys of prestige, the number of Nobel Laureates and other markers of academic status.

It is not that these indicators are not useful and informative. But government ministries are placing too much faith in a paradigm that is not achievable or useful for the economic and socio-economic mobility needs of their countries. They aim for some subset of their universities to inch up the scale of this or that ranking by building accountability systems that influence the behavior of university leaders, and ultimately faculty. Some of this is good, creating incentives to reshape the internal culture of some national university systems that have weak internal quality and accountability policies and practices. But it also induces gaming by university leaders and arguably is pushing institutional behaviors toward a vague model of global competitiveness that is not in the best interests of the nations they serve.

THE FLAGSHIP UNIVERSITY

In a forthcoming book with Palgrave Macmillan, I attempt to advocate the notion of the *Flagship University* as a more relevant ideal – a model for public institutions and perhaps some private institutions, one that could replace, or perhaps supplement and

E. Reale & E. Primeri (Eds.), The Transformation of University Institutional and Organizational Boundaries, 29–39.

alter the perceptions, behaviors, and goals of ministries and universities in their drive for status and influence on society. It is a model that does not ignore international standards of excellence focused largely on research productivity, but is grounded in national and regional service, and with a specific set of characteristics and responsibilities that, admittedly, do not lend themselves to ranking regimes. Indeed, one goal here is to articulate a path, and the language of a *Flagship University*, that de-emphasizes rankings and that helps broaden the focus beyond research. *Flagship Universities* are research-intensive institutions, or in the process of becoming so, but have wider recognized goals.

After a long period of governments and their ministries attempting to shape the mission and activities of universities, including various accountability schemes and demands focused on the normative World Class University (WCU) model, we need to enter a period in which institutions themselves gain greater autonomy and financial ability to create or sustain an internal culture of self-improvement and evidence-based management. The great challenge for the network of universities that are truly leaders in their own national systems of higher education is to shape their missions and ultimately to meaningfully increase their role in the societies that gave them life and purpose. The *Flagship University* profile I offer includes an outline of the mission, culture and operational features and is intended as a possible construct for this cause.

The objective is not to create a single template or a checklist, but a list of characteristics and practices that connect a selective group of universities to the socioeconomic environment in which they must participate and shape – a model that others might expand on and indigenize. Further, the *Flagship University* ideal is not, and could never be, a wholesale repudiation of rankings and global metrics, or the desire for a global presence. The model here is compatible with the WCU focus almost exclusively statistical analysis of research productivity, but aims much higher to, in some form, the soul and culture of the institution.

There are a few key assumptions to allow the *Flagship University* to exist and mature:

- *Mission differentiation* – National systems of higher education require some form of mission differentiation among its network of postsecondary institutions, and including a limited number of research-intensive universities, some of which might be *Flagship Universities*.
- *The Flagship ethos* – Either by government identification or self-appointment, *Flagship Universities* aspire to support regional and national socioeconomic mobility and economic development, educating the societal and business leaders of the future, and understanding and seeking a role in supporting other segments of a nation's education system. As noted, they also have or seek a culture of self-improvement. The best universities are always looking to get better at what they do to positively influence society at large.

But to pursue this ethos, they need the political, financial and policy support of their national governments in a manner that aligns with the overall management of a national higher education system and that meets the needs of various stakeholders – from students and their families, to business interests, and local and national governments. While the *Flagship Model* is largely focused on internal cultures and behaviors, government plays a critical role in a variety of ways, including:

– Using funding to steer the higher education sector to respond to labor market requirements and human welfare needs;
– Incentivizing research and innovation in selected universities.
– Pursuing a close link between national and regional economic policy development and higher education planning.

• *A comprehensive array of academic programs – Flagship Universities* have or aspire to offer degree programs across the disciplines, including professional fields such as engineering, law, medicine, education (including teacher education) and social welfare.
• *A sufficient "academic core"* – Universities that exude the values of the *Flagship Model* can do so only if they have sufficient funding and a baseline of Core characteristics, including manageable student-to-faculty ratios, a significant population of permanent faculty with doctoral degrees, sufficient numbers of masters and in particular doctoral students, and evidence of sufficient graduation rates and research productivity.

Research and analysis on a group of sub-Saharan African universities by the Center for Higher Education Transformation (CHET) based in Cape Town outlined the Academic Core concept first in 2011. CHET's baseline criteria focused on the developmental needs of African Universities; but they provide a useful framework for all universities that are early in the stages of maturation, and often in developing economies. The Academic Core includes input and output variables that link an institution's capacity to positively influence regional economic and social development with its capacity for knowledge production.

The important point is that there is a healthy balance in the various ratios of first degree and graduate students, permanent faculty, and a general assessment of productivity in graduates and research output. A key additional concept is the crucial importance of proper incentives and expectations for academic staff, along with the conditions in which they must work.

• *Institutionally driven Quality Assurance* – While ministries of education can positively or negatively influence the quality of university academic programs and activities, ultimately top tier institutions require sufficient independence to develop internal cultures of quality and excellence *and* incentives. This must include merit-based academic personnel policies. If there is any one major theme that helps determine what are the most effective universities, it is the quality of the faculty, their ability to carry out their duties, high expectations regarding their talents, duties, and performance, and driven by a process of peer and post-tenure review. The quality of students, and to a large degree their academic and other forms of engagement, follow.

An ancillary assumption: government policy regimes and induced efforts to improve the quality and performance of all or a select group of national universities reflect doubt about the ability of their universities to become top, globally competitive institutions, and often with good reason; but ministries should view such government requirements and often one-size-fits all policies (such as national policies on academic advancement) as simply an initial stage in the goal of achieving high-performing *Flagship* universities, with the next and more important stage focused on sufficient autonomy to support *a culture of campus based institutional self-improvement.*

Flagship Universities are mindful of their global interaction and impact (including journal citations) *and* their regional responsibilities and influence in areas such as economic development and socio-economic mobility. They are mindful of ranking systems that essentially encourage them to be what one might call "universities of the cosmos" (for example, with research and quality goals that are not tied to location or more directly to societal needs), but they must remain grounded in a set of values and activities that make them essential to the societies they must operate in and serve.

SEEKING A FLAGSHIP PROFILE

In the forthcoming book with Palgrave Macmillan, I offer a "profile" of the *Flagship University*, organized in four categories, summarized in Figure 1 with each related to the institutions external responsibilities and internal operations. The idea is that, within the context of a larger national higher education system, *Flagship* institutions have a set of goals, shared good practices, logics and the resources to pursue them. Generally, the sequence is from the larger external context, to the mission of the institutions and goals, to the management structure to make it happen. Put another way, my effort here simply attempts to help create coherency, and to provide some guides and examples, for what many universities are already doing or are thinking of doing, but with emphasis on internal culture and processes for evaluation and self-improvement.

The expanded version of the profile provides a path to comprehend the vast array of values and activities that characterize the modern, research-intensive university. Universities are complex organizations that purposefully pursue mutually supportive activities that do not lend themselves easily to separate categories – in a vibrant university, teaching, research, and public service are symbiotic activities, built on a model of institutional revenue sharing and mutual

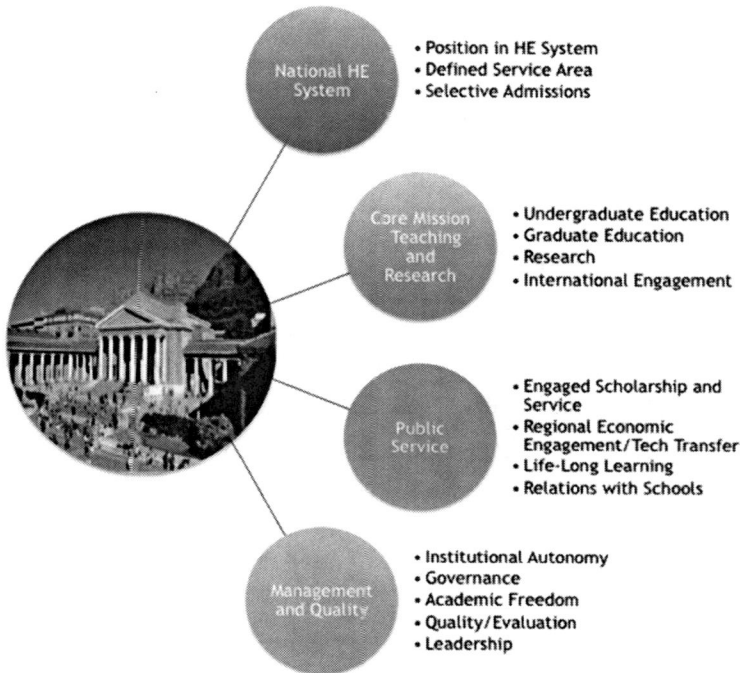

• Position in HE System
• Defined Service Area
• Selective Admissions

• Undergraduate Education
• Graduate Education
• Research
• International Engagement

• Engaged Scholarship and Service
• Regional Economic Engagement/Tech Transfer
• Life-Long Learning
• Relations with Schools

• Institutional Autonomy
• Governance
• Academic Freedom
• Quality/Evaluation
• Leadership

Figure 1. A flagship university profile: Four spheres of policies and practices

support. Hence, there is some redundancy in how I have organized the Profile of *Flagship Universities*.

The following provides an example of one of the policy areas under the Public Service sphere.

PUBLIC SERVICE – Engaged Scholarship and Public Service – *Flagship Universities* promote public service in various forms by faculty, students and staff via formal programs and incentives. This form of "outreach" is extremely important, providing a significant impact on local and regional communities, opportunities for learning and experimentation, and direct evidence of priorities. "Publicly Engaged" universities, as one observer has stated, "can make serious headway against social problems. As civic engagement elevates the quality of university teaching and learning, it produces millions of university graduates with both hands-on competence in their fields and a personal commitment to being agents of social change. And increasing public goodwill for universities can make government and private funders more generous in their financial support".

Figure 2 provides an outline of the traditional view of academic scholarship and the scholarship of Public engagement.

Traditional Scholarship	*Scholarship of Public Engagement*
Breaks new ground in the discipline	*Breaks new ground in the discipline and has a direct application to broader public issues*
Answers significant questions in the discipline	*Answers significant questions in the discipline, which have relevance to public or community issues*
Is reviewed and validated by qualified peers in the discipline	*Is reviewed and validated by qualified peers in the discipline and members of the community*
Is based on a solid theoretical basis	*Is based on solid theoretical and practical bases*
Applies appropriate investigative methods	*Applies appropriate investigative methods*
Is disseminated to appropriate audiences	*Is disseminated to appropriate audiences*
Makes significant advances in knowledge and understanding of the discipline	*Makes significant advances in knowledge and understanding of the discipline and public social issues* *Applies the knowledge to address social issues in the local community*

Figure 2. Traditional views on academic scholarship versus the scholarship of public engagement

In some form, all universities, and more specifically their students, faculty, and staff, are involved in various forms of public service and engagement, but the key is how coherent those efforts are and how are they valued within the institution. Most if not all major public US universities have developed over the past two decades or more the idea of "service learning." This often includes efforts to leverage and expand existing university led activities to support local communities and businesses, including the development of credit bearing courses for undergraduates engaged in formal internships with specified academic and public service outcomes. The University of Michigan, for example, has an endowed a center for engagement, focusing on student service-learning and partnerships and producing a refereed journal of scholarly work.

Similarly, UCLA created the Center for Community Partnerships – reflecting the high priority the campus places on engagement with its surrounding community. This was not the beginning of UCLA's involvement in the community; the university has been engaged in the Los Angeles area for many years, though not in a systematic way. One goal of the Center is to promote campus discourse on what it means to be involved in the surrounding community.

Several factors help explain for relatively high levels of engaged scholarship in America's leading public research universities. One is the expectation that students applying to universities at the undergraduate level have some public service experience, broadly defined. When they enter the university, they already have experience and interest in the student volunteerism and different forms of community engagement. A second factor relates to expectations placed on faculty and an academic culture that has long valued community service and engagement with local business and governments – although with differences among the disciplines. This includes various forms of engaged scholarship incorporated as a formal part of faculty review of their performance and promotion. And a third factor is the growing number of campus organizations targeted toward community engagement – like UCLA's Center for Community Partnerships.

Generally, this is a new concept for most international universities, many who have only recently expanding their missions to include more concerted efforts at integrating community engagement with their teaching and research programs. The Talloires Network, a relatively new international association of institutions, is one example of a global promotion of public service as a central universities mission, providing examples of best practices.

Many Latin American Universities have articulated aspects of the idea of service learning and community engagement, but the coherency of these efforts have been limited, and not clearly articulated in, for example, the faculty advancement process. The following provides avenues and examples on how *Flagship Universities* are or can pursue this central part of their mission – an incomplete but useful way of articulating institutional mission and values with actual programs and activities.

- *Community Volunteering* – faculty, students, and staff at most universities interact informally as individuals in various forms of community service. But Flagship Universities should include formal mechanisms, such as "community service centers" that attempt to identify and link the university community with opportunities for volunteer work. Various forms of civic engagement provide an important path for universities to contributor to local needs – in schools, in hospitals, local social services, charities and similar community based activities. It also raises the visibility, and the value, of the university within the communities they reside in – further proof of their value to local government and populations.
- *Service Learning* – Service-learning is a pedagogical approach; it is academic and integrated into the curriculum. It focuses on student learning through action that benefits the community, but it is mutually rewarding because it can be transformational for students as well, connecting them with their role in a democratic society.

Universities should offer opportunities for undergraduate and graduate students alike to engage in learning opportunities, including course requirements and course credits, which support public service objectives. This is a form of experiential education in which students engage in activities that address human and community needs together with structured opportunities intentionally designed to promote student learning and development. This should not be viewed as a distraction from the traditional academic experience linked almost solely to coursework; rather, that some, indeed, most students gain experiences that support their general edification and is part of the disciplinary based learning. Figure 3 provides examples of "service learning" programs. Below is an outline of objectives for Service Learning experiences:

- Increase retention, particularly among first-generation college students.
- Increase diversity of local enrollment as a form of outreach.
- Enhance achievement of core learning goals and has an effect on progress to degree.
- Make learning more relevant to students, helping them clarify their talents and interests at an early stage of their academic career; it often impacts choice of major selection and eventual career.
- Develop students' social, civic, and leadership skills.

- **University of Minnesota – Service Learning Courses and Scholars Program**

Each semester, the University of Minnesota offers some 50 courses, most for credit, that have service learning components in a wide range of disciplines that enroll approximately 2,000 students. This class-related community involvement enhances students' understanding of course materials. While deepening the learning process in this way, students build a sense of civic responsibility. Support for most service-learning classes is provided by the Community Service-Learning Center which also sponsors a Community Engagement Scholars Program that requires at least 400 hour of community engagement work such as volunteering and a final project, called the Intergrative Community Engagement Project ICEP that is noted on student transcripts for graduate school and employment applications.

- **University of Glasgow – Service Learning Program**

Service-learning at the University of Glasgow combines academic coursework with voluntary work in the community, to help you experience policy in practice. It is part of the Public Policy Honours curriculum, and an accredited course for visiting students. Program requirements includes one academic course in semester 1: Service in the Community 20 credits, an 8 week placement at 6 hours per week, in a welfare agency in Glasgow, and a 3,000 word reflective journal by the student.

- **Texas A&M – Service Learning Courses and Scholars Program**

Service-Learning Fellows program with up to 6 faculty selected via a competitive review process who receive a $3,000 faculty development award for integrating service-learning into their teaching, research, and public service while becoming recognized campus leaders in service-learning pedagogy and community engagement. The program is a partnership between the Center for Teaching Excellence CTE, Office of the Associate Provost for Undergraduate Studies US, and the Department of Student Activities Leadership and Service Center SA-LSC.

Figure 3. CASE EXAMPLES: Service learning programs

- Strengthen undergraduate research skills and capabilities.
- Encourage students to be productive participants in the community by connecting them to their surroundings.

- *Faculty Engaged Policy Research – Flagship Universities* look for ways to encourage academically relevant work that simultaneously meets campus goals as well as community needs. In essence, it is a scholarly agenda that integrates community issues as a value for faculty. In this definition community is broadly defined to include audiences external to the campus that are part of a collaborative process to contribute to the public good.

The following outlines some of the benefits that can be derived by a systematic approach to promoting and supporting engaged scholarship and civic engagement.

- *Bolster the links between research and teaching.* Research indicates that learning is enhanced by real-world experiences that broaden a student's perspective and connect theory with practice. In addition, research that is informed by community participation can have a uniquely meaningful impact that is locally visible.
- *Improve diversity, student retention, and progress to degree.* A university that more fully integrates community engagement into its research and teaching endeavors develops stronger ties to multiple communities and may be better able to attract and engage a diverse student body. In addition, research shows that engaged students remain in school and progress to degree at a greater rate than students who are not engaged.
- *Re-energize faculty around engaged scholarship.* Creating a civic engagement initiative and providing a supportive infrastructure may re-energize faculty teaching and research by providing a fresh perspective on the value their work brings to society.
- *Connect the university to policymakers.* Universities are being questioned about their relevance, lack of transparency, and high costs. Bringing more visibility to the value that the university provides the public through community-based teaching and research is one way to "live" the public mission and reinforce the important role that the university plays in serving the public good.
- *Build transdisciplinary and interdisciplinary research capacity.* The problems of society are complex, and addressing them requires expertise as well as research that crosses disciplinary lines. These capacities should be supported among faculty and nurtured in students.
- *Building a research community around Societies most challenging policy issues.* Focusing on issues that are of local and national public concern brings the unique strengths of a research university to bear on the most pressing challenges that face the state. This can enhance public knowledge of and appreciation for the university system, thereby making more tangible the return on public investment in higher education.

- *Bringing in new resources and funding.* Both government and private funders are calling for more collaborative approaches to projects as a condition of funding. In addition, local and regional funders who may not normally contribute to other university endeavors may have greater interest in investing in projects with clear public purposes and applications.
- *Build social capital among students, faculty, and communities.* Academic inquiry not only addresses critical research questions but also enhances the ability of students, faculty, and communities to take action and build ongoing relationships that yield multiple benefits. The development of such social capital has been shown by research to strengthen communities, making them more resilient and healthy. New networks of trust and cooperation are likely to emerge and create new academic partnerships for scholarly work.

A MORE HOLISTIC MODEL

The *Flagship* Profile I have partially outlined here purposefully provides an alternative conceptual and aspirational approach to the vague World Class University paradigm that now dominates much of the international discussion, and in academic conferences and journal articles. Yet the goal here is more ambitious: to support the ethos and an institutional culture among a select group of institutions, self-identified or formally so by national or even regional governments, and rooted in an ethos of national and regional relevancy and supported by internally derived accountability activities and behaviors.

The best universities are ones that are striving to get better, and not simply in the realm of research, the primary concern of the rhetoric and policy initiatives associated with achieving the World Class designation via international rankings. It is a much broader charge that includes teaching, and public service, and internal mechanisms for supporting quality and excellence.

In this exploratory effort, I have not sought to generate some elaborate scheme to measure outcomes – what many ministries thirst for. While some sort of framework for assessing the success of a *Flagship* can undoubtedly be created, like all existing outcome models it could only offer a partial understanding of the complex benefits and costs of what a highly productive university brings to the world.

Instead, my focus has been on the void in understanding what defines leading universities and what their aspirations should be. Thus far, the WCU rhetoric is the driving force, influencing government policy (not all bad) and institutional behaviors (not all bad) that have, in my view, an exceedingly limited vision, indeed a constraining force, on what major national universities should be and can achieve.

The *Flagship University*, and the exploratory profile is a supplemental and, certainly, more holistic model applicable to some sub-group of major universities. While governments and other stakeholders have a legitimate claim to influence and shape the operations and missions of their universities, the *Flagship* model may provide a path for some universities to explain and seek greater institutional identity, a stronger internal culture of self-improvement, and, ultimately, a greater contribution to economic development and socioeconomic mobility that all societies seek. For that to happen, some group of institutions will need to embrace on their own terms some version of the model and articulate it clearly and loudly.

NOTE

[1]   This essay is adopted from the pending book The New Flagship University, Palgrave Macmillan.

John Aubrey Douglass
Senior Research Fellow – Public Policy and Higher Education
Center for Studies in Higher Education
University of California – Berkeley

SECTION 1

TRANSFORMING UNIVERSITIES INSTITUTIONAL AND ORGANIZATIONAL BOUNDARIES

Changing Functions, Objectives, and Scope of Higher Education and Research Institutions

MAARJA BEERKENS

1. AGENCIFICATION CHALLENGES IN HIGHER EDUCATION QUALITY ASSURANCE

INTRODUCTION

The 1990s were characterized by the rise of quality assurance in higher education (Dill, 1995). Over the last two decades, quality assurance systems in Europe have changed and evolved significantly. There is now much variety in how countries regulate academic quality (Dill & Beerkens, 2010; Schwartz & Westerheijden, 2007), but despite of the variety we can see increasing convergence in the organizational structure that countries use for quality assurance. A great majority of European countries rely on semi-independent or formally autonomous quality assurance agencies. A survey of the European Association for Quality Assurance (ENQA) reports that the number of independent higher education quality agencies in Europe is consistently increasing; moreover, their tasks are widening and they use a greater number of different evaluation instruments (ENQA, 2008). This organizational form is also strongly promoted by the European Standards and Guidelines for Quality Assurance (ENQA, 2005). As a result, within only a decade countries with very different starting points and approaches to academic quality assurance have adopted a rather similar model of regulatory agencies.

The model of independent quality assurance agencies is often promoted from a sector-specific rationale in higher education. Quality assurance must be independent from the political control in order to assure its legitimacy in the eyes of universities, and it must be independent from universities to avoid 'regulatory capture' (Dill & Beerkens, 2013). However, the trend towards independent regulatory agencies cannot be seen apart from the same trend in other policy sectors. An 'agencification' fever characterized public sector reforms in many European countries from 1990s onwards (Pollitt et al., 2001). Agencies were expected to increase the level of expertise among regulators, make them more effective by separating them from policy-making, and increase legitimacy of regulation in the eyes of regulatees (see Laegreid & Verhoest, 2010).

Quality assurance agencies have thus become an interesting element in thinking about universities' organizational boundaries. They play an important role in the changing dynamics between state and universities. Universities have become more autonomous from state but as a response to the autonomy they must demonstrate performance and accountability. Quality assurance agencies fill an important mediation function in this relationship. Regulatory agencies are a defining factor

E. Reale & E. Primeri (Eds.), The Transformation of University Institutional and Organizational Boundaries, 43–61.

of the 'regulatoy state', a state where government does not provide services but delegates the tasks to private entities and uses regulation for steering the entities (Majone, 1997). Regulation takes place in the triangle of the political demand (parliament, government), regulator (agencies) and regulatees (universities). In this relationship, independent regulatory agencies tend to obtain considerable policy-making power and they become an actor with their own interests.

This chapter focuses on potential challenges of 'agencification' in the higher education. Accumulating literature from other sectors points to some weaknesses of 'agencification', most notably to fragmentation in the system and to a loss of political steering capacity. In this chapter we will first discuss how the changing dynamics between universities and state connects to independent regulatory agencies, i.e., the 'regulatory state' model. Thereafter we examine how the quality assurance agencies have evolved in the four countries, to demonstrate the highly varied trajectory to the rather homogenous model. And finally we explore tensions within the systems from the point of view of 'agencification' literature.

REGULATION AND AUTONOMY: THE RISE OF AGENCIES

A tension between autonomy and accountability, or deregulation and regulation, is a constant issue in many sectors of public administration. The higher education sector may have some specificity, due to the notion of academic freedom and historical distrust of government intervention, but the autonomy-accountability dilemma is nevertheless highly visible. Influenced by the public sector reform agenda, higher education systems in most European countries have experienced substantial changes in the level of organizational autonomy and the nature of government control.

Autonomy and Control

Higher education is an illustrative case about a shift from the 'positive state' to the 'regulatory state' in Europe (Majone, 1997). Over the 1990s and 2000s the traditional relationship between universities and state are critically revised in many countries. As a general rule, universities have become more autonomous: free from line-itemized budgets, input control, detailed prescriptions on curricula, and staff restrictions (Santiago et al., 2008). Reforms in public sector management show, however, that de-regulation goes rarely without some kind of re-regulation. A push towards greater managerial autonomy in the New Public Management (NPM) agenda produces also its 'mirror image' in the form of ex-post control and performance evaluation (Hood et al., 1999). Similarly the greater autonomy given to universities is balanced by new accountability mechanisms (Santiago et al., 2008). Detailed rules and line-item budgets ex ante are replaced with accountability post factum, input control is replaced with ex post quality control, and historically derived budgets are replaced by performance-based funding, etc.

Higher education quality assurance was one area that was strongly affected by the NPM agenda in the public sector. Academic quality assurance entered the scene in Europe and Australasia for the most part in the 1980s and 1990s (Dill, 1995). From a theoretical perspective, higher education quality requires a government intervention on several reasons (e.g., Blackmur, 2008; Dill & Soo, 2004). One set of arguments is linked to market failure issues. First, regulation is needed for consumer protection. Since a higher education degree is a considerable expense for students in terms of money, time and opportunity cost, society needs a warranty that the degree meets some basic standards. Higher education is an experience good: it is impossible to estimate the 'quality of the product' before 'buying' it, which causes a serious information asymmetry between a 'consumer' and a 'producer'. Secondly, higher education is believed to have important social externality. The role of government regulation is linked to safeguarding the quality of education so that it can fill the societal function, not only respond to the private interest of students or of university staff.

When we turn from a 'theoretical' perspective to the historical reality, we can identify three main triggers behind intensified quality control (Dill, 2010; Van Vught & Westerheijden, 1994). First, massification of higher education and related increase in public expenditure drew attention to quality issues in the system. A rapid increase in student numbers led to starting new programs in existing institutions and creating new (also private) providers. This rapid proliferation raised concerns of whether universities have sufficient resources to maintain high quality education and whether the new programs expect equally high academic standards. Since the expansion of the sector meant also a greater burden on public funds, governments became more alert to the efficient functioning of the sector. Secondly, the New Public Management agenda entered also the higher education sector. As a result, greater accountability mechanisms, particularly in the form of ex-post evaluation and output monitoring were introduced. Higher education thus entered the 'evaluative state', as famously stated by Neave (1988). Furthermore, explicit attention to quality is one characteristic of the NPM agenda (Pollitt & Bouckaert, 2004). Thirdly, internationalization (and globalization) increased the need for internationally comparable and recognized degrees and a transparent evaluation system is a precondition for such a comparability.

Quality assurance agencies were not an immediate response to the growing attention to quality regulation. Quality assurance tasks were originally filled by a variety of organizations, either affiliated with government or university associations. The rise of independent quality assurance agencies originates from a shift in the dominant model of public sector governance.

Regulatory Agencies and 'Agencification'

In the last decade or two we have experienced an explosion of public sector organizations in a variety of sectors (Pollitt & Talbot, 2004). Much of the actual policy implementation, control and regulation has been transferred to autonomous agencies, separated from the core administration. Such single-purpose organizations have disaggregated the traditional core-administration into smaller parts, both vertically and horizontally (Pollitt et al., 2004). While the trend is rather wide-spread, the agencies are far from homogenous. It is well documented that the agencies come in a great variety of form and size (Pollitt et al., 2001). Talbot (2004) defines agencies quite narrowly, as a body that is formally separated from the ministry, carries out public tasks on a permanent basis, is financed mainly by the state budget, is staffed by public servants and subject to public legal procedures.

There are two main rationales for creating autonomous regulatory agencies in the public sector (Majone, 1996). First, they help to separate politics and administration (Lægreid & Verhoest, 2010). Furthermore, regulatory agencies can be perceived as more credible because of their independence from politicians. Secondly, agencies were seen as a mechanism towards greater specialization, which was believed to lead to greater efficiency (Hood, 1991). Enjoying a greater degree of freedom was believed to lead to more efficient management, due to the benefits of specialization, professionalization, flexibility, transparency, and openness to stakeholders (Pollitt et al., 2001).

Using autonomous agencies in the academic quality assurance is widely spread and strongly promoted by several influential international organizations. 'Standards and Guidelines for Quality Assurance in the European Higher Education Area', a document prepared by the European Association for Quality Assurance (ENQA) and adopted by the education ministers during their meeting in Bergen in 2005, gives much attention to the independence of quality assurance agencies (ENQA, 2005, para 3.6):

> Agencies should be independent to the extent both that they have autonomous responsibility for their operations and that the conclusions and recommendations made in their reports cannot be influenced by third parties such as higher education institutions, ministries or other stakeholders. [...] The definition and operation of its procedures and methods, the nomination and appointment of external experts and the determination of the outcomes of its quality assurance processes are undertaken autonomously and independently from governments, higher education institutions, and organs of political influence. (para 3.6 & 3.8)

The number of external higher education quality assurance agencies in Europe has grown rapidly since the early 1990s (ENQA, 2003). Also their profile and the nature of their work have expanded. In the 2000s such agencies use not only a greater number of quality assurance methods but they are also more likely to advise governments and higher education institutions about quality related issues (ENQA, 2003). While the ENQA guidelines specify the need for autonomy, the formal level of autonomy and the distance from the central government varies among quality agencies (ENQA, 2008). Some quality assurance agencies are formally more distant from the government, often more closely linked to university associations than to the central government and their staff is not necessarily civil servants.

There is not much discussion or empirical evidence available about the benefit of autonomy in the case of higher education quality assurance agencies. From the Standards and Guidelines cited above it appears that the main concern is the objectivity of the process, which requires independence from politicians as well as from universities (see also Dill & Beerkens, 2013). Ewell (2008) is one of the few that discusses the advantages of autonomous agencies in the quality assurance. In the US context he sees two main reasons why independent agencies are more effective than direct state intervention. States are severely challenged by resource shortfall and therefore could not support extensive quality programs or fund performance based schemes sufficiently. Secondly, in a context of short-term policy agenda and severe partisanship it would be difficult to sustain a long-term consistent policy agenda. While strong state initiatives such as performance-based funding proved to be short-lived and did not make much impact under the top administrative level, pressuring accreditation organizations to pursue governments' agenda has been more effective. When the federal government gradually increased pressure on accreditation organizations to focus on student learning outcomes and this was indeed reflected increasingly in their reviews, the majority of institutions had by the end of the 1990s developed the kind of assessment infrastructure originally intended but not accomplished by the state mandates. There thus seems to be a benefit of distancing quality assurance somewhat from the politics, not only for legitimacy but also for credible commitment.

The agency model also seems to correspond well with the reforms that redefine the relationship between universities and government. As universities became 'autonomous' organizations, their regulation was now often seen as a non-political task and therefore not part of the state's 'core business' (Westerheijden, 2008). Outsourcing the task to intermediary bodies (such as quality assurance agencies) was thus a logical step.

'Agencification' in the higher education sector goes well beyond the quality regulation sector. Several tasks are often delegated to various single-purpose agencies, such as student support system, distributing public funding to institutions, institutional and student data collection, etc. A review by the Better Regulation Taskforce in the UK observed in one point that universities have to report to over 100 public agencies and departments, charities and professional bodies for some aspect of their performance (Better Regulation Taskforce, 2000).

Agencification Challenges

As observed in the recent public administration literature, 'agencification' tends to lead to some problems (Bouckaert et al., 2010). On the one hand, delegating responsibilities to highly specialized (semi-) independent agencies leads to coordination problems, particularly in cases where issues cross the borders of one specific agency. On the other hand, separating implementation from the political center makes the latter incapable for steering processes. In the words of Lægreid and Verhoest (2010: 2), "The narrow task definition of agencies, their focus on organizational performance targets, their drive for autonomy, and the decoupling of implementation from policy design creates centrifugal forces, with central and parent departments perceiving a loss of coordination capacity". Furthermore, this has created a situation where programs and organizations are much better able to resists coordination efforts (Lægreid & Verhoest, 2010).

As the problems of fragmentation are coming up, the post-NPM agenda returns its attention to control and coordination (Christensen et al., 2007). We can see examples of 'rationalization' where several agencies have been merged, the control of the center is strengthened via changes in the legal structure, and innovative coordinating mechanisms hope to address the fragmentation issues.

In the next section we will have a closer look at four countries that according to the ENQA 1998 Report (ENQA, 1998) were planning significant changes in their quality framework in the nearest future: the Netherlands, the United Kingdom, Norway, and Denmark. We will analyse their trajectory to an independent quality assurance agency and thereafter examine whether their recent changes and issues can be linked to the known 'agencification' problems.

FOUR CASES

In all four cases we first examine the change in the government-university relations because it is a key shift in the 'regulatory state' model that explains the spread of independent agencies. Then we examine how the regulatory agency has evolved from the 2000s onwards and whether the changes and issues can enlighten us about potential 'agencification' problems.

The Netherlands

The Netherlands was among the forerunners in giving greater autonomy to higher education institutions. In the 1980s, the Netherlands introduced a new steering philosophy that aimed at 'steering at a distance' while requiring ex-post accountability from universities (Neave & van Vught, 1991). The reform was triggered first of all by the expansion of the system. It became clear that it is difficult to manage such a massive sector. Furthermore, the 1970s and early 1980s in the Netherlands were characterized by a doubt that the government is able to plan and steer public sector through a detailed oversight (Huisman & Toonen, 2004). There was thus a feeling that higher education environment has become more complex and dynamic and higher education institutions need more freedom and flexibility in order to adapt to the new environment.

Already in 1983 a conditional funding policy introduced a peer review of research activities (Jeliazkova & Westerheijden, 2004). The 1985 policy paper *Higher Education: Autonomy and Quality*, extended the idea of quality assurance also to teaching. As a result of negotiations between universities and government, universities' professional associations *The Association of Universities (VSNU) and The Association of Universities of Applied Sciences (HBO-Raad)* became the focal point of organizing quality assurance. With this step universities were able to avoid the role of the Ministry's Inspectorate of Education which was known for its highly technical approach and performance indicators at lower levels of education (Huisman, 2003).

Since the end of the 1980s, the core of quality assurance is program evaluation, organized after each 6 years (research universities) or 8 years (universities of applied science), and originally managed by the university umbrella organizations. There were no clear sanctions linked to the assessment results. Enforcement of assessment took place through the Inspectorate for Education under the Ministry of Education, Culture and Science (as currently named), who monitored the evaluation reports and the follow-up activities by universities.

In 2003 a new quality assurance system was established in the Netherlands which introduced both an organizational change and a change in the approach to quality assurance. The old program evaluation was replaced with a program accreditation. A discussion about an accreditation scheme started already in the late 1990s. The previous evaluation system offered a list of comments and recommendations but it did not offer a clear conclusion in the end about the quality of a program. There was a political demand for a stronger accountability instrument. Furthermore, with a transition to the new Bachelor-Master degree structure there was a stronger need to demonstrate the 'proven quality' of Dutch higher education both domestically and abroad (Jeliazkova & Westerheijden, 2004). There was also a need for a more explicit reference framework for judging the level of quality, not to rely only on ad hoc comparisons between programs.

The transition to an accreditation scheme brought along a change in the organizational structure. An independent accreditation body was established, NVAO (the Accreditation Organisation of the Netherlands and Flanders), originally NAO without the Flemish component. NVAO was granted the status of an autonomous administrative body with legal rights according to Dutch legislation (*Zelfstandig bestuursorgan*). It does not report to a particular minister or the Committee of Ministers and the latter has no power over NVAO's operations or decision-making. However, the Committee of Ministers appoints the Board that has the supervisory authority over the organization and the Committee approves its budget, the annual report and the annual accounts.

The process of quality assurance, however, did not change as much as might appear from the reform. The previous process of quality evaluation stayed to a large extent in place. NVAO has a responsibility for making accreditation decisions but the decisions are based on evaluation reports done by other bodies. Although VSNU does not organize the evaluation any more as it did before, it created a separate body QANU to continue with the evaluation work. There are also other organizations on the market that provide the evaluation service to universities. NVAO produces a list of quality agencies that satisfy the requirements of expertise and since 2011 it formally certifies evaluation coordinators.

While the procedure is not so different in its operation, the new system is of course a significant change in its approach to quality. Previously to a large extent the system was evaluating itself, even if there was independent oversight on an ex post basis from the Inspectorate of Education (NVAO Review Report, 2007). In order to strengthen the former system of external review, and to make it internationally more acceptable, the system was revised in several important aspects "by making the system more independent and better aligned with external benchmarks and standards, by having the outcome result in explicit and clear judgements and by strengthening the power of possible sanctions" (NVAO Review Report, 2007).

The year 2011 brought additional changes to the existing quality assurance framework. The change aimed at a more focused and substantive assessment on the one hand, and a lighter accreditation with less paperwork on the other hand (NVAO, 2010). In addition to the program accreditation, institutions may request NVAO to conduct a so-called institutional quality assurance assessment. Should such a thorough audit at the institutional level reveal that an institution's internal quality assurance is in a good order, programmes can get accredited via a 'light' version of the accreditation procedure. The new system constitutes a compromise as universities wished to attain a self-accrediting status and abolish program accreditations as such.

In the summer 2010 the topic of higher education quality assurance reached the front pages of the national media in the Netherlands. One of the largest universities of applied sciences in the country was accused in examination fraud. The reaction from the Minister of Education, Culture and Science was quick and strong. The Ministry's Education Inspectorate was ordered to carry out an investigation. Based on the inspection report, the Vice-Minister responsible for higher education concluded that the quality assurance system in the higher education does not work as expected. He states,

> There is too much liberty in evaluation and quality assurance ... This liberty must go away. Education institutions have a lot of autonomy, but this autonomy comes with responsibility and accountability. Therefore we need to take serious steps in order to restore the trust in the system. (De staatssecretaris ..., 2001)

Next to some specific suggestions for the specific school, the Vice-Minister presented to the Parliament a number of system-wide measures to strengthen control over the sector. The list of suggestions included national examinations in core subjects, external members in examination committees, minimum thresholds for the staff qualifications, etc. Furthermore, the proposal argued that the current evaluation and accreditation system is not sufficient to react effectively on problems and complaints regarding the sector. Regular accreditation by the autonomous Dutch-Flemish accreditation agency (NVAO) should be supplemented by ad hoc inspections by the Ministry's Education Inspectorate.

The new decade introduced a wide social discussion on the future of the Dutch higher education and in 2009 the Minister set up a committee (known as Veerman committee) to review the sustainability of the Dutch higher education. This report, together with the aftermath of the quality scandal, puts another set of proposals on the table. A recently published strategy document "Quality in diversity" (Ministerie ..., 2011) proposes among other a reduction of the student-staff ratio, national standardized tests and external examiners. It proposed a greater role to the Ministry's Inspectorate of Education next to the NVAO in assuring the quality of Dutch degrees. It proposed additional inspections in between the 6 or 8 year accreditation cycle.

Most recently, the Dutch quality agency changed its procedures so that programs are graded on a scale which allows also giving a so-called 'yellow card' without rejecting immediately accreditation. The quality assurance agency earned a high praise from the Parliament for the high number of 'yellow cards' given in the area of Humanities, and a Parliamentarian complemented that 'the agency is doing exactly what it should be doing' (DUB, 2014).

In sum, external quality assurance developed in the Netherlands on the basis of greater autonomy given to universities and in the context of performance and accountability movement. A shift from a 'collegial' evaluation to a 'formal' accreditation brought along also a change in the organizational structure. A professional organization was not any longer fit to fill the task, which led to creating a strictly autonomous public agency with a clear mandate from the Parliament. The relationship between the ministerial inspectorate and the autonomous quality assurance agency is interesting. In case of problems in the system, the Ministry turns to the inspectorate for intervention. While not a typical case of the weakening political core, it refers to some tensions that the distance between the ministry and the agency creates in certain circumstances. We see also a rise in actions that distance the agency from universities and thereby strengthen their legitimacy as guardians of public interest.

While there have been typical responses to fragmentation problems in other areas of higher education, such as mergers of autonomous service units and consolidation of research evaluation schemes, quality assurance system has remained intact. Despite of the concerns of over-evaluation and multiple quality assurance instruments (inc. recently introduced performance contracts), the fragmentation problems have not come up seriously in the agenda.

United Kingdom (England)

Unlike universities in most continental European countries, British universities have had traditionally a high level of autonomy. At the same time, they have a long tradition of professional self-regulation in the form of an external examiner system (Lewis, 2010). In the end of the 1980s, politicians found the self-regulatory approach insufficient in the new environment of an expanding polytechnic and college sector and government Inspectorates started to monitor the quality of polytechnics and colleges (see Brennan & Williams, 2004). In order to avoid a similar strong government inspection, universities gave to their own umbrella body CVCP (Committee of Vice-Chancellors and Principals) a task to set up a quality assurance instrument. The CVCP established an Academic Audit Unit which started to conduct institutional audits of internal quality assurance procedures, on a voluntary, peer-review basis.

The 1988 Education Reform Act and the 1992 Further and Higher Education Act replaced the binary system of universities and polytechnics with a unified higher education system. The Academic Audit Unit was transformed into a separate organization, HEQC (Higher Education Quality Council), still 'owned' by higher education institutions, which continued carrying out academic audits. In parallel, the government established quality assessment committees within Higher Education Funding Councils. A funding council is a non-departmental body (statutory agency) in each part of Britain (England, Wales, Scotland) that distributes public funds to higher education institutions and which have also a statutory responsibility to assess higher education quality. These committees took over the monitoring function of the inspectorates and they also took over many of their staff and evaluation methods. The committee introduced a system of Subject Assessments, a regular subject level teaching quality assessment. The assessment was based on a peer-review and it graded teaching quality on a five-point scale.

In the middle of the 1990s there were thus two major assessment instruments in place, institutional audits and subject assessments, both including a self-evaluation and a peer visit. In addition, universities were subject to the Research Assessment Exercise (again including a peer visit), external examiner control and in some cases to professional accreditation. This system was highly unpopular because it was time and resource consuming. The inspection-like Subject Assessment was particularly unpopular among academics. A joint review by the CVCP and the funding councils examined the issue and as a result a new organization, QAA (Quality Assurance Agency in Higher Education) was established in 1997. QAA is a not-for-profit company and a registered charity. It is jointly 'owned' by university associations and the higher education funding councils, both of which appoint the board of directors. This non-statutory agency took over the two assessment tools – institutional audits and subject assessments. It was claimed that the consolidation of the two activities in one organization would lead to greater efficiency and particularly reduce the burden for universities (Brennan & Williams, 2004).

Concerns regarding over-regulation of the higher education sector continued in the new millennium. The Better Regulation Taskforce in the Blair's cabinet mapped all the regulatory relationships affecting higher education institutions and identified over 100 public agencies and departments, charities and professional bodies to whom the universities are answerable for some aspect of their performance on the basis of statute or contracts (Better Regulation Taskforce, 2000). Government continued to support the idea of subject assessments because of its commitment to competition and consumer choice as an effective regulatory approach in the public sector. Producing and providing information to the public was therefore a major policy direction. Vice-Chancellors proposed that higher education institutions themselves could take greater responsibility for making information public, if freed from the subject assessments (Brennan & Williams, 2004). Subject Assessment was abolished in 2001 and instead a revised institutional audit was launched in 2003. Through the institutional audit process, institutions are expected to demonstrate their commitment to strong internal quality assurance procedures. Institutions are expected to conduct internal reviews of departments or programs, usually involving some inputs from external peers. Institutional audits by the QAA also audit whether universities indeed publicize their various quality reports, such as the internal reviews, external examiner reports, student feedback questionnaires and other sources. The new system was expected to be more 'light touch'.

The quality assurance system in the UK consists of a number of components, such as institutional review audits, Integrated Quality Enhancement and Review (for further education), public information on teaching quality (including National Student Survey), institutions' own internal quality assurance processes, Academic Infrastructure, external examining arrangements, QAA procedure for investigating concerns about standards and quality, and the HEFCE Policy on unsatisfactory quality (QHEG, 2011). To ensure the coherence of such a system, there is a Quality of Higher Education Group, a standing, not time-limited committee in place since 2011. It is jointly owned by the university associations (UUK & GuildHE), HEFCE and the Department of Employment and Learning (UUK et al., 2011). Furthermore, another committee, Higher Education Better Regulation Group, is in place to observe regulation in the sector more broadly. Most recently, England is experimenting with a risk-based approach to quality assurance in higher education, in order to reduce the regulatory burden on universities and focus the quality assurance activities on this part of the system where the quality risks are the biggest (see HEFCE, 2012).

In sum, the evolution towards a quality assurance regime in England, similarly to the Netherlands, is influenced by negotiations between universities and the government, with universities' intention to limit the external control. The nature of the regulatory agency in the UK is somewhat different. It is still strongly linked to the universities but again formally moved away from the universities' umbrella association. Despite of the fact the agency is still close to universities, political steering does not seem to create many problems. Over-burdening of universities with various formats of assessment, however, has been a problem. Still highly fragmented, the system is now coordinated by a standing committee to ensure the coherence of the system.

Norway

Since the early 1990s, a series of reform initiatives in Norway have given more autonomy to universities and strengthened the role of institutional leadership in higher education institutions (Bleiklie et al., 2000, Langfeldt et al., 2008). Unlike many other countries, Norway did not develop a systematic quality assurance system until the 2000s. Nevertheless, an interest in quality issues started to rise already in the 1990s when government experimented with a large-scale five-year evaluation project which aimed at improving educational quality and which came close to formal evaluation exercises introduced in other countries at the same time (Stensaker, 1997). In 1998, government established the Norway Network Council with a task to advise the Minister about higher education issues and to develop a national system for evaluating higher education. Formally, it was a central agency responsible to the Minister and closely linked to the Ministry. Norway retained its traditional system of quality assurance that stood on two pillars: the Ministry regulated the establishment of new programs, and an external examiner system within universities guarded quality standards of higher education programs.

Driven by concerns over increasing student numbers and other challenges facing the higher education sector, the Minister of Education and Research appointed a National Commission, known as the Mjøs-Commission, to assess the Norwegian higher education and offer recommendations for its improvement. Among several other propositions, the Commission suggested establishing a new organization that would accredit higher education programs. According to the commission, such an accreditation agency must be independent (both from the Ministry and institutions) and its Board members should be appointed by the Minister but based on their academic competencies. This suggestion did not get implemented immediately. The Ministry proposed that its own advisory Norway Network Council should be redefined as a quality development organization and given the appropriate tasks and organization. The parliament was on the side of the Mjøs-Commission and wanted to see an independent quality assurance agency written into the new Higher Education Act.

In 2003, a new independent accreditation body, Norwegian Agency for Quality Assurance in Education (NOKUT) was established. It did grow out of the Norway Network Council, hiring many of the same staff and using institutional audits and an improvement-oriented quality assurance system (Stensaker, 2007). It is, however, a professionally independent government agency by its legal status as specified in the Higher Education Act. It is significantly more autonomous than the former Council, and the Ministry can influence its activities only by legal acts. The agency itself can decide the methods and the frequency of accreditation. An important element of the quality assurance system is institutional accreditation. The new system requires that universities have an internal quality assurance system in place, covering all programs, which is evaluated by NOKUT every 6 year. NOKUT and the Research Council of Norway, which assesses research quality, were ordered to try to co-ordinate their evaluation activities in order to minimize the administrative burden on the institutions (Stensaker, 2007).

While NOKUT organizes and conducts the accreditation process both for institutions and for programs, the accreditation decisions are sent to the Minister for the final approval. The double authority shows the separation of an expert decision and political decision. It may well be the case that an expert decision and political decision do not coincide in case of certain nationally relevant context (e.g., regional colleges). Similarly to the Netherlands, the quality assurance agency in Norway also recently strengthened its power and visibility by a tough evaluation round, by rejecting accreditation to a large number of programs (Stensaker, 2011).

In sum, also Norway has created an independent agency but unlike in the UK and in the Netherlands it evolved from a ministerial unit, not from a university association. An interesting element in Norway is the discussion between the Ministry and the Parliament regarding the extent to which an accreditation agency needs to be autonomous from the Ministry. We can see in Norway that adopting a clear accreditation scheme seems to go hand-in-hand with creating a more separate and an autonomous agency. The new agency is not only more autonomous but also more 'single-purpose'. We also see in the Norway that agencies may establish their status in the eyes of the parliament as well as of universities by showing some 'teeth' in their evaluation exercise.

Denmark

With the new Act of Universities of 1993, Denmark replaced its traditional continental university governance model with a new system. The key words of the reform, as stated by the government, were 'deregulation and decentralization, combined with mechanisms to ensure quality' (Thune, 2001). With this act the Ministry of Education transferred a significant authority to higher education institutions and aimed to strengthen the managerial structure of higher education institutions.

The Danish government started to regulate higher education quality quite early compared to its European counterparts. In 1992 it established the Danish Centre for Quality Assurance and Evaluation of Higher Education that was required to evaluate all higher education programs on a regular and systematic basis. The Center grew out of an initiative of the chairmen of the advisory bodies in higher education in the end of the 1980s. The chairmen had initiated a series of pilot evaluations of higher education programs and in the early 1990s they encouraged the Minister of Education to set up an organization to proceed with this work on a more formal basis (Thune, 2001). The new center was formally independent from the Ministry and from universities. It started to evaluate all higher education programs in an interval of seven years, but the evaluations were not part of formal program recognition.

In 1999 the Quality Assurance and Evaluation Center was transformed into the Danish Evaluation Institute (EVA). The new institute maintained its tasks to systematically evaluate education, carry out specific requests from the relevant Ministries, and function as an expertise center in educational evaluation. As a main change its activities were extended to all levels of education. It is an independent organization under the responsibility of the Ministry of Education. It has its board, which is nominated by the Minister, and a high level of autonomy. It is independent in deciding what and how to evaluate but its annual plan is approved by the Minister.

Since its creation, EVA has been experimenting with different evaluation formats. Initially it continued its predecessor's work of regular program evaluations but in 2004 it switched to the format of institutional audits, which emphasizes the role of proper internal quality assurance mechanisms.

In the year 2007 the Parliament passed the Danish Accreditation of Higher Education Act, which introduced a new element in the quality assurance structure. Since then all new and existing university programs need to be regularly evaluated and accredited. The change seems to have a strong international motivation. The accompanying letter to the legal proposal states that "The Danish system for quality assurance of study programs does not fully meet the joint European quality assurance standards" (Explanatory ..., na). It also refers to the OECD's country review of 2005 which points out that the quality assurance of Danish university study programs needs to be strengthened. With the new system universities are expected to be better equipped to document and demonstrate the quality of their programs, both domestically and abroad.

With this act the parliament established also a new accreditation agency – ACE Denmark. This is an independent institution within the public administration, responsible for accrediting all higher education programs. The accreditation decision is based on program evaluations, which are conducted by ACE for Master level degrees (long-cycle programs) and by EVA for lower level studies. Universities may also choose another accreditation agency at their own cost. With this change the Minister's authority to approve study programs was transferred to the accreditation unit and as stated explicitly in the letter to the parliament, "a systematic external element will be introduced in the quality assurance of Danish higher education" (Explanatory ..., na).

In Denmark we can see an interesting transformation of the quality assurance agency. Already in the beginning of the 1990s the task of quality evaluation was given to an independent agency, which had also a somewhat wider responsibility for developing evaluation approaches and evaluation culture. This center was broadened further. After demonstrating its capacity and success in higher education quality evaluation, its repertoire was extended to other educational sectors. A few years ago, however, a separate single-purpose agency was created which is solely responsible for accreditation decisions and evaluating Master level education programs. While the new system is thoroughly justified in a letter to the Parliament, a need for a new agency to carry on the task (as opposed to EVA) is not touched at all.

DISCUSSION

The four countries studied in this paper vary with respect to their higher education system and approach to quality assurance but in all cases a semi-independent agency stands at a central position in the system. Interestingly, the trajectory to the rather similar organizational form has been very different. The quality assurance systems in all the four countries have had some changes in the organizational structure since the

2000s, or at least since the late 1990s, and in all cases these developments strengthen the idea of an autonomous agency as a most effective regulatory structure. The development pattern is also interesting. In all cases the current agency format has been reached through one or more reiterations. In Denmark, the evaluation tasks were originally given to an autonomous agency, which had somewhat broader mission including policy advice. With implementing a formal accreditation scheme, government created a new, single-purpose accreditation agency. In Norway, on the other hand, the movement towards an autonomous agency has been via a council that was part of the central government. Again, with a new accreditation scheme also a new accreditation agency emerged which was both autonomous and 'single-purpose'. In the UK and in the Netherlands the agencies have taken over the tasks from university umbrella organizations.

While the evolution of the quality assurance system has been different in the four countries, there seems to be quite a convergence in the final outcome, perhaps with an exception of the UK. The agencies are commissioned by the Parliament for quality assurance tasks. They are not in a hierarchical structure of the Ministry but they are linked to the Minister via a Board that is nominated by the Minister in charge of higher education. The Minister is also responsible for overseeing the general performance of the agency, requiring regular external evaluations. There are of course functional differences: some accredit institutions, not programs; some conduct the evaluations themselves while others rely on external partners, etc. Nevertheless, the organizational structure and procedures are surprisingly similar.

There seems to be also a link between introducing a new instrument and revising the existing agency structure. A more hierarchical evaluation system (e.g., accreditation) expectedly requires more autonomy from professional organizations (i.e., regulatees) than a collegial peer-oriented evaluation. While cooperation with professional associations seems to work well in case of 'softer' type assessments, harder instruments such as accreditation or formal subject assessments seem to require a greater distance but also a clearer legal mandate.

Does the agency model create problems for higher education quality regulation? We can indeed see some signs that may require awareness and caution in the future. One generic problem of agencification is fragmentation: it is more difficult to coordinate activities of independent agencies. In many countries there are different evaluation instruments in place. Universities have had to accommodate several site visits, provide data to multiple evaluation schemes and organizations, and report to several organizations. The fragmentation issue in the UK is perhaps most visible and it has been explicitly addressed by policy changes. A new quality assurance agency was established to combine two assessment tools, previously under two different organizations. Current fragmentation issues are addressed by a standing committee whose task is to ensure coherence and offer suggestions for improvement if necessary. On the other hand, it is difficult to make a claim that fragmentation problems and evaluation overload originate from the independence of the agencies. Tensions seem to appear often from the fact that universities face different demands from different stakeholder groups: external quality assurance is expected to ensure minimum standards but also work as a transparency tool, it should offer incentives for internal quality improvement but also secure political legitimacy, etc. (Beerkens, 2015). An independent agency may also have a positive role because it allows focussing on one core purpose without blurring responsibilities.

Higher education quality assurance has become a mature regulatory field where autonomous agencies form one corner of the regulatory triangle, together with policy makers (parliament, government) and universities. Complaints about regulatory burden have encouraged many agencies to search for a more 'light-touch' quality assurance mechanism. This pressure tends to lead towards institutional audits as a dominant quality assurance approach. On the other hand, there is a political demand for stricter instruments that serve the goals of accountability and political legitimacy. To respond to these demands and secure their own position in the quality assurance system, agencies offer more critical and publicly visible judgments. These reactions are familiar from the point of view of 'regulatory capture' (Baldwin et al., 2011). Regulatory capture means that regulation may serve more the interests of the regulatees than the public interest. A simple argumentation would claim that agencies serve the interests of universities because of their very strong links with universities, via expertise, career mobility, common interactions, shared history, etc. A more strategic approach to regulatory capture assumes that regulators soften their rules in order to avoid strong criticism from the side of the regulatees. The criticism is likely to reach politicians through universities' 'lobby' and thereby threaten the future of the regulatory agencies. On the other hand, when quality issues are high on the political agenda, tough control and regulation is also in the interest of politicians. Balancing the support of the regulatees and maintaining legitimacy in the eyes of the political principals is the every-day reality of regulatory agencies.

The second generic problem of agencification concerns the weakening political core: policy makers cannot steer independent agencies as closely as they can steer their own departments. This may also create accountability problems. Political executives may feel that they lose control since the public holds them responsible for problems but yet they are not supposed to interfere in agencies' activities (Christensen & Laegreid, 2006). In the Netherlands, a quality scandal indeed brought up questions about the role of the autonomous agency vs the role of the ministerial inspectorate. Even though the agency was not held accountable for the problems, the actions and the proposals give an impression that the ministry sees a need for a more 'operational' force in the form of its own inspectorate.

The political steering capacity of quality assurance agencies is affected also by the rise of the European dimension in quality assurance. The European association of quality assurance agencies is a strong network that strengthens the independence of the agencies. The 'mimetic' and 'normative' isomorphism (see DiMaggio & Powell, 1983) through shared experiences and professional expertise, as well as 'coercive' isomorphism through the European Standards and Guidelines weaken the influence of the national policy on agencies. The agencification at the European level, furthermore, defines quality assurance primarily as a technical, expertise-based exercise as opposed to a political exercise where public goals and objectives are an important starting point.

In conclusion, higher education quality assurance has become a mature regulatory field. Independent quality assurance agencies in higher education are praised for their legitimacy, expertise and credible commitment. At the same time it is helpful to be aware of the weaknesses the agency model may produce. Under certain circumstances agencification may lead to fragmented, uncoordinated policy instruments, it may lead to technical, expertise-based approach to quality assurance that is cut off from political steering, and it may create accountability challenges in the eyes of the public. Most importantly, agencies have become a core actor in higher education quality regulation, an actor with their own identity and strategic interests.

REFERENCES

Baldwin, R., Cave, M., & Lodge, M. (2011). *Understanding regulation: Theory, strategy, and practice.* Oxford, England: Oxford University Press.

Beerkens, M. (2015). Quality assurance in the political context: In the midst of different expectations and conflicting goals. *Quality in Higher Education* (forthcoming).

Better Regulation Taskforce. (2000). *Higher education: Easing the burden.* Retrieved from http://archive.cabinetoffice.gov.uk/brc/publications/2002.html

Blackmur, D. (2008). The public regulation of Higher Education qualities: Rationale, processes and outcomes. In D. F. Westerheijden, B. Stensaker, & M. João Rosa (Eds.), *Quality assurance in higher education: Trends in regulation, translation and transformation.* Dordrecht, The Netherlands: Springer.

Bleiklie, I., Hostaker, R., & Vabo, A. (2000). *Policy and practice in higher education: Reforming Norwegian universities.* London, UK: Jessica Kingsley.

Bouckaert, G., Peters, B. G., & Verhoest, K. (2010) *The coordination of public sector organizations: Shifting patterns of public management.* Basingstoke, England: Palgrave Macmillan.

Brennan, J., & Williams, R. (2007). Accreditation and related regulatory matters in the United Kingdom. In S. Schwarz & D. F. Westerheijden (Eds.), *Accreditation and evaluation in the European higher education area.* Dordrecht, The Netherlands: Kluwer Academic Publishers.

Christensen, T., & Lægreid, P. (Eds.). (2006). *Autonomy and regulation: Copying with agencies in the modern state.* Cheltenham, England: Edward Elgar.

Christensen, T., Lie, A., & Lægreid, P. (2007). Still fragmented government or reassertion of the center. In T. Christensen & P. Lægreid (Eds.), *Transcending new public management: the transformation of public sector reform.* Aldershot, England: Ashgate.

De staatssecretaris van Onderwijs, Cultuur en Wetenschap. (2011). *Beleidsreactie op de eindrapporten alternatieve afstudeertrajecten.* aan de voorzitter van de Tweede Kamer der Staten-Generaal. 20 mei 2011. Retrieved from http://www.rijksoverheid.nl/documenten-en-publicaties/kamerstukken/2011/05/20/beleidsreactie-op-de-eindrapporten-alternatieve-afstudeertrajecten.html

Dill, D. D. (1995). Through Deming's eyes: A cross-national analysis of quality assurance policies in higher education. *Quality in Higher Education, 1*(1), 95–110.

Dill, D. D. (2010). Quality assurance in higher education: Practices and issues. In B. McGaw, E. Baker, & P. P. Peterson (Eds.), *International encyclopedia of education* (3rd ed.). Dordrecht, The Netherlands: Elsevier Publications.

Dill, D. D., & Beerkens, M. (Eds.). (2010). *Public policies for academic quality: Analyses of innovative policy instruments.* Dordrecht, The Netherlands: Springer.

Dill, D. D., & Beerkens, M. (2013). Designing the framework conditions for assuring academic standards: Lessons learned about professional, market, and government regulation of academic quality. *Higher Education, 65*(3), 341–357.

Dill, D. D., & Soo, M. (2004). Transparency and quality in higher education markets. In P. Teixeira, B. Jongbloed, D. Dill, & A. Amaral (Eds.), *Markets in higher education: Rhetoric or reality?* Dordrecht, The Netherlands: Kluwer.

DiMaggio, P. J., & Powell, W. W. (1983). The iron cage revisited: Institutional isomorphism and collective rationality in organizational fields. *American Sociological Review, 48*(2), 147–160.

DUB. (2014). *Tweede Kamer: keuringsstelsel hoger onderwijs functioneert prima.* Retrieved September 4, 2014, from http://www.dub.uu.nl/artikel/nieuws/tweede-kamer-keuringsstelsel-hoger-onderwijs-functioneert-prima.html

Enders, J., & Westerheijden, D. (2011). Policies for quality in higher education – coordination and consistency in EU-policymaking 2000–2010. *European Journal of Higher Education, 1*(4), 297–314.

ENQA. (2003). *Quality procedures in European higher education: An ENQA survey.* ENQA Occasional Papers 5. Retrieved from http://enqa.eu/files/procedures.pdf

ENQA. (2005). *Standards and guidelines for quality assurance in the European higher education area.* Retrieved from http://www.enqa.eu/files/ENQA%20Bergen%20Report.pdf

ENQA. (2008). *Quality procedures in the European higher education area and beyond: Second ENQA survey.* ENQA Occasional Papers 14.

ENQA / Danish Centre for Quality Assurance and Evaluation. (1998). *Evaluation of European higher education: A status report of 1998.*

Ewell, P. (2008). The "quality game": External review and institutional reaction over three decades in the United States. In D. F. Westerheijden, B. Stensaker, & M. João Rosa (Eds.), *Quality assurance in higher education: Trends in regulation, translation and transformation.* Dordrecht, The Netherlands: Springer.

Explanatory Notes to the Draft Bill on the Accreditation Agency for Higher Education (The Accreditation Act). *L294 – Explanatory.* Retrieved from http://acedenmark.eu/fileadmin/user_upload/dokumenter/ Engelske_tekster/Engelsk_oversaettelse_af_bemaerkninger_til_Akkrediteringsloven.pdf

Frazer, M. (1992). Quality assurance in higher education. In A. Z. Craft (Ed.), *Quality assurance in higher education.* London, UK: Falmer Press.

HEFCE. (2012). A risk-based approach to quality assurance: Outcomes of consultation and next steps. Retrieved October 27, 2012, from http://www.hefce.ac.uk/media/hefce/content/pubs/2012/201227/ Risk-based%20quality%20assurance%20consultation%20outcomes.pdf

Hood, C. (1991). A public management for all seasons. *Public Administration, 69*(1), 3–19.

Hood, C., Scott, C., James, O., Jones, G., & Travers, T. (1999). *Regulation inside government: Waste-watchers, quality police, and sleaze-busters.* Oxford, England: Oxford University Press.

Huisman, J. (2003). Institutional reform in higher education: Forever changes? In B. Denters, O. van Heffen, J. Huisman, & P.-J. Klok (Eds.), *Interactive governance and market mechanisms.* Dordrecht, The Netherlands: Kluwer.

Huisman, J., & Toonen, T. (2004). Higher education and university research in the Netherlands: A mixed pattern of control. In C. Hood, O. James, B. G. Peters, & C. Scott (Eds.), *Controlling modern government: Variety, commonality and change.* Cheltenham, England: Edward Elgar.

Jeliazkova, M., & Westerheijden, D. F. (2004). The Netherlands: A leader in quality assurance follows the accreditation trend. In S. Schwarz & D. F. Westerheijden (Eds.), *Accreditation and evaluation in the European higher education area.* Dordrecht, The Netherlands: Kluwer Academic Publishers.

Lægreid, P., & Verhoest, K. (2010). Introduction: Reforming public sector organizations. In P. Lægreid & K. Verhoest (Eds.), *Governance of public sector organizations: Proliferation, autonomy and performance.* Basingstoke, England: Palgrave Maxmillan.

Langfeldt, L., Harvey, L., Huisman, J., Westerheijden, D., & Stensaker, B. (2008). *Evaluation of NOKUT – The Norwegian agency for quality assurance in education, Report 2: NOKUT's national role.* Norway, Europe: Norwegian Ministry of Education and Research.

Lewis, R. (2010). The external examiner system in the United Kingdom. In D. D. Dill & M. Beerkens (Eds.), *Public policies for academic quality: Analyses of innovative policy instruments*. Dordrecht, The Netherlands: Springer.

Majone, G. (1997). From the positive to the regulatory state: Causes and consequences of changes in the mode of governance. *Journal of Public Policy, 17*(2), 139–167.

Ministerie van OCW, Ministerie van ELI. (2011). *Kwaliteit in verscheidenheid: Strategische Agenda Hoger Onderwijs, Onderzoek en Wetenschap.*

Neave, G. (1988). On the cultivation of quality, efficiency and enterprise: An overview of recent trends in higher education in Western Europe, 1986–1988. *European Journal of Education, 23*(1/2), 7–23.

Neave, G., & van Vught, F. (1991). *Prometheus bound: The changing relationship between government and higher education in Western Europe*. Oxford, England: Pergamon Press.

Pollitt, C., & Bouckaert, G. (2004). *Public management reform: A comparative analysis* (2nd ed.). Oxford, England: Oxford University Press.

Pollitt, C., & Talbot, C. (Eds.). (2004). *Unbundled government: A critical analysis of the global trend to agencies, quangos and contractualisation*. London, UK: Routledge.

Pollitt, C., Bathgate, K., Caulfield, J., Smullen, A., & Talbot, C. (2001). Agency fever? Analysis of an international policy fashion. *Journal of Comparative Policy Analysis, 3*(3), 271–290.

Pollitt, C., Talbot, C., Caufield, J., & Smullen, A. (2004). *Agencies: How governments do things through semi-autonomous organizations*. New York, NY: Palgrave Macmillan.

Report of the committee for the review of the Accreditation Organization of The Netherlands and Flanders (NVAO). (2007, September). Retrieved from http://www.enqa.eu/files/NVAO%20review%20report.pdf

Santiago, P., Tremblay, K., Basri, E., & Arnal, E. (2008). *Tertiary education for the knowledge society: Governance, funding, quality* (Vol. 1). Paris, France: OECD.

Schwarz, S., & Westerheijden, D. F. (Eds.). (2007). *Accreditation and evaluation in the European higher education area*. Dordrecht, The Netherlands: Kluwer Academic Publishers.

Stensaker, B. (1997). From accountability to opportunity: The role of quality assessments in Norway. *Quality in Higher Education, 3*(3), 277–284.

Stensaker, B. (2007). The blurring boundaries between accreditation and audit: The case of Norway. In S. Schwarz & D. F. Westerheijden (Eds.), *Accreditationa and evaluation in the European higher education area*. Dordrecht, The Netherlands: Springer.

Stensaker, B. (2011). Accreditation of higher education in Europe – moving towards the US model? *Journal of Education Policy, 26*(6), 757–769.

Talbot, C. (2004). The agency idea: Sometimes old, sometimes new, sometimes borrowed, sometimes untrue. In C. Pollitt & C. Talbot (Eds.), *Unbundled government: A critical analysis of the global trend to agencies, quangos and contractualisation*. London, UK: Routledge.

Thune, C. (2001). Quality assurance of higher education in Denmark. In D. Dunkerly & W. S. Wong (Eds.), *Global perspectives on quality in higher education*. Aldershot, England: Ashgate Publishers.

UUK, HEFCE, GuildHE, DELNI. (2011). *Terms of reference for the quality in higher education group*. Retrieved from http://www.universitiesuk.ac.uk/PolicyAndResearch/Guidance/AccommodationCodeofPractice/Documents/QHEG-2011-01a%20terms%20of%20reference.pdf

van Vught, F. A., & Westerheijden, D. F. (1994). Towards a general model of quality assessment in higher education. *Higher Education, 28*(3), 355–371.

Westerheijden, D. F. (2008). States and Europe and quality of higher education. In D. F. Westerheijden, B. Stensaker, & M. João Rosa (Eds.), *Quality assurance in higher education: Trends in regulation, translation and transformation*. Dordrecht, The Netherlands: Springer.

Maarja Beerkens
Institute of Public Administration
Leiden University

TATYANA KORYAKINA, CLÁUDIA S. SARRICO AND
PEDRO N. TEIXEIRA

2. UNIVERSITIES' THIRD MISSION ACTIVITIES

Challenges To Extending Boundaries

INTRODUCTION

In the context of accelerated international competition on the one hand and financial austerity on the other, economic aspects of knowledge have gained an unprecedented significance. Along with universities' traditional missions of teaching and research, an economic development mission has become an important strategic and policy issue for universities, governments and local authorities (Etzkowitz & Leydesdorff, 1997; Laredo, 2007). While there is no singular definition of what "third mission" means, it can be broadly defined as a third role beyond teaching and research that centres specifically on the contribution to regional development (Jongbloed et al., 2008) or as a wide range of activities involving the generation, use, application and exploitation of knowledge and other university capabilities outside academic environments (Tuunainen, 2005). For universities, cooperation with the external environment has been a way to demonstrate their relevance and secure additional funding. Governments and local authorities look at universities as engines of economic growth and expect them to play major roles in the transition to a knowledge economy. There has been an especially strong emphasis on entrepreneurship, knowledge transfer and collaboration with the business and industrial sectors at national, as well as European Union (EU) levels (European Commission, 2007, 2011). The influence of the EU on European governments can be dated back to the Lisbon strategy, in which heads of EU member states committed themselves to becoming 'the most competitive and dynamic knowledge-based economy in the world'. One of the goals of the Lisbon strategy, reinforced in the Europe 2020 strategy (European Commission, 2010), was to increase investment in research and development to 3 per cent of GDP, with two thirds of this investment being provided by private funding, and to invest 2 per cent of GDP into higher education.[1] Subsequent EU policy documents encouraged universities to develop more external interactions with industry and society and modernize institutional governance arrangements in order to promote innovation and assist change (European Commission, 2008).

A recent communication from the European Commission stressed that the contribution of higher education to growth and jobs can be enhanced through 'close,

E. Reale & E. Primeri (Eds.), The Transformation of University Institutional and Organizational Boundaries, 63–82.

effective links between education, research and business – the three sides of the same "knowledge triangle", and, furthermore, partnership and cooperation with business should be viewed as a "core activity" of higher education institutions' (European Commission, 2011).

Besides explicit policy imperatives for universities to engage in cooperation with industry and business, third mission activities are an important part of the income diversification efforts of European universities in the current climate of financial austerity (Johnstone & Marcucci, 2010). Income diversification has been defined as generation of revenue beyond government appropriation through commercialization of research, technology transfer, consulting, life-long learning and customized courses, generating funds from assets and alterations in financial decision-making and management as well as other activities (Ziderman & Albrecht, 1995). Recent studies into the changing nature of university income have demonstrated that institutions all over Europe have taken considerable steps towards income diversification (Shattock, 2008).

In order to respond to this complex external environment, higher education institutions all over Europe have been adapting their internal goals, strategies and structures, professionalizing their services, developing new skills and institutionalising their existing practices. As the weakness of Europe in the face of a globalized economy has been identified in the lack of efficient knowledge transfer between research institutions, including universities, and industry and business (European Commission, 2007; van der Wende, 2009), it is important to know what barriers exist at the national level and what institutional features are considered as impediments to greater success in third mission activities.

This chapter examines universities top and middle managers' perceptions at two Portuguese universities on relations with the external environment. It aims at contributing to and improving current knowledge about an emergent phenomenon of income diversification and institutionalisation of third mission of universities, as considerable knowledge gaps still exist with respect to universities' engagement with the external environment and its impact on internal governance and management. Therefore, we will try to answer the following research questions:

- What do university managers perceive as external barriers towards third mission activities?
- What do university managers identify as internal barriers?
- What are different and converging elements between different universities?

In the next section we present governance changes that paved the ground for organisational transformations towards entrepreneurial governance and discuss organisational tensions regarding this transformation. Then, we briefly outline the methodological choices of the study and the Portuguese higher education landscape. We proceed with the main results of the study and in the end, we draw some conclusions.

THEORETICAL FRAMEWORK

Changes in University Governance and Internal Transformations of Universities

In recent years, especially in Continental Europe, the traditional forms of university governance have come under pressure (Paradeise et al., 2009; Shattock, 2014). There has been a considerable loss of confidence in the capacity for self-governance by the academic community. At the same time, strong state regulation has become subject to a fundamental ideological critique, in higher education as in other domains. In Europe, New Public Management reforms (Pollitt, 1990; Hood, 1991) have led to changing modes of inter-organizational steering as well as institutional governance of universities. According to Paradeise et al. (2009), the reforms focused on changing beliefs, whereby public agencies were induced to change from a bureaucratic mode to an entrepreneurial one and started operating as business enterprises in the market. It was believed that implementation of business techniques in higher education would provide the incentive for universities to improve the quality of education and research, to improve academic productivity, to encourage innovation and, in general to improve the services the system offers to society (Dill, 1997).

There are several aspects of higher education governance that have been redefined in the course of reforms in various European countries. One of the most significant reforms observed in the past decades has been the increased autonomy given to higher education institutions (de Boer & File, 2009). The state has been increasingly taking a more supervisory and 'steering at a distance' role by delegating its decision-making power to the institutional leadership and governance (Van Vught, 1994). At the same time the government has tightened control over higher education performance, shifting from *a priori* evaluation to *a posteriori* evaluation regime (Neave, 2012).

Another aspect worth mentioning is the proliferation of policy actors in general and the diversification of policy instruments in particular which has suggested that the relationship between the state and other non-state actors in higher education delivery and financing has changed from "hierarchical" to a "network" relationship (Bleiklie et al., 2011). In this context the concept of a stakeholder has become especially prominent in recent decades. According to Jongbloed et al. (2008), the term *stakeholder* points to a major shift in the roles assigned to those who participate in higher education institutions' decision-making as representatives of external society, just as it points to an equally major shift in the obligations to render accounts to the general public or to agencies acting in its name.

As the direct role of the state is reduced and the autonomy of the individual universities increases, universities are becoming "organisational actors" (Kruecken & Meier, 2006), i.e., integrated, goal-oriented entities that deliberately choose their own actions. Stensaker et al. (2014) argue that many reform attempts in the public sector have incorporated globalized ideas about how modern organisations should look. Such modern organisations are often said to emphasize leadership, communication, result achievement, proper decision-making structures, and an active and engaged board setting out the strategic direction of the organization (Schultz et al., 2000). One such globalized idea or templates for higher education institutions has been that of the entrepreneurial university (Clark, 1998; Etzkowitz, 2003).

Entrepreneurs in a business world are individuals who are innovative, independent, and willing to assume proportionately high risks for the potential of big returns:

> The function of entrepreneurs is to reform or revolutionize the pattern of production by exploiting an invention, or more generally, an untried technological possibility for producing a new commodity or producing an old one in a new way... To undertake such new things is difficult and constitutes a distinct economic function, first because they lie outside of the routine tasks which everybody understands, and secondly, because the environment resists in many ways. (Schumpeter, 1942, p. 13)

The contemporary notion of entrepreneurship is distinguished from previous usage in a sense that it brings with it a shift from serendipitous and individual to organised and social. For example, in higher education, entrepreneurialism can be defined neither in pure economic forms, nor as an individual undertaking only. As non-profit organisations, public higher education institutions cannot risk taxpayers' money in the hope of big monetary returns. They also use generated income for strategic development of activities of failed markets, or recycle it into entrepreneurial academic activity, i.e., use the surplus as a start-up capital for new ventures (Buckland, 2009).

Thus, central to the idea of the entrepreneurial university is its proactive and opportunistic attitude (Clark, 1998). The entrepreneurial university exploits its strengths in order to achieve maximum political and financial gains in the marketplace, relying on the initiative and risk-taking of individuals and groups in different parts of the institution and a clear managerial framework from the top. According to Shattock (2005), entrepreneurialism stimulates external collaboration notably with industry and commerce, and reinforces academic performance by attracting additional resources and widening the research and teaching agenda. Such activity produces self-reliance and less dependence on the state. Therefore, entrepreneurial forms of management are most likely to be found when the institution needs to generate income or to enhance its reputation in a variety of different ways in order to prosper or to survive (Shattock, 2008; Etzkowitz, 2003). Although there is no clear cut answer for what entrepreneurial management should be, as, in the words of Clark (2004) "... complex universities operating in complex environments require complex differentiated solutions"; there are some common features that have been mentioned by authors studying entrepreneurial universities (Clark, 1998; Sporn, 1999; Shattock, 2008):

- *clear mission statements and goals*

There is a growing tendency of universities to define their "own" organisational goals which has become apparent through the development of mission statements, university strategies and the implementation of strategic planning and related management practices (Kruecken & Meier, 2006; Machado et al., 2008). According to Eastman (2006), as institutions move away from the state towards the market, their goals become narrower, their administrative hierarchies become more pronounced and the power of their faculty diminishes.

- *committed leadership*

It has been observed that when income is derived from many sources, institutional management must be sufficiently flexible to respond to opportunities that arise, but at the same time contained by a broader university strategy for the institution not to lose the sense of purpose (Williams, 1992). These requirements have led in many cases to strengthening the role of central administration (Bleiklie & Kogan, 2007; Clark, 1998; Williams, 1992). Strong central leadership is seen as the key to institutional success and this leadership is as likely to be managerial as academic. The increased autonomy of institutions also gives more power to institutional leaders to become agents of change.

- *entrepreneurial culture*

Successful implementation of third stream activities also depends on the entrepreneurial spirit of members of the institution and on cultural and organisational conditions necessary to support these ventures (Clark, 1998). Senior administrators can be essential to these initiatives. In particular, they can establish what Clark (ibid.) calls the "steering core" for entrepreneurial efforts. Developing and sustaining a culture supportive of change requires leaders who are oriented to problem solving, operate on trust and with openness, are self-critical, are internally responsive and flexible, and provide expert attention (Davies, 2001).

The above mentioned organisational features are usually associated with the ability of higher education institutions to successfully engage in third mission activities. However, despite isomorphic pressures for entrepreneurial transformation, cooperation with society has been a rather complex process (Pinheiro et al., 2012; Whitley, 2008), not least due to inherent characteristics of universities, as well as broader features of political economy. In the next section we present some of the reasons for this complexity.

Tensions and Ambiguities within Universities

Pinheiro et al. (2012) argue that there has been a readiness within existing analyses to assume that universities are simple, strategic actors able to respond to a well-articulated set of regional or societal needs. However, they posit, the reality is that universities are enormously diverse entities: the very idea of a university rests on its capacity to balance competing tensions and hold together diverse constituencies in ways that help to address multiple goals. The authors distinguish five ambiguities through which the complexity of universities as organisations and institutions can be described: of intention; of understanding, of history, of structure and of meaning.

First of all, universities have been conceived as having relatively ill-defined and multiple goals that are often at odds with one another. The decision-making power inside universities is spread over a large number of units and actors. Universities are compared to federal systems, rather than centralised ones: semi-autonomous departments and schools, chairs and faculties act like small sovereign states as they pursue distinctive self-interests and stand over against the authority of the whole (Clark, 1983).

Second, the results of teaching and research are difficult to predict in advance, which creates an *ambiguity of understanding*. The role of universities in regional development, for example, showed considerable different results from locality to locality, even in cases where universities have similar sizes, institutional profiles and core competencies (Pinheiro et al., 2012). Whitley (2008) also points out to inherent uncertainty of public scientific research and the prevalent role of international scientific communities in establishing research priorities and evaluating the research results. Thus, the universities have limited discretion over setting collective objectives, division of scientific labour and achieving organisational goals. This characteristic suggests that central coordination of third stream activities based on exploitation of scientific research would be highly constrained (Musselin, 2014).

The *ambiguity of history* pertains to university structures being largely shaped by path dependencies or past trajectories, resulting from the interplay between local traditions and environmental adaptations. Kruecken (2011) assumes that universities, which in the past showed a great degree of openness toward their social environments, will incorporate new organisational templates (e.g., entrepreneurial university) easier than those whose organisational history was mainly based on a sense of elitism. The ambiguity of history can be applied to a national context as well, as culture and history vary considerably in different national settings, namely regarding funding mechanisms, academic labour markets, and governance arrangements. The *ambiguity of structure* term is used to describe a specific way in which universities are organised. Organisational structures have reflected the claims of professional control by joining discipline-based departments into faculties and thus forming the building blocks of higher education institutions. Reflecting this arrangement, higher education institutions were called "loosely-coupled systems" (Weick, 1976). This term implies a relative lack of coordination; a relative absence of regulations; little linkage between the concerns of senior staff as managers and those involved in the processes of teaching and research; a lack of congruence between structure and activity; differences in methods, aims and even missions between departments; little lateral interdependence among departments; infrequent inspection; and the "invisibility" of much that happens (McNay, 1995; Musselin, 2007).

Finally, the *ambiguity of meaning* is related to the notion that universities are highly symbolic entities characterised by a prevalence of various sub-cultures and their respective norms, identities and traditions (DiMaggio & Powell, 1983). Among other things, this implies that internal stakeholder groups not only sense external dynamics differently, but also disagree in the ways in which university structures, functions and traditions ought to be locally adapted (Pinheiro et al., 2012).

Based on the theoretical framework, we may conclude that third mission of universities has both isomorphic and diversifying forces. On the one hand universities are placing higher priority on local and regional needs in order to gain external legitimacy and mediate funding dependencies. On the other hand, inherent institutional characteristics of higher education institutions and individual organizational profiles may lead to different outcomes.

Keeping in mind these tensions and ambiguities we will proceed with the analyses of the Portuguese universities and the challenges that income diversification and third mission activities present for university governance and management in the perception of the institutional leadership.

METHODOLOGY

To analyse the perceptions of university managers of the relations with the external environment, a case-study approach was chosen and two case studies were conducted at Portuguese public universities. The two sampled universities differ in size, location, age and study programmes offer. Their organisational structures are also different: University A has a flat management structure without intermediate units (faculties), while University B is organised into autonomous faculties and institutes some of which are subdivided into departments. University A has an explicit regional mandate and adopted a foundation status in 2009. University B is a classical university located in a large metropolitan area.

A total of 28 semi-structured interviews with top management (vice-rectors, pro-rectors, and administrators) and middle management (faculty deans, heads of departments) were conducted during 2010–2011. Academics in management positions were selected because they are the ones in charge of formal decisions, they have a broader view of organisational processes and they assume a role of a buffer between government and their institution and between institutional administration and academics. The interviews were analysed with the help of content analysis software, resulting in a grid with different dimensions and categories which were developed from two main sources: interview data and theoretical framework. The categories included the following titles: strategy, success factors, constraints, incentives, motivations and environmental context. The data from the interviews were confirmed and completed by documentary analysis. The interviews were coded in the following way: UA – University A; UB – University B; TM – top manager; HD – the Head of Department, FD – Faculty Dean. Additionally, each interview was assigned a number.

NATIONAL HIGHER EDUCATION LANDSCAPE

Portuguese higher education governance has experienced considerable transformations in the past years. The major organisational changes were prompted by a higher education governance reform. Following the OECD report of December 2006 and its recommendations, a reform of the legal-juridical system of higher education was prepared and subsequently approved by the Parliament in the autumn of 2007 (Law, 62/2007). The Law (RJIES – acronym in Portuguese) recognised the principle of diversity of internal organisation and enabled each higher education institution to develop its own statutes within a broad framework. This broad framework included a number of significant changes: fewer members in the main governing body – General Council, obligatory participation of external members and more power to rectors. One of the main changes introduced by this law is the possibility of a public institution to adopt a status of a public foundation governed by private law. One of the underlying conditions to become a foundation university was the ability to raise 50% of its income from other than government block grant sources. University foundation has potentially the following advantages: borrow and raise funds; full control of budgets to achieve objectives; set administrative and management procedures; create own academic careers; set salaries and reward systems; set criteria and size of student enrolments. They are funded according to 5-year strategic plans presented to the Ministry. The governance bodies of the foundation are the Board of Trustees and the Auditor. The government appoints the Board of Trustees, following the proposal and the approval of the General Council of the university. The Board of Trustees is composed of external stakeholders recognised as highly qualified and with relevant professional experience.

Overall, the reform was aimed at making universities more flexible, strategic actors, able to connect to their external environments. Although it is too early to determine the impact of these changes at the institutional level on the ability of higher education institutions to expand their third stream activities and income diversification, they may serve as catalysts for change in this direction.

The Portuguese governance reform was implemented in the environment of financial austerity and Europe-wide economic crisis. Since 2001 Portugal has experienced a fiscal crisis, breaching the stability pact in that year and leading to the adoption of painful budgetary measures. This has led several governments to freeze promotions and salaries in the public sector (including public higher education), to cut higher education's budget and to restrict higher education institutions' level of expenditure (even when using their own resources). Thus, the last years were characterised by significant financial difficulties for public higher education institutions. These budgetary cuts have been even more complex because staff expenditures have continued to present a strong tendency to grow due to the increasing qualification of the staff (especially the academics) and the financial addition that it encompassed. Furthermore, since 2007 the institutions were also obliged to pay deductions to the pension fund (7.5% – 11% of the total amount of salaries), which aggravated their financial standing. This situation has led higher education institutions to pursuing non-government revenue streams, as well as competitive public funds, both national and international.

The main source among earned income has been rising tuition fees, although other areas such as research funding, EU programmes and the commercialization of services have all gained increasing relevance (Teixeira et al., 2014).

MAIN RESULTS

The results are part of an exploratory study on the impact of income diversification on Portuguese universities' governance and management. Although third stream activities comprise multiple forms of engagement with diverse stakeholders, we only analysed third stream activities that were mentioned by the interviewees in relation to income diversification.

Challenges of Academic Career Regulations

From the perspective of the universities' top and middle managers, quality of teaching and research was the most important factor for successful income generation. As tuition fees and research grants are the largest income streams in universities' budgets, having top academics and outstanding reputation has become a prerequisite for financial sustainability:

> I usually say that contrary to a firm, a university's capital is not the land where it is installed, not the buildings, not the machines; its capital is its human capital. (UAHD9)

This result corroborates findings of Liefner (2003) whose respondents in six US and European universities identified the quality of academics as a key determinant in university success. Di Gregorio and Shane (2003, cited in Rossi, 2009) suggest that intellectual eminence plays an important role in the universities' ability to commercially exploit their research.

Following the national legislative changes, political commitments in the European context and the OECD directives both universities established an internal quality assurance system, which allows a regular collection, processing and comparing of standardised data regarding various activities. In both universities an internal quality assurance system monitors, in the first place, teaching and learning. The quality of research is assessed through the external evaluation coordinated by the National Science and Technology Foundation (FCT) At the time of interviews, there were no formal quality practices concerning third mission activities (e.g., technology transfer) and no regular data gathering at the central level which means that information on initiatives developed by different basic units cannot be used for strategic planning. However, some change can be expected as the academic employment statutes were changed in 2009 (Decree-Law, 205/2009). Among other aspects the new statutes foresaw the need for each university to promote regular evaluations of its staff, based on four criteria: quality of teaching; research performance; contribution to third mission activities and participation in the management of academic activities. At University A the proposed criteria and their weights in the overall evaluation were: teaching – 0%–60%; research – 20%–60%; knowledge transfer – 0%–20%; university management – depending on professional category, 0%–100% (0% for assistant and associate professors; 100% for positions that require exclusive dedication to university management, for example, the Rector). At University B indicators for quality assessment of entrepreneurial activities were also suggested: patents filed; value of research and technology transfer contracts in connection with intellectual property; number and success of start-ups (measured by employment and business volume). There were also plans to evaluate the technology transfer office as well according to the following indicators: support to researchers, stimulation, dissemination and training activities, and the outcomes of the above activities.

The new Statutes also intend to make mobility between sectors easier, namely to enable university professors to move to companies to develop projects. The preamble of the reviewed statutes indicates "the creation of conditions for the cooperation between universities and other organizations" as an important reason for the reform. In the new framework university professors may be freed from their university duties, for specified periods, to carry out extension services or research projects outside their university. The effectiveness of these new mechanisms will depend on the regulations set up internally by each institution and also on the way they will be implemented in practice.

The evaluation of academic performance is related to the question of career progression. The rules for career assessment and progression have been cited as one of the major constraints for a larger involvement of academic staff in cooperation with industry, business companies and the society at large. There is no tradition, in Portugal, of differentiation in remuneration of the academic staff (such as merit-pay), other than what concerns the different categories of academic staff, salaries being rigidly fixed according to these categories and to the number of years of work in each one of these.

A career assessment situation occurs only at particular moments centered around a process of promotion, a public competition for a vacant position or at the end of a temporary contract, to be changed into a permanent one. The distribution of importance of each activity (teaching, research, management) has been usually skewed towards research performance. Thus, the main driver for an academic career progression is research performance. Such activities as consultancy work, contract research for industry or business companies, service provision for the local community have had no or very little impact on career assessment:

There is an area that I think is fundamental and where there should be a significant alteration for this question of valorization [of the service mission] to make sense, that is the question of academic career statutes. (UATM11)

From the point of view of a scientific career, this type of work [service to community] in many cases does not count in terms of evaluation and thus represents an additional effort asked of an academic.

We are talking about providing services... this line in the curriculum vitae has an absolutely marginal or null value from the point of view of public competition evaluators. (UAHD13)

These findings are confirmed by Jongbloed et al. (2008) who point out that criteria of academic performance largely do not take into account engagement with non-academic communities. While *publish or perish* culture may be found in the prestigious universities, the academic workload and teaching responsibilities determine the terms of employment in the more teaching oriented institutions. A case-study analysis of Norwegian, Finnish and South African universities by Pinheiro (2012) also revealed an absence of macro- (government) and meso- (university) level mechanisms motivating academics to become actively involved with third stream activities.

Cultural Challenges

Culture can be defined as a pattern of basic assumptions, invented, developed or discovered by a given group, as it learns to cope with its problems of external adaptation and internal integration that has worked enough to be considered valid (Schein, 1992). The strength of an organisational culture is a function of the stability of the group, the length of time that the group has existed, the intensity of the group's experiences of learning and the strength and clarity of the assumptions held by the founders and leaders of the group (Schein, 1990).

The integrated entrepreneurial culture is one of the components of Clark's constituents of universities' transformation (1998). The entrepreneurial culture is generally characterised not only by the willingness to take risks and to experiment with new things, but by the ability to evaluate those ventures, learn collectively from experience, and transfer the essence of experience across the university (Davies, 2001).

The importance of the organisational culture has been emphasized by almost one third of participants. At University A, organisational culture was considered by interviewees as propitious to income diversification.

> The university has always tried to be innovative and pioneering. I know that this is very subjective but I feel that this culture exists, our own culture. (UATM1)

> I think we can say that in our DNA there already exists, is implicit to almost all of our professors, researchers, students, a notion that we exist, we work, or we research, or we teach because in a way we want to contribute to society. (UATM11)

On the contrary, interviewees at University B mainly spoke of the lack of entrepreneurial culture, both inside the institution and generally in Portugal.

> Maybe our problem is not having an internal appreciation of entrepreneurial activities; in our [organisational] culture. (UBHD8)
> The first step to success is becoming aware of the fact that we are looking for new income streams. However, in Portuguese culture, this awareness is not common and immediate. (UBTM2)

One faculty's director related that pro-activity in terms of knowledge valorisation is not part of the university's academic culture yet. He reflected on the role of the technology transfer office, for example:

> Technology transfer office cannot be based on the American model in a sense that its staff can stay in their office and the scientist will go there and knock on the door. Here they have to be more active, they have to talk and try to excite the scientists. And it is not easy. (UBFD4)

Nevertheless, respondents from University B pointed out that organisational culture is changing and there is a greater proximity between academics and external environment. It has also to be mentioned that due to its size and decentralized structure, the extent to which organisational changes are being implemented varies from faculty to faculty. It may be suggested that a higher degree of "academic capitalism" regime can be noted in some research units and institutes, as well as in interface units.

Successful cooperation between industry and the university requires a special kind of synergy. To achieve a successful cooperation agreement, both parties need to be aware of each other's interests and objectives as well as each other's complementary strengths. The interviewees in our study have mentioned the importance of such awareness:

> Some academics want a perfect intervention. A perfect intervention usually bypasses the needs of companies and therefore there is a misunderstanding and a mismatch of expectations between the actors. It leads, from the internal and the external point of view, to a certain devaluation [of cooperation]. (UATM1)

> I believe that what we do not yet feel on the part of companies is that they treat this relationship with a certain humility and sustainability. The companies have many problems and come very biased, money-oriented to be able to pay salaries [to their employees] and support their own company. (UAHD12)

The respondents also highlighted the limits to how closely higher education and industry can work together and significant cultural differences between the two.

> Sometimes it may not be compatible. I can get money through business and at the same time do research with them. They do not like it very much, they want results for yesterday, very fast things and science is something that takes time, it has a very special pace. (UAHD16)

The university scientist usually uses a long-term approach to research and is devoted to academic freedom and publication. Faculty members are typically concerned with career progression which heavily depends on research performance. In some academic departments, applied research may not be rewarded as much as teaching or basic research. On the other hand, the industry culture emphasizes applied research, secrecy, protection through patents and typically employs a product-driven approach.

Another cultural aspect worth mentioning is the perceived lack of scientific culture in small and medium enterprises, which represent the major part of the Portuguese economy. In the words of one head of department:

> The Portuguese society is not prepared to finance education, the training of its staff. Therefore, American models are very interesting but in Portugal maybe 30 years from now the society will get there. (UAHD13)

It was recognized by the interviewees though that despite existing cultural differences, universities, industry and business are moving towards each other. There is an understanding that practical and theoretical knowledge can and should complement each other. In the words of one of the interviewed: 'the gap that existed in the past is beginning to narrow a little' (UAHD13). Our findings show that cultural empathy and trust are key success factors in knowledge transfer. Hatakenaka (2004) in her work about university-industry partnerships states that developing partnerships is about developing a rationale for joint action. The more the rationale is shared and understood by both parties across boundaries, the more robust the partnership will be. And according to our results we may add that this rationale is developed through personal relations, through successful networking and good communication.

Managerial Challenges

An increased importance of management and administrative staff has been noticed at both universities. It was reported that there is a lack of a new type of professionals who can "interpret" scientific knowledge for industrialists and other external audiences, so that it makes sense to them. These professionals are not simply administrators, academics or managers – they are all three at once. They understand the motives and interests of all three communities. At both universities, respondents mentioned the need of such professionals and an attempt to create such a new "breed" of administrative staff:

He needs to have a grasp on technology that is being analysed, knowledge of the market, management skills, financial and economic skills, interpersonal communication skills, negotiation skills, let alone the knowledge of legislation. Even though it is not us who will write the contract, we have to be able to tell how the contract should be elaborated. Here there are seven or eight characteristics that we would have if we had seven or eight people working together, but a knowledge manager has to have them all. (UATM 11)

Other skills that interviewees felt to be lacking or needed more development are international research project management, marketing and fund raising.

Another factor reported by the interviewees is the poor communication within universities. This relates to communication at different levels: between the centre and the academic units (departments at University A and faculties at University B); between different academic units; between research centres and between individuals. At University A the complaints were mainly from department heads in relation to the central administration. At University B, the lack of communication was noticed more between different faculties. As the university has a decentralized structure, the interviewees admitted the existence of a "protective", "non-sharing" culture at faculty level.

Interviewees also referred to poor communication in terms of data collection about research and entrepreneurial activities at each academic unit and its dissemination among university community as well as insufficient information about funding opportunities. They feel better communication would facilitate collaborative research within the institution and improve individual and research groups' funding opportunities.

The problem of communication can be related with still weak strategic steering of third stream activities. While both universities had an overall institutional strategy or strategic documents, there were no formal income diversification strategies at the institutional level. There were strategic lines that included income diversification as one of other priorities and there were talks at the management meetings about the need to supplement government block grant with additional income sources:

UB has various basic units and each one of them has its own specificity. We have a meeting with faculties' directors once a month. We cannot tell them what they have to do to have their own revenue. It is impossible. Each director decides what has to be done. We can only tell them that they have to look for additional revenue. (UBTM3)

As a consequence, there was no tight control over the income diversification process at the central level. The top managers often referred to income diversification as a process that was developed locally, at the basic unit and individual levels. Each faculty, department and research unit seemed to work autonomously in this direction.

Funding Pressures

According to the respondents from both universities, funding changes have powerfully influenced the university responses to seeking additional resources. The main changes pointed out relate to diminishing state funding to higher education institutions in relative terms and the increased funding for research available on a competitive basis.

> There is much more access to competitive funding, both from competitive projects of FCT and AdI (Innovation Agency), as well as from projects funded by the European Union. Thus, in relation to the past if not ten years, but definitely, 25 years, the situation has changed radically. (UAHD9)

However, income diversification is not only revenue from research contracts. Another important stream relates to the service mission of the university. In this respect the role of the state has arguably been far less significant. It is felt that while cooperation between university and society is high on the agenda a regulatory framework for this cooperation is missing, probably meaning that there are few opportunities for state funding.

The economic crisis that started in 2008 was perceived by the interviewees to be a threat to generating revenue from third stream activities:

> It is a lot more difficult to obtain other kinds of funding either through the state, local administration or through other foundations. Because these sources also eventually run out of money. And with a crisis that we are experiencing now, I am afraid we will suffer from the decrease in financial availability of these entities. (UBFD9)

The interviewees demonstrated preoccupation with the private sector's ability to support higher education in the current economic climate. The top managers at University B reported that, for example, the funding base of private companies and philanthropic foundations has been affected by the economic crisis, which had an impact on their donating capacity.

As public funding represents the biggest share of universities' budgets, fluctuations in public allocations were perceived as having the biggest impact. From the perspective of top managers at University A, there was a minimum threshold of public funding that guaranteed the university's normal operations. They estimated it as at least 50% of the total university budget. It has been noted that high levels of uncertainty in obtaining financial resources negatively affect the establishment of medium- and long-term scientific agendas, attractiveness of human resources and in some cases—in the experimental sciences—the maintenance of conditions to develop research and teaching activities (Horta, 2008).

> It is necessary to have investments, to have equipment. If there is no equipment, what can we do? We are very conditioned in this respect. To buy equipment

nowadays is very complicated, only through research units or special investment programs. (UAHD6)

The interviewees also mentioned that annual budget allocation complicates long-term strategic planning. Top managers at both universities preferred multi-annual funding, which presupposes a higher degree of financial autonomy. They also advocated for a public funding allocation system which includes incentives for certain outcomes.

CONCLUDING REMARKS

This chapter focused on academic managers' perceptions regarding barriers towards development of third income activities. By presenting an evidence-based account of this issue, we seek to contribute to an on-going debate regarding organisational transformations due to various environmental pressures (Paradeise et al., 2009; Whitley & Glaeser, 2014). The analysis of the interviews showed that according to the respondents, there are more external than internal challenges for developing third mission activities. The major obstacle was related to the structure of the academic career, in particular, to the evaluation of academic staff's work and its influence on career advancement. The absence of reward and incentive systems impedes tighter coupling of third mission activities with the primary activities of teaching and research (Pinheiro, 2012). In relation to this, career incentives need to be changed and the third mission activities such as consulting, services to the community, contracts with industry and business enterprises need to be valued. The tight career regulations by the state point out to weak academic and staffing autonomy. According to a study by the EUA (Estermann et al., 2011), Portugal occupies 21st place out of 28 European countries in terms of academic autonomy, which includes the ability of higher education institutions to decide on overall student numbers, admission mechanisms, and capacity to introduce and terminate programmes among others. It is in 18th place in terms of staffing autonomy which relates to capacity to decide on recruitment procedures, dismissals, promotions and salary levels.

Financial pressures were another major challenge for university managers. Funding allocation mechanisms and current financial situation of Portuguese higher education do not allow room for financial maneuvering, making it difficult for higher education institutions to respond to emerging opportunities or maintain existing commitments (Whitley, 2008). If universities do not receive additional resources there is little incentive for them to set up organizational structures that promote entrepreneurial activity (Williams & Kitaev, 2005). Funding of third mission activities raises a lot of questions. Are these activities an end in itself as part of the move towards the knowledge society and therefore part of mainstream activities? Or do universities seek third stream income in order to generate a surplus for "traditional missions" of teaching and research run better? (ibid.) Our case studies suggest that financial stringency has been the main driver for third stream activities. However, a great part of complementary funding, especially for research, comes from public sources, national or international. Therefore, there can be observed a paradoxical relationship between funding and third stream activities that needs to be clarified by clearer government policies and regulations.

Despite similarity of norms, values, and regulations in the institutional context, there can be observed a certain degree of differentiation in the way third mission activities are institutionalized within each university. There is still a great amount of ambiguity in relation to third stream activities and income diversification. The ambiguity of history was revealed in the role of path dependencies in the process of cooperation with the external environment. UA and UB have different institutional profiles, location, size and history which influenced their orientation in relation to third mission activities. UA is strongly marked by its region while UB's central location provides it with opportunities to cater for mostly service oriented public and private companies in the areas of law, geography and territorial planning, and arts and humanities. Thus, stereotyping institutions by type of third mission activities could be a mistake as both universities engage in various types of cooperation.

Although there were changes towards more centralisation and more managerial control over research, third stream activities are scattered across the academic and research units, showing different degrees of involvement. It seems that these activities are still conducted in a somewhat ad hoc manner by enthusiastic academics, without formal procedures being in place, such as reward mechanisms and quality assurance, for example, which confirms universities' structural ambiguity. In terms of ambiguity of meaning, we found a co-existence of two kinds of normative demands within the universities. One set of norms relates to complying with the imperative of the day, becoming more entrepreneurial and market-oriented in order to obtain legitimacy and to conform to the outside pressures. Another set of norms relates to maintaining and supporting traditional academic roles and activities which hold a great value to the interviewees. However, at UA the organisational culture was perceived by the respondents as propitious to the development of third stream activities. The interviewees were unanimous about the innovative spirit of their institution and about its uniqueness in the national higher education landscape. The university managed to create an entrepreneurial narrative, which is supported by different organisational levels. At UB, a weak entrepreneurial culture was mostly referred to as a barrier for successful income diversification.

The role of institutional leadership seems to be important as it is up to university leaders to consolidate their organisations around common goals, communicate university's skills to the outside community, and create spaces for interaction and patterns for replication of successful partnerships. The literature suggests that the success of income diversification activities and their sustainability is in the ability to replicate or institutionalise existing initiatives and turn them into institutional templates (Etzkowitz, 2003). To do so, an analysis of what is being done inside the institution is required, as well as priority setting and communication among the actors. Insufficient communication between the top and middle management was reported at both universities.

This chapter presented results of a small-scale study with a statistically non-representative sample. However, the study had an explorative character and its results can inform future research. For example, other levels within each institution which may present further insights into the nature of university third stream activities and income diversification can be addressed. Further research into variations of change among individual academics, basic and research units and disciplines can also add to the overall picture. Additionally, perspectives of external stakeholders can be studied.

NOTE

¹   The EU's spending on research (1.9 percent of GDP) compared unfavorably with that of the US, Japan, and South Korea who were all close to three percent thanks to much higher investments by industry. Higher education spending in the EU at 1.1 percent of GDP also compared badly with US and South Korea, both of whom spent 2.7 percent, again due to differences in private investments.

REFERENCES

Aghion, P., Dewatripont, M., Hoxby, C., Mas-Colell, A., & Sapir, A. (2010). The governance and performance of universities: Evidence from Europe and the US. *Economic Policy, 25*, 7–59.

Bleiklie, I., & Kogan, M. (2007). Organisation and governance of universities. *Higher Education Policy, 20*(4), 477–493.

Bleiklie, I., Enders, J., Lepori, B., & Musselin, C. (2011). NPM, Network governance and the university as a changing professional organisation. In T. Christensen & P. Laegreid (Eds.), *The ashgate research companion to new public management.* Surrey, UK: Ashgate Publishing Limited.

Buckland, R. (2009). Diversifying the funding base of the UK university. In M. Mano, F. Almeida, L. M. Ramos, M. C. Marques, & S. Nolan (Eds.), *Governance and management models in higher education: A global perspective.* Porto, Portugal: Vida Economica.

Clark, B. (1983). *The higher education system: Academic organization in cross-national perspective.* Berkeley, CA: University of California Press.

Clark, B. (1998). *Creating entrepreneurial universities: Organizational pathways of transformation.* Oxford, England: Pergamon.

Clark, B. (2004). *Sustaining change in universities: Continuities in case studies and concepts.* Maidenhead, England: SRHE & Open University Press.

Davies, J. (2001). The emergence of entrepreneurial cultures in European universities. *Higher Education Management, 13*(2), 25–43.

de Boer, H., & File, J. (2009). *Higher education governance reforms across Europe.* Brussels, Belgium, Europe: ESMU.

Dill, D. (1997). Higher education markets and public policy. *Higher Education Policy, 10*(3/4), 167–185.

DiMaggio, P., & Powell, W. (1983). The iron cage revisited: Institutional isomorphism and collective rationality in organizational fields. *American Sociological Review, 48*, 147–160.

Eastman, J. (2006). Revenue generation and organisational change in higher education: Insights from Canada. *Higher Education Management and Policy, 18*(3), 55–82.

Estermann, T., & Nokkala, T. (2009). *University autonomy in Europe I.* Brussels, Belgium, Europe: EUA.

Estermann, T., & Pruvot, E. (2011). *Financially sustainable universities II: European universities diversifying income streams.* Brussels, Belgium, Europe: EUA.

Estermann, T., Nokkala, T., & Steinel, M. (2011). *University autonomy in Europe II: The scorecard.* Brussels, Belgium, Europe: EUA.

Etzkowitz, H. (2003). The European entrepreneurial university: An alternative to the US model. *Industry and Higher Education, 17*(5), 325–335.

Etzkowitz, H., & Leydesdorff, L. (1997). *Universities and the global knowledge economy, a triple helix of university-industry-government.* London, UK: Pinter.

EUA. (2008). *Financially sustainable universities: Towards full costing in European universities.* Brussels, Belgium, Europe: EUA.

European Commission. (2007). *Improving knowledge transfer between research institutions and industry across Europe: Embracing open innovation.* Brussels, Belgium, Europe: European Commission.

European Commission. (2008). *Delivering on the modernisation agenda for universities: Education, research and innovation.* Brussels, Belgium, Europe: European Commission.

European Commission. (2010). *Europe 2020: A strategy for smart, sustainable and inclusive growth.* Brussels, Belgium, Europe: European Commission.

European Commission. (2011). *Innovation union competitiveness report.* Luxembourg, Europe: Publications Office of the European Union.

Hatakenaka, S. (2004). *University-industry partnerships in MIT, Cambridge and Tokyo: Storytelling across boundaries.* New York, NY: RoutledgeFalmer.

Horta, H. (2008). On improving the university research base: The technical university of Lisbon case in perspective. *Higher Education Policy, 21,* 123–146.

Jongbloed, B., Enders, J., & Salerno, C. (2008). Higher education and its communities: Interconnections, interdependencies and a research agenda. *Higher Education, 56,* 303–324.

Johnstone, B., & Marcucci, P. (2010). *Financing higher education worldwide: Who pays? Who should pay?* Baltimore, MD: The John Hopkins University Press.

Kruecken, G. (2011). *A European perspective on new modes of university governance and actorhood.* CSHE. Retrieved November 17, from http://www.cshe.berkeley.edu/european-perspective-new-modes-university-governance-and-actorhood

Kruecken G., & Meier, F. (2006). Turning the university into an organizational actor. In G. Drori, H. Hwang, & J. Meyer (Eds.), *Globalization and organization: World society and organizational change.* Oxford, England: Oxford University Press.

Kwiek, M. (2012). The growing complexity of the academic enterprise in Europe: A panoramic view. *European Journal of Higher Education, 2*(2–3), 112–131.

Laredo, P. (2007). Revisiting the third mission of universities: Toward a renewed categorization of university activities? *Higher Education Policy, 20*(4), 441–456.

Liefner, I. (2003). Funding, resource allocation and performance in higher education systems. *Higher Education, 46,* 469–489.

Machado, M., Taylor, J., & Peterson, M. (2008). Leadership and strategic management: Keys to institutional priorities and planning. *European Journal of Education, 43*(3), 369–386.

McNay, I. (1995). From the collegial academy to corporate enterprise: The changing cultures of universities. In T. Schuller (Ed.), *The changing university?* Buckingham, England: The Society for Research into Higher Education and Open University Press.

Musselin, C. (2014). Empowering of french universities by funding and evaluation agencies. In R. Whitley & J. Glaeser (Eds.), *Organizational transformation and scientific change: The impact of institutional restructuring on universities and intellectual innovation.* Bingley, UK: Emerald Group Publishing Limited.

Musselin, C. (2007). Are universities specific organizations? In G. Kruecken, A. Kozmuetzky, & M. Torka (Eds.), *Towards a multiversity? Universities between global trends and national traditions* (pp. 63–84). Bielefeld, Germany: Transcript Verlag.

Neave, G. (2012). *The evaluative state, institutional autonomy and re-engineering higher education in Western Europe: The prince and his pleasure.* Hampshire, UK: Palgrave McMillan

OECD. (2004). *Internationalization and trade in higher education: Opportunities and challenges.* Paris, France: OECD.

Paradeise, C., Reale, E., Bleiklie, I., & Ferlie, E. (Eds.). (2009). *University governance: Western European comparative perspectives.* Dordrecht, The Netherlands: Springer.

Pinheiro, R. (2012). University ambiguity and institutionalization: A tale of three regions. In R. Pinheiro, P. Benneworth, & G. A. Jones (Eds.), *Universities and regional development: A critical assessment of tensions and contradictions*. Abingdon, England: Routledge.

Pinheiro, R., Benneworth, P., & Jones, G. A. (Eds.). (2012). *Universities and regional development: A critical assessment of tensions and contradictions*. Abingdon, England: Routledge.

Rossi, F. (2009). Universities' access to research funds: Do institutional features and strategies matter? *Tertiary Education and Management, 15*(2), 113–135.

Schein, E. (1990). Organizational culture. *American Psychologist, 45*(2), 109–119.

Schein, E.(1992). *Organizational culture and leadership: A dynamic view* (2nd ed.). San Francisco, CA: Jossey-Bass.

Schultz, M., Hatch, M. J., & Larsen, H. (Eds.). (2000). *The expressive organization: Linking identity, reputation and the corporate brand*. Oxford, England: Oxford University Press.

Schumpeter, J. A. (1942). *Capitalism, socialism and democracy*. New York, NY: Harper and Row.

Shattock, M. (2000). Strategic management in European universities in an age of increasing institutional self-reliance. *Tertiary Education and Management, 6*(2), 93–103.

Shattock, M. (2003). *Managing successful universities*. Buckingham, England: The Society for Research into Higher Education and Open University Press.

Shattock, M. (2005). European universities for entrepreneurship: Their role in the Europe of knowledge – The theoretical context. *Higher Eduucation Management and Policy, 17*(3), 13–25.

Shattock, M. (Ed.). (2008). *Entrepreneurialism in universities and the knowledge economy: Diversification and organizational change in European higher education*. Maidenhead, England: McGraw Hill, Society for Research into Higher Education, Open University Press.

Shattock, M. (2014). The context of modernising reforms in university governance. In M. Shattock (Ed.), *International trends in university governance: Autonomy, self-government and the distribution of authority*. Oxon, England: Routledge.

Sporn, B. (1999). *Adaptive university structures: An analysis of adaptation to socioeconomic environments of US and European universities*. London, UK and Philadelphia, PA: Jessica Kingsley Publishers.

Stensaker, B., Frolich, N., Huisman, J., Waagene, E., Scordato, L., & Botas, P. (2014). Factors affecting strategic change in higher education. *Journal of Strategy and Management, 7*(2), 193–207.

Teixeira, P. N., Rocha, V., Biscaia, R., & Cardoso, M. (2014). Revenue diversification in public higher educaiton: Comparing the university and polytechnic sectors. *Public Administration Review, 74*(3), 398–412.

Tuunainen, J. (2005). Hybrid practices? Contributions to the debate on the mutation of science and university. *Higher Education, 50*, 275–298.

van der Wende, M. (2009). *European responses to global competitiveness in higher education*. Berkley, CA: CSHE.

Van Vught, F. (1994). Autonomy and accountability in government/university relations. In J. Salmi & A. Verspoor (Eds.), *Revitalising higher education*. Oxford, England: Pergamon Press.

Weick, K. (1976). Educational organizations as loosely-coupled systems. *Administrative Science Quarterly, 21*, 1–19.

Whitley, R. (2008). Constructing universities as strategic actors: Limitations and variations. In L. Engwall & D. Weaire (Eds.), *The university in the market*. London, UK: Portland Press Ltd.

Whitley, R., & Glaeser, J. (Eds.). (2014). *Organizational transformation and scientific change: The impact of institutional restructuring on universities and intellectual innovation*. Bingley, UK: Emerald Group Publishing Limited.

Williams, G. (1992). *Changing patterns of finance in higher education*. Buckingham, England: Society for Research into Higher Education and Open University Press.

Williams, G., & Kitaev, I. (2005). Overview of national policy contexts for entrepreneurialism in higher educaiton institutions. *Higher Education Management and Policy, 17*(3), 125–140.

Ziderman, A., & Albrecht, D. (1995). *Financing universities in developing countries*. Washington, DC: The Falmer Press.

ANDREW KRETZ AND CRESO M. SÁ

3. STUDENTS AND STARTUPS

How New Forms of Entrepreneurial Learning and
Practice Redraw University Boundaries

INTRODUCTION

The promotion of entrepreneurship in higher education is often studied as a subset of third stream activity, or put differently, as one of the means through which universities contribute to innovation and economic development. Entrepreneurship involves the use of business strategies to initiate, grow, and sustain innovative activities, such as through new venture creation, with the ultimate goal of generating wealth (Mars, 2013). The efforts of universities to nurture and grow spinoff companies have thus long been investigated from the perspective of faculty involvement in commercial activities, with the associated implications for academic norms, practices, and identities; from the 'entrepreneurial university' viewpoint of a secular evolution of academic missions and roles towards greater engagement with the marketplace; and from an economic perspective on the outcomes and impacts of academic entrepreneurship.

In this chapter we view of entrepreneurship in higher education as a broad socio-cultural phenomenon, rather than just a response to market opportunities, commercial logics, and pushes for third stream activity (Sá & Kretz, 2015). As they develop courses and programs to teach entrepreneurship, universities are joined not only by governments intent on spurring innovation, but also philanthropists and non-profit organizations dedicated to the virtues of entrepreneurship, students from across disciplinary fields with interest in creating ventures, and entrepreneurs from the local community motivated by the desire to support the regional entrepreneurship ecosystem and the next generation of startups. In this sense, the field of entrepreneurship education straddles the boundaries of universities. The greater involvement of universities in supporting student entrepreneurship has spread entrepreneurial ideas and practices across academic disciplines, inside and outside the classroom. Furthermore, this development has brought together higher education institutions with a range of external actors and organizations. Although, the objectives and functions of entrepreneurship education may vary across disciplines, curricular and extra-curricular entrepreneurship activities are united in internalizing the thinking and modus operandi of the broader entrepreneurship field.

E. Reale & E. Primeri (Eds.), The Transformation of University Institutional and
Organizational Boundaries, 83–105.

To put it simply, entrepreneurship education encourages proactive and opportunistic behaviour that generates value or meaningful change. This involves experiential, hands-on opportunities that have students applying learning to real-world scenarios, while interacting with potential users, beneficiaries, and partners in the development of an idea. Hence, the field of entrepreneurship education redraws university boundaries in multiple ways: it (a) straddles academic fields of study with the dissemination and adaptation of entrepreneurship as a subject; (b) brings a range of external actors as participants in the conception, implementation and operation of entrepreneurship programs; and (c) spans academic learning and practice through a range of curricular and extra-curricular activities.

Our analysis of how entrepreneurship education has redrawn higher education boundaries is guided by grounded-theory in that we aim to construct a conceptual understanding of the problem through inductive, comparative, and iterative strategies (Charmaz, 2006; Corbin & Strauss, 2008). We use data from two research projects on entrepreneurial education at universities and colleges in the United States and Canada. From the first project, we draw on qualitative data collected from entrepreneurship initiatives at nine universities in both countries.[1] We gathered this data through three means: (1) site visits to university entrepreneurship centres and programs, (2) interviews with administrators and students involved with entrepreneurship education courses and programs, and (3) the examination of documents (e.g., reports, press releases, brochures) specific to each university's entrepreneurship education programs. From the second project, we draw from a dataset of all entrepreneurship education opportunities, both curricular and extra-curricular, available in colleges and universities in the Canadian province of Ontario. Findings from this project were included in our final report (Sá, Kretz, & Sigurdson, 2014), and we cite this document when referencing it below. Data collection entailed an examination of institutional websites and catalogues and a survey of all entrepreneurship education personnel from programs identified in the province. During these two data collection phases, we sought information connected to a program's origins and pedagogy, management and operation, purpose and priorities, and impact. Over the course of these projects we examined policies and institutional efforts towards supporting student entrepreneurship, and we draw from our observations of these initiatives in our discussion below.

BACKGROUND

Traditionally, academic researchers and scholars have viewed the commingling of higher education and commercial activity with serious misgiving. A primary rationale for this opposition is that market-oriented and entrepreneurial values represent an intrusion into academic practices and standards (Bok, 2003; Eckel, 2003; Etzkowitz, Webster, & Healey, 1998; Kirp, 2003; Slaughter, Campbell, Holleman, & Morgan, 2002; Slaughter & Rhoades, 2004; Washburn, 2006). Along with this resistance to entrepreneurship education, scholars in business schools have also been sceptical as to whether institutions of higher education should or even could teach entrepreneurship (Vesper & McMullan, 1988).

Unease about the presence of entrepreneurial activities within institutions of higher education has eroded over time. Today, successes of faculty and students in launching start-up companies are commonly celebrated on campuses. Entrepreneurship education in universities has gained legitimacy, in part, through public expectations of the economic and social relevancy of higher education. The positive attention garnered by entrepreneurs is a consequence of their perceived role in advancing innovation (Mars, 2013). Indeed, entrepreneurship is central to theories for economic development (Audretsch, Grilo, & Thurik, 2007), and many policy makers believe that promoting entrepreneurship education will have a dramatic role in creating new industries and revitalizing economies (Competition Policy Review Panel, 2008; Ontario, 2013; White House, 2011).

Indeed, entrepreneurship education has rapidly expanded on college and university campuses in the United States and Canada since the 1980s (Katz, 2003, 2008; Menzies, 2004, 2009; Solomon & Fernald Jr., 1991). Many observers even cite entrepreneurship as one of the fastest growing subjects in higher education (Finkle, Kuratko, & Goldsby, 2006; Katz, 2003; Kauffman Foundation, 2009; Kuratko, 2005; MBA Roundtable, 2012; Menzies, 2009), which is now a worldwide phenomenon (Potter, 2008). In Europe, policymakers have encouraged higher education institutions to support entrepreneurial education and innovation since 2000 (European Commission, 2001, 2004, 2006, 2013).

Following the growing number of courses and programs on the topic, the scope and range of entrepreneurship education offerings in universities has expanded considerably. Courses traditionally offered in business schools to their own students are increasingly offered in academic departments from the arts to the sciences (European Commission, 2008; Morris, Kuratko, & Cornwall, 2013; Streeter & Jaquette Jr., 2004). Accompanying the diffusion of courses is the emergence of incubators, accelerators and other programs aimed at stimulating start-up activity among students (Morris et al., 2013; Sá, Kretz, & Sigurdson, 2014).

THE FIELD OF ENTREPRENEURSHIP EDUCATION

This chapter frames entrepreneurship education as a field—a shared socio-structural context consisting of practices and interests recognized and rewarded by a community of actors (Bourdieu, 1977; Bourdieu & Wacquant, 1992). Although the subject of business creation is typically found within business schools, the expectations, processes, support structures, and outcomes of entrepreneurship education are distinct from their traditional academic homes (Gartner & Vesper, 1994; Katz, 2008; Kuratko, 2005; Solomon & Fernald Jr., 1991). Experts and practitioners in the field of entrepreneurship education uphold values, orientations, and identities that set them apart from traditional management education.

85

Moreover, the field involves a variety of stakeholders with varying responsibilities in promoting entrepreneurship. Such stakeholders include non-profit organizations evangelizing the virtues of entrepreneurship, philanthropists dedicated to building the field, consultants and think tanks specialized on the topic, public agencies providing services to entrepreneurs, and agents involved in supporting, capitalizing, and transacting with startup companies (Sá & Kretz, 2015). In sum, entrepreneurship education is a field consisting of a community of students, academic staff, entrepreneurs, alumni, and government and non-government organizations.

Boundary spanners maintain and grow the entrepreneurship education field in universities. These are both individuals and organizations that straddle the boundaries of different fields, operating across different sets of norms, values, orientations (Levina & Vaast, 2005; Tushman & Scanlan, 1981). In established fields, they maintain and shape the shared context in which activities take place (Levina & Vaast, 2014). The work of boundary spanners is facilitated by institutional cultures and rewards that legitimize their activities and priorities. Boundary spanners are empowered by symbolic capital (Bourdieu, 1998), which comprise prestige, honours, positive attention, and social recognition. These supports are significant for promoting entrepreneurship education, as they enhance the desirability of entrepreneurship courses and programs.

In what follows, we provide an account of approaches to fostering student entrepreneurship on campuses, whether in terms of engendering entrepreneurial mindsets or the development of actual business startups. Our discussion is organized into three parts that follow the form of our theoretically arrived at conceptualization of entrepreneurship education's impact on higher education. The first section includes a discussion of the broad coalition of entrepreneurship education advocates that promote, legitimate, and diffuse entrepreneurship within higher education institutions. The second section identifies the boundary-spanning actors and organizational structures that bring together academic and entrepreneurial communities. The third section characterizes entrepreneurship education as a new field of practice within higher education that is shared by entrepreneurs and academic staff. We conclude the paper with a brief summary and reflect on the implications of our findings for higher education.

STAKEHOLDER SUPPORT FOR ENTREPRENEURSHIP EDUCATION

In contrast to prior conceptualizations of academic entrepreneurship (Slaughter & Rhoades, 2004; Zummuto, 1984), the trend towards greater support for student entrepreneurship is not driven entirely by financial incentives. Rather, it is the result of a pervasive socio-cultural movement backed by various stakeholders. Whereas curricular and pedagogical priorities have generally been the traditional prerogative of the academic community, the forces behind the growth of entrepreneurship education include actors beyond the boundaries of higher education institutions. The endorsement of entrepreneurship education by governments and university associations, the financial support of individuals and groups external to higher education institutions, and expectations from students have provided powerful incentives for universities to embrace entrepreneurship.

Government

Our review of policy documents show that support for entrepreneurship is often part of broader policy initiatives to stimulate innovation, but it is also linked to efforts for enhancing regional economic development and increasing employment. For this reason, policies and initiatives to encourage entrepreneurship may be found at various levels of government and across agencies, departments, and ministries. The importance of science, technology, and business education for initiatives aimed at fostering entrepreneurship has made universities key to entrepreneurship policies.

In some jurisdictions, policymakers have attempted to steer institutions of higher education towards the greater promotion of entrepreneurship education. In Canada, Ontario's Ministry of Training, Colleges and Universities has highlighted the importance of entrepreneurial activity as a means by which colleges and universities might distinguish themselves (Ministry of Training, Colleges and Universities, 2013). In the US, legislatures in Oregon, Florida, and New York have authorized institutions of higher education to establish venture development funds to create incubator facilities for budding entrepreneurs on college and university campuses (State Science & Technology Institute, 2014).

New government programs also exist to support the development of entrepreneurship in higher education. In Canada, the government of Ontario has devoted $20 million (CAD) to support university or college campus-based business accelerators and other on-campus entrepreneurship activities. One of the goals of provincial initiatives such as this, according to Ontario's minister of research and innovation, is to "build the most entrepreneurial post-secondary system in North America" (Kula, 2015). In Nova Scotia, the Department of Labour and Advanced Education, together with the federal government's Atlantic Canada Opportunities Agency, has funded spaces on university and college campuses from which to foster and support student entrepreneurship (Premier's Office, 2014). In the US, the National Science Foundation has established its Innovation Corps program (I-Corps), an effort to teach NSF-funded university researchers and their students how to build profitable startups around their technologies. The program began at three universities—Stanford University, the University of Michigan, and the Georgia Institute of Technology—and has subsequently expanded to include 16 additional universities across 12 states.

University Associations

Organizations representing the senior leadership of universities have aligned themselves with public priorities and have positioned their institutions to support entrepreneurship education. Fostering a culture of entrepreneurship on campus and developing students' entrepreneurial skills and mindsets is recognized as essential for promoting innovation and for preparing students for life after graduation. Through efforts of the American Association of Universities (AAU) and the Association of Public Land Grant Universities (APLU) in the United States, academic leaders at 142 universities endorsed recommendations for how government, universities, and the private sector could partner to advance university-based innovation and entrepreneurship. Similar efforts to foster entrepreneurship have been pursued by the National Association of Community College Entrepreneurship (NACCE) and the Historically Black Colleges and Universities (HBCU) community, through the work of the United Negro College Fund and the HBCU Business School Deans (Office of Innovation and Entrepreneurship, 2013). In Ontario, the Council of Ontario Universities has supported the integration of entrepreneurship into core curriculum, as well as into extra-curricular opportunities (COU, 2011), and has celebrated those universities with entrepreneurship programs (COU, 2013).

Philanthropy & Evangelizers

In addition to policy pressure and endorsement by higher education leaders, the growth of entrepreneurship education in the US and Canada is largely attributed to financial support from successful entrepreneurs and private foundations. A number of non-profit organizations actively promote entrepreneurship in higher education as well. Many are networks involving university faculty, administrators and staff.

The Global Consortium of Entrepreneurship Centers (GCEC), for one, plays multiple roles in promoting entrepreneurship: it hosts an annual conference and an awards program, and is home to the 21st Century Entrepreneurship Research Fellows. Venture Well is another major national organization. The organization began as a project of the Lemelson Foundation to support student inventors and help them take their ideas to market. Today the organization operates several programs aimed at supporting entrepreneurship on colleges and university campuses. For instance, VentureWell provides faculty with funding for courses and programs in technology-based entrepreneurship and supports "Student Ambassadors" as they work to host events and boost the presence of entrepreneurship on their campuses. In Canada, the Next36 is a private initiative that selects 36 postsecondary students from across Canada for a nine-month program at the University of Toronto, in which they receive mentorship and seed capital in support of their ventures. In promoting student entrepreneurship, the Next36 seeks to address Canada's so-called deficit of high impact entrepreneurs.

More generally, philanthropy has helped fuel the growth of entrepreneurship education. Observing 142 university entrepreneurship centres in the US, Mars (2007) found that about 44 percent were named based on private sector gifts. Surveys of entrepreneurship centres in the US indicate that roughly 43 percent of operating budges come from endowments and donations (Bowers, Bowers, & Ivan,

2006; Finkle, Menzies, Kuratko, & Goldsby, 2012). Moreover, there are hundreds of endowed positions in entrepreneurship (Katz, 2004). Foundations have played a significant role in supporting the curricular integration of entrepreneurship into general undergraduate education, quite prominently in the case of the Ewing Marion Kauffman Foundation, which has supported the creation of new interdisciplinary entrepreneurship education programs at American universities and colleges (Torrance, 2013). Likewise, the Coleman Foundation's Faculty Entrepreneurship Fellows Program contributes to the diffusion of entrepreneurship across higher education institutions by sponsoring faculty who teach in disciplines outside business schools. In Canada, private donors are also critical to entrepreneurship program budgets in universities (Menzies, 2000). The John Dobson Foundation, for instance, promotes entrepreneurial activities and education in Canada, and supports entrepreneurship at sixteen Canadian universities. The motivation of foundations for supporting university and college entrepreneurship education generally stems from goals of promoting values like self-sufficiency, individual initiative, and community engagement, while individual philanthropists are often proponents of entrepreneurship and are often alumni of the institutions receiving their gifts.

Students

The popularity of entrepreneurship among students has also compelled institutions of higher education to support entrepreneurship. In the US, roughly 43 percent of incoming freshman report that becoming successful in a business of their own is essential or very important (Pryor & Reedy, 2009), and several studies have demonstrated that students from diverse disciplinary backgrounds are interested in learning about entrepreneurship (Levenburg, Lane, & Schwarz, 2006; Mayhew, Simonoff, Baumol, Wiesenfeld, & Klein, 2012; Shinner, Pruett, & Toney, 2009). Similar survey results are found in Canada, where 46 percent of surveyed postsecondary students see themselves starting a business after graduation (Hire Prospects, OAYEC, D-Code, 2008; BMO, 2013).

Student interest in entrepreneurship has manifested in a growing number of student-run entrepreneurship clubs. In addition to creating a community of student entrepreneurs, such clubs also typically host guest lecturers and panel discussions, as well as sponsor and run workshops, competitions, and networking events (Brown & Kant, 2009; Pittaway, Gazzard, Shore, & Williamson, 2012; Pittaway, Rodriguez-Falcon, Aiyegbayo, & King, 2011). These clubs may be formed independently by students following their own interests or established as a chapter or affiliate of a external organization that supports local chapters and host national and regional conferences and expositions, competitions, and awards (Pittaway et al., 2012). Examples of national student organizations include Enactus, Collegiate Entrepreneurs' Organization, Enterprize Canada, Collegiate DECA (formerly Delta Epsilon Chi), and the entrepreneurship honours society Sigma Nu Tau.

Considering the entrepreneurial aspirations and interests of the college-going cohort, several sources have recently begun ranking university and college entrepreneurship programs (Examples include *U.S. News and World Report, Entrepreneur Magazine, Success Magazine, Financial Times*, and *UBI Index*). Although numerous scholars have raised concerns about the validity and importance of rankings, students and academic leaders use them to make decisions—the perceived benefits of being associated with a successful university or program may attract students, donor income, and industry funding (Marginson, 2006; Morphew & Swanson, 2011; Hazelkorn, 2011; Locke, 2011). In this context, higher education leaders tend to find it in their interest to adapt to the entrepreneurial interests of today's students.

To recap, the endorsement of entrepreneurship education by academic leaders, the financial support of individuals and groups external to higher education institutions, and the expectations from governments and students have provided incentives for promoting entrepreneurship education. Boundary spanners leverage these incentives in their support for entrepreneurship education. Their activities are discussed below.

BOUNDARY SPANNERS

Boundary spanners facilitate the development of university entrepreneurship programs, initiatives, and communities of practice. They bring ideas, practices, organizational models, expertise, and other resources related to entrepreneurship into the university. They also navigate academic norms and structures to adjust and blend entrepreneurial offerings into higher education institutions. Additionally, new organizational units and programs foster connections between universities and the start-up community, while forging new spaces on campus for entrepreneurship. These organizations originate inside and outside of the university.

Entrepreneur Volunteers

Seasoned entrepreneurs play various roles in the operation of university entrepreneurship programs such as clinical faculty, entrepreneurs-in-residence, or volunteer mentors. These entrepreneurs supplement the work of academic staff by teaching courses, facilitating workshops, and advising programs and students while operating their own startups and established businesses. Furthermore, entrepreneurship programs generally require the support of volunteers from local business communities. Apart from mentoring students in all aspects of starting and growing a new venture, these community entrepreneurs also lecture, judge business plan and new venture competitions, host student interns, serve as board members on student startups, and evaluate educational programs (Morris et al., 2013).

Volunteers also serve on advisory boards established by entrepreneurship centres and programs. These boards reflect the integration of entrepreneurial practice and university education, and are comprised of advocates for entrepreneurship, representing industry, business, finance, and the not-for-profit sector. Board members provide strategic and tactical support, fund raise, use personal networks to increase collaboration across higher education and business communities, and help bolster a program's reputation. For instance, the Conrad Business, Entrepreneurship, and Technology Centre in the Faculty of Engineering at the University of Waterloo draws on the expertise of its advisory council predominantly composed of entrepreneurs and leaders of technology-driven companies, but also includes a partner in a law firm, a CEO of a community foundation, a university technology transfer director, and the managing director of Ontario Centres of Excellence.

Entrepreneurship Centres

Entrepreneurship centres in universities usually facilitate education program administration and delivery. Although they have long been housed within business schools in service of business students, entrepreneurship centres are becoming increasingly focused on the integration of programs and activities aimed at fostering student entrepreneurship and venture creation across disciplines (Morris et al., 2013). Most centres are located within business schools, although a growing number are becoming established within engineering schools as well as the arts. Others are independent units serving campus-wide entrepreneurship education for students across disciplines. Many support a variety of complimentary activities like business plan competitions, internships, student clubs, venture capital funds, seminars/ workshops, and guest speakers (Finkle et al., 2006; Finkle et al., 2012; Menzies, 2000, 2009). Entrepreneurship centres also interface with surrounding communities of entrepreneurs. At the San Diego State University, for example, the Lavin Entrepreneurship Center provides a focal point from which to recruit entrepreneurs to serve as guest speakers and mentors, while also providing a source of talent for local start-ups in need of interns.

Business professionals with entrepreneurial experience are often hired as directors of entrepreneurship centres. It is not unusual for directors to have a background in marketing and even running their own start-up. In addition to bringing their experience and networks, these entrepreneurs tend to operate in entrepreneurial centres as if they are part of a start-up (Morris et al., 2013). Many cultivate a brand by hiring marketing and communications staff to write press releases and maintain a visible web presence, and bootstrap existing resources while seeking external funding. In this way, entrepreneurship centres are embedded within the start-up culture of entrepreneurship communities. Indeed, one survey of 122 entrepreneurship centres in the United States revealed that, on average, 27 percent of a centre's budget is funded by universities, the rest come largely from endowments, grants, and donations (Finkle et al., 2012).[2] Similarly, our survey of extra-curricular entrepreneurship programs in the province of Ontario, revealed that universities and colleges only supplied 38 percent of program funding, with the rest provided by external sources (Sá et al., 2014). Multiple sources of funding not only reflects the broad range of entrepreneurship education supporters, it also incentives entrepreneurial behaviour and engagement with actors and stakeholders outside of academe.

Some entrepreneurship centres coordinate and receive support from their institutions' Technology Transfer Office (TTO), which generally have experience in starting new enterprises from university technology. At universities without a strong legacy of entrepreneurship education in faculties of business, TTOs have become campus champions of student business creation. Because they are established outside the academic bureaucracy, TTOs may serve as a natural focal point of entrepreneurship on campus, connecting students and faculty from across departments. Moreover, the relatively autonomous status of TTO's give it greater flexibility than academic units to form partnerships with outside organizations and to apply for external funding. At the Arizona State University, for example, the Entrepreneurship and Innovation Group was formed as a joint initiative of the university's Office of Knowledge Enterprise Development (formerly Office of the Vice President of Research and Economic Affairs) and Arizona Technology Enterprises (the university's technology transfer office) to coordinate and support entrepreneurship opportunities on campus. The technology transfer office at the University of Ottawa provides another example. Observing the growing participation of students in business plan competitions, TTO staff recognized a need on campus for a program to help students transform their ideas into functioning enterprises. With the help of a grant from the province, the TTO leveraged the interests and experience of its staff to provide the university's first extra-curricular entrepreneurship program. The case of the University of Ottawa illustrates how existing administrative units on campus are widening their services to support student entrepreneurship. Other examples of on-campus units taking an interest in fostering student entrepreneurship include career centres, housing departments, travel-abroad offices, and student unions (Sá & Kretz, 2015; Sá et al., 2014). In such cases the driving force is generally a response to student demand.

Start-Up Development Units

A growing number of boundary-spanning units support the practice of entrepreneurship in universities. The most common models are incubators and accelerators. The former provide support to students in the early-stages of venture development, including management guidance, technical assistance and consulting, dedicated workspace, access to shared business services, technology support services, and assistance in securing funding. Accelerators are like incubators, but typically offer a more structured, intensive program for student entrepreneurs who are usually further along with their ventures and have a proven business model. University accelerators adopt many of the core elements of community-based private accelerators: an open, highly competitive application process; pre-seed investments for admitted ventures; run as a cohort model focused on small teams, not individual founders; time-limited support comprising clear goal of funding or growth and periodic assessments or milestones (Miller & Bound, 2011).

The Digital Media Zone at Ryerson University is one prominent incubator in Canada. The DMZ, as it is known, was created in 2010 to help students and alumni develop marketable digital products and services. Students accepted to the DMZ receive four months of free space and services. Like most incubator and accelerator programs, students are required to submit an idea for a business venture in teams. Students who are ready to launch their business have access to seed funding and an accelerator program through Ryerson Futures Inc. (RFI), a for-profit entity associated with the university. The DMZ boasts of incubating 130 start-ups that have raised $40 million (CAD) while creating over 1,200 jobs (Ryerson University, n.d.).

Although typically located on campus, both incubators and accelerators operate through a network of individuals and organizations that extend beyond the university to include community entrepreneurs, industry contacts, venture capitalists, and angel investors (Hackett & Dilts, 2004). As mentioned above, entrepreneurs and others connected to the start-up community typically support such extra-curricular opportunities by serving as mentors, guest speakers, and project evaluators. In fact, incubator and accelerator programs often end with a Demo Day, which involves students presenting their venture to an audience of potential investors, media, sponsors, partners, alumni, and others (Caley, 2013). Moreover, it is not unusual for incubators and accelerators to permit non-student participation, such as by alumni, faculty and staff, and community members. In Ontario, non-students constitute roughly 30% of incubators and accelerators participants (Sá et al., 2014). These alumni, faculty and staff, and community members generally join these start-up programs as members of a team consisting of at least one enrolled student. A last noteworthy connection of these start-up programs with communities outside of higher education is made through program funding. Many of the activities of incubators and accelerators rely on the financial support and volunteerism of entrepreneurs and business leaders. Moreover, in the US, foundations like the Moxie Foundation and the Blackstone Charitable Foundation have stepped in to support these new venture creation programs, while such support in Canada has traditionally come from government initiatives and agencies.

Some campus-based incubators and accelerators are located off-campus within near-by entrepreneurship/innovation centres. These independent (although often publicly supported) centres connect startups, industry, government, and universities in the promotion of innovation and new enterprises. Higher education institutions in the Kitchener-Waterloo region of Ontario, for example, have longstanding relations with the Communitec Digital Media Hub. In addition to co-hosting with local universities and colleges entrepreneurship learning activities for students, such as entrepreneurship-focused workshops and networking events, Communitec houses Wilfred Laurier University's student venture incubator and provides students internships for course credit with a start-up. In other instances, support for student entrepreneurship off-campus is breathing new life into university science parks, many of which have been rebranded as innovation centres (Hansson, Husted, & Vestergaard, 2005). At the Arizona State University, student entrepreneurs receive office space in Skysong, the university and City of Scottsdale's Innovation Center. The University of Florida has recently begun constructing a residence building for a new entrepreneurial-based academic residential community to be located at the university's Innovation Square, a public-private planned community that will include spaces for faculty research, entrepreneurs, and incubators. In all of these cases, student entrepreneurs work in the same setting as other entrepreneurial students and faculty as well as community entrepreneurs, industry, and business support providers.

Entrepreneurship Brokers

Even though some universities have placed responsibility for entrepreneurship under Vice Presidents for Research—often changing titles to become Vice Presidents of *research and innovation*—others have created entirely new positions, such as Vice President and University Dean for Entrepreneurship & Innovation (Arizona State University), Associate Vice Chancellor for Entrepreneurship (University of California at Los Angeles), Special Advisor to the President for Entrepreneurship (University of Waterloo), and Executive Director for Entrepreneurship within the VP Research (University of Ottawa). Universities assign such roles typically in efforts to coordinate entrepreneurship education on campus and make courses and programs visible and accessible to all students across disciplines.

In Ontario, the rise of such positions is in part reaction to new funding for entrepreneurship education that requires cross-campus coordination. The provincial government's Campus-Linked Accelerator Program and On-Campus Entrepreneurship Activities Program have channelled a total of $25 million (CAD) to universities and colleges in support of entrepreneurship programming. To be eligible for this funding institutions needed to formulate a strategy for promoting entrepreneurship, in addition to coordinate with local non-academic entrepreneurship communities (e.g., innovation centres, angle networks, business enterprise centres, etc.). Our interviews with entrepreneurship education leaders at several of the province's universities revealed that institutions were responding to these initiatives by developing new positions and offices from which to coordinate their entrepreneurship education programs and activities.[3]

Overall, boundary spanners, such as entrepreneurs-in-residence, volunteer mentors, entrepreneurship advisory boards, entrepreneurship centres and technology transfer offices, incubators and accelerators, and local and university innovation hubs, connect institutions with surrounding entrepreneurial communities, as well as maintain the field of entrepreneurial learning and practice on campus. Concurrently, some entrepreneurship centres—those independent of a faculty—along with high-level administrative positions responsible for coordinating campus-wide entrepreneurship initiatives serve to connect disciplinary communities on campus, fostering the development of entrepreneurship education for students of varying academic majors.

SHIFTING UNIVERSITY BOUNDARIES

The development of the entrepreneurship education field in universities involves students from multiple disciplinary backgrounds. Accompanying this development are practices unique to entrepreneurship that are used within university campuses.

Entrepreneurship across Academic Boundaries

Entrepreneurship education started in business schools, but much of the recent growth of entrepreneurship courses and programs has occurred to accommodate non-business majors. Entrepreneurship education's growing acceptance across disciplines is facilitated by the multi-disciplinary applicability of entrepreneurial practice and thinking. For instance, proponents of infusing entrepreneurship into non-business courses find value in the subject's emphasis on managing risk, spotting opportunities, and innovating, all of which are generally deemed essential skills and aptitudes favoured in the contemporary economy (Powell & Snellman, 2004; Stam & Garnsey, 2008). Entrepreneurship within engineering and the arts, for example, are perceived as a way to bolster students' skills and labour market competitiveness (Mars, 2007).

Engineering schools generally have the largest number of entrepreneurship courses and programs outside of business schools. More than half of the American Society for Engineering Education's member institutions offer an undergraduate program in entrepreneurship (Gilmartin, Shartrand, Chen, Estrada, & Sheppard, 2014), and in Ontario, roughly 25 percent of undergraduate courses and approximately two-thirds of graduate courses in entrepreneurship are offered through engineering schools. The inclusion of entrepreneurship education in engineering is intended to teach students how to identify opportunities and bring them to life through product design and development, prototyping, technology trends, and market analysis (Nelson & Byers, 2010).

The arts is another field where entrepreneurship has expanded. More than emphasizing the formation of new companies, arts entrepreneurship applies entrepreneurial strategies to teach artists how to reach audiences and seek funding (Roberts, 2013). According to members of the United States Association for Small Business and Entrepreneurship Arts Entrepreneurship Special Interest Group, there are an estimated 450 arts entrepreneurship courses offered at higher education institutions in the US (Roberts, 2013). Some of these institutions support arts entrepreneurship curriculum and programming from within arts administration programs located within business schools, whereas others offer arts entrepreneurship minor degrees from within an arts college or institute (Beckman & Essig, 2012).

A smaller number of universities have established programs that help students develop an arts venture of their own.

The Pave Arts Venture Incubator at Arizona State University is one of eight university arts incubator programs in the US (Essig, 2013). Each year it provides seed funding for up to six teams that receive assistance with the development of a project proposal. Arts venture incubator programs also exist at select institutions in Canada. For instance, at OCAD University, Canada's largest and oldest educational institution for art and design, students have the chance to participate in the Take-It-to-Market incubator, which provides a full-range of venture support services in addition to shared meeting spaces, event/presentation venues, and fabrication/prototyping facilities.

Furthermore, liberal arts scholars have helped the acceptance of entrepreneurship outside of business schools by highlighting the parallels between a liberal arts education and the development of entrepreneurial behaviour. Such scholars have argued that a liberal arts education serves a similar function as an entrepreneurship education. Both teach students to approach problems in novel ways and allow them to tolerate ambiguity (Godwyn, 2009; Ray, 1990; Regele & Neck, 2012; Shaver, 2005). For example, at Wake Forest University, the Innovation, Creativity, and Entrepreneurship program's mission is to "make innovation, creativity and entrepreneurship an integral and enduring part of the liberal arts college experience" (Wake Forest University , n.d.). The program offers liberal arts students' a minor in Entrepreneurship and Social Enterprise, and makes available grants and workspace for students to help develop their ventures. At the University of Texas at Austin, the College of Liberal Arts has launched its Student Ventures program, a series of monthly start-up workshops, to engage Liberal Arts students in innovation and entrepreneurial activities. The university also offers an interdisciplinary certificate in Innovation, Creativity, and Entrepreneurship "that combines courses from Business, Communication, Fine Arts, and Liberal Arts, students will learn how ideas, inventions, talents, and skills are developed and transformed into commercial and social ventures" (The University of Texas at Austin, n.d.).

Elsewhere, entrepreneurship has gained acceptance by resonating with widely accepted notions of action-oriented, interdisciplinary teaching and learning. In the social sciences, entrepreneurship and innovation have been fused with community-based service learning and civic engagement activities to form social entrepreneurship courses and programs (Winfield, 2005). Social entrepreneurship emphasizes the use of economic and market driven solutions for solving social problems (Shaw & Carter, 2007); it is a response to pressures that non-profit organizations and volunteer or charitable initiatives "scale-up" and become "sustainable" (Enos, 2014; Foster & Bradach, 2005). Social entrepreneurship became a topic of study in the early 1990s (Short, Moss, & Lumpkin, 2009), and by 2005, nearly 32 percent of the 47 ranked undergraduate business programs of the 2005 US News and World Report's annual rankings offered either a formal program of study or individual courses in social entrepreneurship (Mars, 2007b). However, according to Ashoka (2014), a leading social entrepreneurship advocacy organization, about half of social entrepreneurship programs are located outside of business schools.

The Entrepreneurship Learning-Practice Boundary

As entrepreneurship education has grown in non-business majors, curricular developments have led to distinctive approaches to entrepreneurship education, moving away from management education. The writing of business plans, for instance, have long been required of business students participating in entrepreneurship courses (Gartner & Vesper, 1994; Gorman, Hanlon, & King, 1997; Hills, 1988; Honig, 2004; Klatt, 1988; Solomon, 2007; Vesper & McMullan, 1988), so much so that hosting and participating in business plan competitions have become the stock in trade of hundreds of business schools (Kauffman Foundation, 2001; Leffel & Hallam, 2008; Ross & Byrd, 2011). Nonetheless, business plans and associated competitions are increasingly being replaced by alternative practices formulated from within the start-up community for teaching and supporting budding entrepreneurs. For instance, "Lean start-up" techniques that favour real-life experimentation and customer feedback over pen-and-paper planning and environmental scan-based decision-making have been popularized by serial-entrepreneur and lecturer in the Program in Entrepreneurship at the Haas School of Business at the University of California at Berkeley, Steve Blank. According to Blank (2013), lean start-up pedagogy has students proposing and testing their assumptions on a weekly basis, discovering whether their desired customers would actually buy or use their products or services, and redesigning their business model accordingly. Through this strategy, students learn about entrepreneurship by becoming entrepreneurs, adapting their venture plan based on their market interactions and in-class mentoring until they find a venture that serves customers.

This entrepreneurship pedagogy ties classroom learning and assessment to interactions with external stakeholders and provides entrepreneurship educators and entrepreneurs with a shared set concepts and strategies. The NSF's I-Corps program's curriculum is based on the lean start-up model, as it is at the National Institutes of Health's (NIH) I-Corps program. Moreover, each year hundreds of university and college instructors are completing Lean LaunchPad seminars offered at a dozen universities across the US and hosted by VentureWell (Blank, 2013). It is common to find entrepreneurship bootcamps, workshops, and incubator programs in the US and Canada using lean start-up techniques in their curriculum. For example, accelerator programs, such as those at the University of British Columbia and New York University ground student entrepreneurs in lean start-up principles, while San Diego State University's LeanModel Start-up Competition has students presenting their start-ups using the business model canvas—a lean start-up strategy for providing a framework that describes how a company will operate.

97

Accompanying innovation in entrepreneurship curriculum is a more diverse ecosystem of business plan competitions and events, growing from the efforts of entrepreneurship centres and other hubs of entrepreneurship on campus. One popular event are pitch competitions, which require students to expeditiously present their inchoate business ideas in a few minutes to successful entrepreneurs, angel investors, and venture capitalists. In addition to mimicking the real-life situation in which an entrepreneur must convey an idea to financiers or customers, these opportunities aim to provide training, mentoring, and networking opportunities to students, as well as the possibility of acquiring seed capital. For instance, at the University of Southern California, students, faculty, and staff have the opportunity to enter the Marshal School of Business' New Venture Seed Competition, a pitch competition supported by several entrepreneur and angel investors that awards cash prizes to selected ventures. Applicants attend workshops where they receive guidance in developing their pitches, including a "pitch deck"—presentation slides. In 2014, 155 student and faculty ventures participated by giving a 10-minute pitch to an audience of students, faculty, entrepreneurs, and investors (University of Southern California, 2014).

Start-up summits, start-up weekends, and hackathons are others nodes in the expanding ecosystem of entrepreneurship education. They provide a hybrid between conference and start-up competition, in which entrepreneurs convene for a period of a few days to network, form teams, develop an idea, and transform it into a product or prototype, and then pitch the idea and demonstrate the product live in front of judges for a chance at some seed capital, services, and other awards. Universities and external organizations sponsor many of these types of events collaboratively. For example, the non-profit organization Startup Weekend helps to facilitate the organisation of weekend-long start-up events. Student groups, on the other hand, are largely responsible for hosting Hackathons. The largest university hackathon purportedly took place at the University of California Los Angeles, where a reported 1,500 university students devoted a weekend to create and present "apps" for prizes and awards (Alagot, 2014). One common element found across pitch competitions, start-up summits and weekends, and hackathons is the inclusion of panel of judges of entrepreneurs and venture capitalists that evaluate student ideas and work who are integrated with the local entrepreneurship community.

The popularity of lean start-up methods and entrepreneurship events reflect the substantial impact actors from within the start-up community have had on university teaching and learning activities. Whereas the writing and presenting of business plans are activities largely confined to business schools, new methods for teaching entrepreneurship that are being introduced to universities by entrepreneurs have moved the learning largely out of the walls of universities, as students engage with potential clients, users, and partners as they develop their businesses. Moreover, whereas business plan competitions are normally the domain of business schools, a more diverse ecosystem of competitions and events are growing from the efforts of entrepreneurship centres and other support units on and off campus. For instance, in Ontario, roughly 42 per cent of all extra-curricular entrepreneurship activities are offered outside of business and engineering schools (Sá et al., 2014). This is all to say that new forms of entrepreneurship learning and practice not only take place outside of traditional departmental boundaries, they have also been heavily influenced by actors outside of universities.

CONCLUSION

In this paper we have provided an analysis of how entrepreneurship education is shifting institutional boundaries in higher education. The involvement of numerous stakeholders in promoting and shaping entrepreneurship education has widened the scope universities and colleges to include engagement with new business venture creation and entrepreneurial communities. In so doing, entrepreneurship education has become a common field for individuals conventionally separated by institutional boundaries. Boundary spanners actively promote and maintain this shared field. They serve as teachers, mentors, advisors, and evaluators, bringing in ideas and practices of the entrepreneurship realm into the university. Entrepreneurship boundary spanners are also responsible for the growing entrepreneurial ecosystem on campuses that includes incubators, workshops, pitch competitions, and start-up events. Furthermore, as their name here indicates, these boundary spanners connect universities with surrounding entrepreneurial communities.

The diffusion of entrepreneurship education across universities is not simply a response to immediate commercial rewards. Instead, it represents an adaptation to social expectations for economic and social relevancy, as expressed in the diffusion of entrepreneurial learning across fields, and in the dissemination of spaces for students to become entrepreneurs. University practices that foster student entrepreneurship and the creation of start-up companies represent and reinforce changes to the traditional functions, objectives, and scope of higher education already forged by the relationship between academic research and industry (Geiger & Sá, 2008; Mowery, Nelson, Sampat, & Ziedonis, 2004). University support for student entrepreneurship signifies the transposition of these previous institutional and organizational changes—namely, the need for economic engagement and relevancy—into the education domain of higher education. Student demand is also an important factor driving this change, which is fuelled by the support of private donors and foundations. A consensus in academic community that university graduates be innovative and adept at applying innovative solutions to real-world settings have helped to embed entrepreneurship learning and practice within higher education.

In addition to the overlapping boundaries of higher education and the entrepreneurship community, the advance of entrepreneurship education in universities has transcended academic boundaries. Indeed, the teaching of entrepreneurship spans departments and disciplines. Even if the specific focus and objective of entrepreneurship education differs across programs, common mindsets, skills, and strategies provide a shared learning context; it is a common practice for students from multiple disciplines to enrol in the same entrepreneurship course and participate together in entrepreneurship activities on campus. Communities outside of the conventional boundaries of higher education play an important role in the education of students in entrepreneurship by not only supporting the provision of educational opportunities but also participating in learning processes as mentors, guest lectures, and even as developers of curriculum.

By analysing student entrepreneurship learning and practice occurring within higher education in the United States and Canada, we have further characterized an under examined domain of higher education. We argued that entrepreneurship education is shifting institutional boundaries in universities, creating shared spaces from which academic and entrepreneurial actors may educate students from across academic departments. The outcomes of this phenomenon may be much less spectacular and more benign than envisioned by promoters and detractors of entrepreneurship education. First, the notion that universities will spur scores of successful start-up companies is easily deflated by the notoriously high failure rate of entrepreneurship (Sá & Kretz, 2015). Second, the promotion of entrepreneurial thinking across fields does not necessarily lead to widespread commercialism, as many entrepreneurship programs seek to engender creativity and resourcefulness in students while empowering them to seek out and apply innovative solutions in their lives and communities. While venture creation is at the roots of the entrepreneurship education field, its dissemination in universities has rested on a broad and malleable interpretation of what constitutes entrepreneurial thinking and practice, which now goes well beyond start-up activity.

NOTES

[1] These include the University of Southern California, Arizona State University, San Diego State University, the University of California at San Diego, the University of Western Ontario, the University of Ottawa, the University of Waterloo, and Ryerson University.
[2] In the United States, the average size of a centre's annual budget was estimated to be near $516,000.
[3] Thirteen confidential interviews with university entrepreneurship education leaders were conducted between October 2013 and March 2014.

REFERENCES

Alagot, C. (2014, April 13). UCLA hosts biggest hackathon in history. *LA Weekly*. Retrieved from http://www.laweekly.com/informer/2014/04/12/ucla-hosts-biggest-hackathon-in-history
Arizona State University. (2010). *A new American university*. Retrieved from http://newamericanuniversity.asu.edu/docs/NAU_Dec10.pdf
Ashoka U. (2014). *Trends in social innovation education*. Arlington, VA: Ashoka.
Audretsch, D. B., Grilo, I., & Thurik, A. R. (2007). Explaining entrepreneurship and the role of policy: A framework. *The handbook of research on entrepreneurship policy* (pp. 1–17). Cheltenham, England and Northampton, MA: Edward Elgar Publishing, Inc.
Beckman, G. D., & Essig, L. (2012). Arts entrepreneurship: A conversation. *Artivate: A Journal of Entrepreneurship in the Arts, 1*(1), 1–8.
Blank, S. (2013). Why the lean start-up changes everything. *Harvard Business Review, 91*(5), 63–72.

BMO. (2013). *Half of Canadian students aspire to start their own business after graduating: BMO survey.* Retrieved from http://globalnews.ca/news/823144/bmo-survey-46-of-students-plan-own-business/

Bok, D. C. (2003). *Universities in the marketplace: The commercialization of higher education.* Princeton, NJ: Princeton University Press.

Bourdieu, P. (1977). *Outline of a theory of practice* (R. Nice, Trans.). Cambridge, England: Cambridge University Press.

Bourdieu, P. (1998). *Practical reason: On the theory of action.* Stanford, CA: Stanford University Press.

Bourdieu, P., & Wacquant, L. J. D. (1992). *An invitation to reflexive sociology.* Chicago, IL: University of Chicago Press.

Bowers, M. R., Bowers, C. M., & Ivan, G. (2006). Academically-based entrepreneurship centers: An exploration of structure and function. *Journal of Entrepreneurship Education, 9,* 1–14.

Brown, J. T., & Kant, A. C. (2009). Creating bioentrepreneurs: How graduate student organisations foster science entrepreneurship. *Journal of Commercial Biotechnology, 15*(2), 125–135.

Caley, E. (2013). *Seeding success: Canada's startup accelerators.* MaRS Data Catalyst. Retrieved from http://www.marsdd.com/app/uploads/2014/04/20130619-datacatalyst-acceleratorreport.pdf

Charmaz, K. (2008). Grounded theory as an emergent method. In S. N. Hesse-Biber & P. Leavy (Eds.), *The handbook of emergent methods* (pp. 155–170). New York, NY: Guilford Press.

Competition Policy Review Panel. (2008). *Compete to win: Final report June 2008.* Ottawa, Canada: Industry Canada.

Conway, T., Mackay, S., & Yorke, D. (1994). Strategic planning in higher education: Who are the customers. *International Journal of Educational Management, 8*(6), 29–36.

Council of Ontario Universities (COU). (2011). *Submission to the expert panel on the review of federal support to research and development, expert panel consultation paper.* Toronto, ON: Council of Ontario Universities.

Council of Ontario Universities (COU). (2013). *Entrepreneurship at Ontario universities: Fuelling success.* Retrieved from http://cou.on.ca/publications/reports/pdfs/entrepreneurship-at-ontario-universities---fuellin

Eckel, P. D. (2003). Capitalizing on the curriculum: The challenge of curricular joint. *American Behavioral Scientist, 46*(7), 865–882.

Enos, S. L. (2014). Review essay: What's all this I hear about social entrepreneurship? *Michigan Journal of Community Service Learning, 21*(1), 91–97.

Essig, L. (2013, June 26). *Arts incubators: 47 and counting.* Creative Infrastructure. Retrieved from http://creativeinfrastructure.org/2013/06/26/arts-incubators-47-and-counting/

Etzkowitz, H., Webster, A., & Healey, P. (1998). *Capitalizing knowledge: New intersections of industry and academia.* New York, NY: SUNY Press.

European Commission. (2001). *The concrete future objectives of education systems.* [COM(2001) 59 final]. Brussels, Belgium, Europe: European Commission.

European Commission. (2004). *Action plan: The European agenda for entrepreneurship.* [COM(2004) 70 final]. Brussels, Belgium, Europe: European Commission.

European Commission. (2006). *Implementing the community Lisbon programme: Fostering entrepreneurial mindsets through education and learning* [COM(2006) 33 final]. Brussels, Belgium, Europe: European Commission.

European Commission. (2008). *Entrepreneurship in higher education, especially within non-business studies.* Brussels, Belgium, Europe: European Commission, Enterprise and Industry Directorate-General.

European Commission. (2013). *Entrepreneurship 2020 action plan: Reigniting the entrepreneurial spirit in Europe.* [COM(2012) 795 final]. Brussels, Belgium, Europe: European Commission.

Finkle, T. A., Kuratko, D. F., & Goldsby, M. G. (2006). An examination of entrepreneurship centers in the United States: A national survey. *Journal of Small Business Management, 44*(2), 184–206.

Finkle, T. A., Menzies, T. V., Kuratko, D. F., & Goldsby, M. G. (2012). Financial activities of entrepreneurship centers in the United States. *Journal of Business and Entrepreneurship, 23*(2), 48–64.

Foster, W., & Bradach, J. L. (2005). Should nonprofits seek profits? *Harvard Business Review, 83*(2), 92–100.

Gartner, W. B., & Vesper, K. H. (1994). Experiments in entrepreneurship education: Success and failures. *Journal of Business Venturing, 9,* 179–187.

Geiger, R. L., & Sá, C. M. (2008). *Tapping the riches of science: Universities and the promise of economic growth.* Cambridge, MA: Harvard University Press.

Gilmartin, S., Shartrand, A., Chen, H., Estrada, S., & Sheppard, S. (2014). U.S.-Based entrepreneurship programs for undergraduate engineers scope, development, goals, and pedagogies. *Epicenter Technical Brief 1.* Stanford, CA and Hadley, MA: National Center for Engineering Pathways to Innovation.

Godwyn, M. (2009). Can the liberal arts and entrepreneurship work together? *Academe, 95*(1), 36–38.

Gorman, G., Hanlon, D., & King, W. (1997). Some research perspectives on entrepreneurship education, enterprise education and education for small business management: A ten-year literature review. *International Small Business Journal, 15*(3), 56–76.

Hackett, S. M., & Dilts, D. M. (2004). A systematic review of business incubation research. *The Journal of Technology Transfer, 29*(1), 55–82.

Hansson, F., Husted, K., & Vestergaard, J. (2005). Second generation science parks: From structural holes jockeys to social capital catalysts of the knowledge society. *Technovation, 25*(9), 1039–1049.

Harris Interactive. (2010). *YouthPulseSM 2010: Kauffman foundation custom report.* Kansas City, MO: Kauffman Foundation.

Hazelkorn, E. (2011). *Rankings and the reshaping of higher education: The battle for world-class excellence.* Basingstoke, UK: Palgrave Macmillan.

Hills, G. E. (1988). Variations in university entrepreneurship education: An empirical study of an evolving field. *Journal of Business Venturing, 3*(2), 109–122.

Hire Prospects, OAYEC, D-Code. (2008). *National youth entrepreneur social attitude and innovation survey.* Retrieved from http://www.firstwork.org/wp/wp-content/uploads/2011/04/National-Youth-Entrepreneur-Social-Attitude-and-Innovation-Study.pdf

Honig, B. (2004). Entrepreneurship education: Toward a model of contingency-based business planning. *Academy of Management Learning & Education, 3*(3), 258–273.

Industry Canada. (2010). *The teaching and practice of entrepreneurship within Canadian higher education institutions.* Ottawa, ON: Industry Canada.

Jongbloed, B., Enders, J., & Salerno, C. (2008). Higher education and its communities: Interconnections, interdependencies and a research agenda. *Higher Education, 56*(3), 303–324.

Katz, J. A. (2003). The chronology and intellectual trajectory of American entrepreneurship education: 1876–1999. *Journal of Business Venturing, 18*(2), 283–300.

Katz, J. A. (2004). *2004 survey of endowed positions in entrepreneurship and related fields in the United States.* Retrieved from http://sites.kauffman.org/pdf/survey_endowed_chairs_04.pdf

Katz, J. A. (2008). Fully mature but not fully legitimate: A different perspective on the state of entrepreneurship education. *Journal of Small Business Management, 46*(4), 550–566.

Kauffman Foundation. (2001). *The growth and advancement of entrepreneurship in higher education: An environmental scan of college initiatives.* Kansas City, MO: Ewing Marion Kauffman Foundation.

Kauffman Foundation. (2009). *Entrepreneurship in American higher education.* Kansas City, MO: Ewing Marion Kauffman Foundation.

Kirp, D. L. (2003). *Shakespeare, Einstein, and the bottom line: The marketing of higher education.* Cambridge, MA: Harvard University Press.

Klatt, L. A. (1988). A study of small business/entrepreneurial education in colleges and universities. *The Journal of Private Enterprise, 4,* 103–108.

Kuratko, D. F. (2005). The emergence of entrepreneurship education: Development, trends, and challenges. *Entrepreneurship Theory and Practice, 29*(5), 577–598.

Leffel, A., & Hallam, C. R. (2008). Stimulating entrepreneurial enterprise development: Business plan competitions are not the answer. In *Association for small business and entrepreneurship 35th annual conference proceedings 1* (pp. 162–188). San Antonio, Texas, TX: University of Texas at San Antonio, College of Business.

Levenburg, N. M., Lane, P. M., & Schwarz, T. V. (2006). Interdisciplinary dimensions in entrepreneurship. *Journal of Education for Business, 81*(5), 275–281.

Levina, N., & Vaast, E. (2005). The emergence of boundary spanning competence in practice: Implications for implementation and use of information systems. *MIS quarterly, 29*(2), 335–363.

Levina, N., & Vaast, E. (2014). A field-of-practice view of boundary-spanning in and across organizations: Transactive and transformative boundary-spanning practices. In J. L. Fox & C. Cooper (Eds.), *Boundary spanning in organizations: Networks, influence, and conflict* (pp. 285–307). New York, NY: Routledge.

Marginson, S. (2006). Dynamics of national and global competition in higher education. *Higher Education, 52*(1), 1–39.

Mars, M. M. (2007a). Exploring the privatized dimension of entrepreneurship education and its link to the emergence of the college student entrepreneur. In J. A. Sandlin & P. McLaren (Eds.), *Critical pedagogies of consumption: Living and learning in the shadow of the "shopocalypse."* New York, NY: Routledge.

Mars, M. M. (2007b). The diverse agendas of faculty within an institutionalized model of entrepreneurship education. *Journal of Entrepreneurship Education, 10*(1), 43–62.

Mars, M. M. (2013). Framing the conceptual meaning and fundamental principles of innovation. In M. M. Mars & S. Hoskinson (Eds.), *A cross-disciplinary primer on the meaning and principles of innovation* (pp. 1–12). Emerald Group Pub Limited.

Mars, M. M., & Metcalfe, A. S. (2009). Entrepreneurship in the contemporary academy. *ASHE Higher Education Report, 34*(5), 1–111.

Mars, M., Slaughter, S., & Rhoades, G. (2008). The state-sponsored student entrepreneur. *The Journal of Higher Education, 79*(6), 638–670.

Mayhew, M. J., Simonoff, J. S., Baumol, W. J., Wiesenfeld, B. M., & Klein, M. W. (2012). Exploring innovative entrepreneurship and its ties to higher educational experiences. *Research in Higher Education, 53*, 831–859.

MBA Roundtable. (2012). *Curricular innovation study.* Retrieved from http://www.mbaroundtable.org/curricular_innovation_study

Menzies, T. V. (2000). An exploratory study of university entrepreneurship centers in Canada. *Journal of Small Business and Entrepreneurship, 15*(3), 15–38.

Menzies, T. V. (2004). *Entrepreneurship and the Canadian university.* St. Catharines, ON: Brock University.

Menzies, T. V. (2009). *Entrepreneurship and the Canadian universities: Strategies and best practices of entrepreneurship centres.* St. Catharines, Ontario: Faculty of Business, Brock University; Canada: John Dobson Foundation.

Merriam, S. B. (2009). *Qualitative research: A guide to design and implementation.* San Francisco, CA: Jossey-Bass.

Miller, P., & Bound, K. (2011). *The startup factories: The rise of accelerator programmes to support new technology ventures.* Retrieved from NESTA website: http://www.nesta.org.uk/sites/default/files/the_startup_factories_0.pdf

Ministry of Training, Colleges and Universities. (2013). *Ontario's differentiation policy framework for postsecondary education.* Toronto, ON: Queen's Printer for Ontario.

Morphew, C. C., & Swanson, C. (2011). On the efficacy of raising your university's ranking. In J. C. Shin, R. K. Toutkoushian, & U. Teichler (Eds.), *University rankings: Theoretical basis, methodology and impacts on global higher education* (pp. 185–199). Dordrecht, The Netherlands: Springer.

Morris, M. H., Kuratko, D. F., & Cornwall, J. R. (2013). *Entrepreneurship programs and the modern university.* Northampton, MA: Edward Elgar Pub.

Mowery, D. C., Nelson, R., Sampat, B., & Ziedonis, A. (2004). *Ivory tower and industrial innovation: University-industry technology transfer before and after the Bayh-Dole act in the United States.* Stanford, CA: Stanford University Press.

Nelson, A. J., & Byers, T. (2010). *Challenges in university technology transfer and the promising role of entrepreneurship education.* Kansas City, MO: The Ewing Marion Kauffman Foundation.

Office of Innovation and Entrepreneurship. (2013). *The innovative and entrepreneurial university: Higher education, innovation, and entrepreneurship in focus.* US Department of Commerce.

Ontario. (2013). *Seizing global opportunities: Ontario's innovation agenda.* Toronto, ON: Ministry of Research and Innovation.

Pittaway, L., Rodriguez-Falcon, E., Aiyegbayo, O., & King, A. (2011). The role of entrepreneurship clubs and societies in entrepreneurial learning. *International Small Business Journal, 29*(1), 37–57.

Pittaway, L., Gazzard, J., Shore, A., & Williamson, T. (2012). Entrepreneurial learning through experience: The hidden role of student clubs in management education. *Center for Entrepreneurial Learning and Leadership,* 1–32.

Powell, W. W., & Snellman, K. (2004). The knowledge economy. *Annual Review of Sociology, 30*(1), 199–220.

Premier's Office. (2014, March 19). *Sandboxes encourage innovation, entrepreneurship.* Retrieved from http://novascotia.ca/news/release/?id=20140319003

Pryor, J. H., & Reedy, E. J. (2009). *Trends in business interest among US college students: An early exploration of data available from the cooperative institutional research program.* Kansas City, MO: Ewing Marion Kauffman Foundation.

Ray, D. (1990). Liberal arts for entrepreneurs. *Entrepreneurship Theory & Practice, 15*(2), 79–93.

Regele, M. D., & Neck, H. M. (2012). The entrepreneurship education sub-ecosystem in the United States: Opportunities to increase entrepreneurial activity. *Journal of Business & Entrepreneurship, Winter,* 25–47.

Roberts, S. (2013). Infusing entrepreneurship within non-business disciplines: Preparing artists and others for self-employment and entrepreneurship. *Artivate: A Journal of Entrepreneurship in the Arts, 1*(2).

Ross, L. W., & Byrd, K. A. (2011). Business plan competitions: Start-up idols and their twenty-first century launch pads. *Journal of Higher Education Theory and Practice, 11*(4), 53–64.

Ryerson University. (n.d.). *About the DMZ.* Retrieved from http://digitalmediazone.ryerson.ca/about/

Sá, C., & Kretz, A. (2015). *The entrepreneurship movement and the university.* New York, NY: Palgrave MacMillan.

Sá, C., Kretz, A., & Sigurdson, K. (2014). *The state of entrepreneurship education in Ontario's colleges and universities.* Ontario, Canada: Higher Education Quality Council of Ontario.

Shaver, K. G. (2005). Reflections on a new academic path: Entrepreneurship in the arts and sciences. *Peer Review, 7*(3), 21–23.

Shaw, E., & Carter, S. (2007). Social entrepreneurship: Theoretical antecedents and empirical analysis of entrepreneurial processes and outcomes. *Journal of Small Business and Enterprise Development, 14*(3), 418–434.

Shinner, R., Pruett, M., & Toney, B. (2009). Entrepreneurship education attitudes across campus. *Journal of Education for Business, 84*(3), 151–158.

Short, J. C., Moss, T. W., & Lumpkin, T. (2009). Research in social entrepreneurship: Past contributions and future opportunities. *Strategic Entrepreneurship Journal, 3*(2), 161–194.

Slaughter, S., & Rhoades, G. (2004). *Academic capitalism and the new economy: Markets, state, and higher education.* Maryland, MD: The Johns Hopkins University Press.

Slaughter, S., Campbell, T., Holleman, M., & Morgan, E. (2002). The traffic in graduate students: Graduate students as tokens of exchange between academe and industry. *Science, Technology & Human Values, 27*(2), 282–312.

Solomon, G. (2007). An examination of entrepreneurship education in the United States. *Journal of Small Business and Enterprise Development, 14*(2), 168–182.

Solomn, G. T., & Fernald, Jr., L. W. (1991). Trends in small business management and entrepreneurship education in the United States. *Entrepreneurship Theory and Practice, 15*(3), 25–39.

Stam, E., & Garnsey, E. W. (2008). Entrepreneurship in the knowledge economy. In J. Bessant & T. Venables (Eds.), *Creating wealth from knowledge* (pp. 145–176). Cheltenham, England: Edward Elgar Publishing Limited.

State Science & Technology Institute. (2014). *Trends in tech-based economic development: Local, state, and federal action in 2013.* Retrieved from http://ssti.org/report-archive/trends2013.pdf

Streeter, D. H., & Jaquette, Jr., J. P. (2004). University-wide entrepreneurship education: Alternative models and current trend. *The Southern Rural Sociological Association, 20*(2), 44–71.

The University of Texas at Austin. (n.d.). *Innovation, creativity, & entrepreneurship: Bridging disciplines programs*. Retrieved from http://www.utexas.edu/ugs/bdp/programs/ice

The White House. (2011). *Startup America*. Retrieved from http://www.whitehouse.gov/economy/business/startupamerica (Accessed March 20, 2013)

Torrance, W. (2013). *Entrepreneurship campuses: Action, impact, and lessons learned from the Kauffman campus initiative*. Kansas City, MO: Ewing Marion Kauffman Foundation.

Tornatzky, L. G., Waugaman, P. G., Gray, D. O., Southern, T. T., & Southern, G. G. P. (2002). *Innovation U: New university roles in a knowledge economy*. Research Triangle Park, NC: Southern Technology Council.

Tushman, M. L., & Scanlan, T. J. (1981). Boundary spanning individuals: Their role in information transfer and their antecedents. *The Academy of Management Journal, 24*(2), 289–305.

University of Southern California. (2014). *2014 New venture seed competition*. Retrieved from http://www.marshall.usc.edu/news/releases/2014/2014-new-venture-seed-competition

University of Waterloo. (2013). *A distinguished past – A distinctive future: University of Waterloo strategic plan*. Retrieved from https://uwaterloo.ca/strategic-plan/sites/ca.strategic-plan/files/uploads/files/c002637_strategicplan2013.sept3_.lowres_final-s.pdf

Vesper, K. H., & McMullan, W. E. (1988). Entrepreneurship: Today courses, tomorrow degrees. *Entrepreneurship Theory and Policy, 13*(1), 7–13.

Wake Forest University About. (n.d.). *Innovation, creativity and entrepreneurship program*. Retrieved from http://entrepreneurship.wfu.edu/about-us/vision

Washburn, J. (2006). *University, Inc.: The corporate corruption of higher education*. New York, NY: Basic Books.

Winfield, I. (2005). Fostering social entrepreneurship through liberal learning in the social sciences. *Peer Review*, Spring, 15–17.

Zammuto, R. F. (1984). Are the liberal arts an endangered species? *Journal of Higher Education, 55*(2), 184–211.

Andrew Kretz
Ontario Institute for Studies in Education of the University of Toronto

Creso M. Sá
Associate Professor of Higher Education
Ontario Institute for Studies in Education of the University of Toronto

105

DIMITRI GAGLIARDI, DEBORAH COX AND YANCHAO LI

4. INSTITUTIONAL INERTIA AND BARRIERS TO THE ADOPTION OF OPEN SCIENCE

INTRODUCTION

The advance of networking and computing technologies offers unprecedented opportunities for the implementation of principles and practices of Open Science. Yet its uptake entails factors beyond merely technological circumstances. Substantial conditions relate to stakeholder attitudes and institutional arrangements. Based upon an e-survey and a workshop involving a wide range of important stakeholders, this chapter makes an early contribution to understanding the significant factors enabling or hindering the uptake of open science practices, in the immediate research areas involving research professionals and research organisations. We found that key drivers to the uptake of open science practices include the usefulness of publicly available research outcomes in developing personal lines of research; nonetheless, the propensity of research professionals to openly share their contributions is not high. Operational barriers such as difficulties in assessing the quality and rigour of research contributions, lack of skills and/or time to contribute to the open science movement are slowing the uptake of open science. More importantly still, there are institutional barriers linked to systemic issues such as the inadequacy of the current funding schemes. In particular, we found that institutional inertia plays a significant role in inhibiting the further opening up of the scientific process. This exploration has revealed some very promising insights for a roadmap for further research.

TRENDS TOWARDS OPEN SCIENCE

The institutional arrangements and the organisation of undertaking scientific research that have developed since the Renaissance have changed little throughout the 20th Century. In the 21st Century, the diffusion of Information and Communication Technologies (ICT) and new web-based tools have created a range of new possibilities for conducting knowledge creation activities by exploiting the large investments in cyber infrastructure and the networking capabilities of rich web technologies. New technologies and investments in ICTs have supported a variety of new collaborative initiatives in conducting science, these initiatives are typically described by the term Science 2.0 whereby the organisation of science is moving towards a more open process, termed appropriately Open Science.[1] Whilst we recognise that this is still an evolving domain, a great deal of research has been conducted on the various

E. Reale & E. Primeri (Eds.), The Transformation of University Institutional and Organizational Boundaries, 107–133.

aspects of open science (David, 2004; Priem et al., 2010; Nielsen, 2011; Bartling & Friesike, 2014 amongst others). In trying to define this phenomenon we observe that open science is not only an uptake of Web 2.0 technologies nor only the adoption of strategic behaviours typical of the Web 2.0 revolution into scientific practices. It is also the attitudes of research performers and their organisations towards the technological infrastructure upon which these new approaches to undertaking science are based and the resultant expanding networked organisations that arise from the greater connectivity of scientists.

In this essay we define Open Science as a 'movement' that involves scientists, research organisations, funding bodies, businesses and the general public in the domain of science affecting the way scientific work is carried out and characterised by wide collaborative effort at each stage of the research process. Open science implies an overall focus on openness in science, be it to publications or research data; new methods of publication of scientific findings or processes, the growing readership of scientists' blogs and the growing number of citizen scientists taking part in scientific research projects (Peters, 2010; Peters & Robert, 2011; Bartling & Friesike, 2014).

The trends that are emerging from this evolutionary process point towards the increasing reliance on large databases and increased computational power, the organisation of scientific practices being increasingly bundled within collaborative teams who are operating on technological platforms and research findings that are communicated *in itinere,* via means which are much faster and accessible than the traditional publication channels. Indicators of this trend are many and diverse; three notable interrelating macro trends in science are:

- a new way of doing science: data-intensive science enabled by the availability of large-scale datasets, processed through simulation software and enabled by high performance computing;
- an explosion of science/research output, including not only open science/access to scientific data but also replicability of scientific discovery, which implies access to methods, tools, data, and articles, and also new ways of conducting scientific collaborations and
- a diversification and increase in the number of actors producing scientific deliverables. These include, amongst others, citizens scientists (Burgelman et al., 2010).

The objective of this essay is to investigate the existing institutional arrangements and the adoption of new methods, highlighting conflicting interests of stakeholders that may hinder the cultural changes necessary for embracing the principles and the practices of open science. In particular, this paper explores our thoughts on addressing and analysing drivers and barriers to the adoption of open science with a focus on the roles of the research performing stakeholders in the scientific process. We focus our attention on the research performing side comprising researchers, managers, support staff and other professionals including research organisation leaders, research practitioners and communicators and the institutions within which they operate. Our aim is also to reflect on the policy implications deriving from the emergence of open science and its adoption within the existing organisational settings.

Whilst it has to be understood that this study should be considered exploratory rather than conclusive, from our analysis we can certainly infer that institutional inertia plays a significant role in inhibiting the further opening up of the scientific process. Undeniably, there are constraining factors linked to the quality of research, as fully open science features may impair appropriate evaluation or assessment of research findings but research funding methods and the absence of alternative reputation systems for scientists and scientists' performance do constitute a major barrier to open science. Research output assessment practices, adaptive research funding methods, discipline dependent practices and alternative reputation systems are certainly worth deliberation as the tools and methods of open science and its approach have proven extremely useful for conducting research at a faster pace, with results that manifest greater effect and impact.

The chapter develops along the following lines. In section 1) the idea that progressing open science as a facilitator of superior and more effective research is explored from the relevant academic literature. In section 2) we describe the methodological approach adopted in carrying out this research. In section 3) we highlight the results obtained from analysing the data collected through the e-survey and in section 4) we provide the discussion of the findings, some limitations of the current research and the conclusions highlighting promising research areas.

SOME REFLECTIONS FROM THE LITERATURE

Open science is the result of a long term evolutionary process in conducting science, in recent years it has found a new and greater emphasis due to the introduction of networking information and communication technologies including pervasive Web 2.0 technologies and newer rich web technologies (known as Web 3.0 or semantic Web). This renewed emphasis can be attributed to the scientific community and policy makers identifying the megatrends described above and consequently raising questions upon the current status and potential evolutionary paths that the organisation of science might take in the future. This, albeit reductive, justification of the interests in the state of the organisation of science is easily explained by the enormous commitments that governments, public and private organisations have in terms of their remit to pursue social and economic progress, current outlays in scientific endeavours and their economic and social outcomes. In other words, the vested interests of the modern patrons of science – be they public or private – and of the scientific community, is to understand whether, and to what extent the ways of conducting science can be honed to 'bear more fruit'. This logic is now particularly cogent given the tightening of the public and private budgets for science and research.

A synthesis of the theoretical underpinning of the arguments for open science is certainly not in the remit of this paper, however in this brief review is perhaps necessary to remind the reader that pioneer work on the nature and practices of science are still the yardstick for what we now understand as science and scientific practices.

The discussion on open science has a long standing tradition that is still shaping the current debate. Its theoretical basis can be found in the works of Merton (1942), Popper (1935, English ed., 1959) and Polanyi (1962).[2]

Science does not only involve the stock of knowledge, but also the methods established to create and verify new knowledge. It involves the social and cultural values governing the production and dissemination of knowledge. Within this definition of science, Merton (1973) develops the institutional 'imperatives' that characterise modern science. Polanyi (1962) lays out 'ground rules' or professional standards involving scientists' motivations to contribute to the corpus of knowledge. Popper (1935) offers a justification of the current peer review system.

Modern investigations in the 'modes of science' do not invalidate the principles set out *inter alia* by Popper, Merton and Polanyi. The following contributions highlight organisational changes in the traditional process of undertaking science and novel forms of organisation of knowledge production that are emerging. Compared to traditional science, which is confined within the remit of the academe and organised in a hierarchical fashion, compartmentalised in homogeneous disciplines, Gibbons et al. (1994) and Nowotny at al. (2001) introduce and discuss the new production of knowledge as characterised by application-centred investigation, transdisciplinarity, heterogeneity and organisational diversity, social accountability and reflexivity (Mode 2 of knowledge production). More recently, Carayannis and Campbell (2006) and Wagner (2008) describing perhaps a Mode 3 of knowledge production, highlight how scientific endeavours are increasingly characterised by multilevel and networked clusters of knowledge production.

Core to the scientific process, from the more traditional form of organisation to the modern networked science is the dyad 'creation' and 'dissemination' of knowledge; the first driven by curiosity, ingenuity and ethics, the second validated by sceptical peers and diffused by the available means of communication.

The process is undertaken under the aegis of a patron. Eamon (1985) and David (2004, 2005) argue that public knowledge or open science derives from the Scientific Revolution where, departing from the dominant regime of secrecy in the pursuit of Nature's secrets, scientists recognised the invaluable contribution to science that a collaborative approach might allow. Notwithstanding the complementarities and idiosyncrasies that confidentiality and openness present in relation to the dissemination of science, the principle of priority of attribution constitutes a strong incentive to disclosure and as a consequence, accumulation of knowledge increases at a faster rate and more organically than if it were undertaken in secrecy[3] (David, 2004).

Given the support of the State to the promotion of science, opening the scientific process became an aspirational target which experienced different fortune throughout the years. Recently, however, it has found renewed vigour especially since successful examples of some open science initiatives ensuing on the diffusion of networking technologies.

Fecher and Friesike (2014) present a concise synthesis of the current debate on open science; they identify five streams, or schools of thought, informing the contemporary discourse. The authors term these 1) 'public school' concerned with the public engagement and understanding of knowledge; 2) the 'democratic school' which is mainly concerned with public access to knowledge; 3) the 'pragmatic school' which stresses the importance of collaborative research for an efficient use of resources; 4) the 'measurement school' which is concerned with the assessment of the 'quality' of the research output and looks at alternative metrics for the evaluation of scientific contributions and personal contribution to sciences; and finally 5) the 'infrastructure school' which is mostly concerned with the technological aspects of open science and the role of new information and communication technologies in fostering open science.

As Fecher and Friesike (2014) point out, the discourse on open science is complex as it develops along many intertwined domains, entailing many different stakeholders interacting at different levels. We can argue that science is a systemic occurrence and that it directly involves a variety of stakeholders with interests and stakes in the process which are rarely aligned. The attention of scientists and research professionals, research organisations, research funders and policy makers has long been focussed on the various expressions of open science notably, open access to publications, e-infrastructures, data repositories and other practices. A synthesis and relevant references of the key features of open science is presented in the Table 1 below.

The first steps towards opening up the outcomes of the scientific process have entailed the dissemination of publications through open access to publications and diffusion of the data from which such research originates. Open access to publication, as we shall see below, has been at the centre of a lively debate since the mid-1990s whilst the first inroads in open data were made at the beginning of the current century.

To have a perspective on the scale of the current *open access* publishing industry, the Directory of Open Access Journals (DOAJ), one of the most important associations of open access publishers by number of publications, consists of some 10,000 journals in all disciplines. To date the number of articles published by journals listed in the DOAJ is about 1.7 million. Adding to these, traditional subscription-based journals have, since the early 2000s, opened up to the possibility of publishing in open access mode and many traditional publishing houses are developing their open access catalogues of journals.

The argument at the basis of the open access to publications debate originates from the observation that the public is actually paying twice for the production of knowledge, once in the form of public research funding and a second time to access the knowledge that has been produced. The possibilities offered by electronic

Table 1. Key features of open science practices

Open Science practices	Key features	Literature/source
Open access to publications/open access publishing	Publications that use a funding model that does not charge readers or their institutions for access. Such publications may be further redistributed and reused for research, education and other purposes.	Directory of Open Access Journals (DOAJ)[4] Dallmeier-Tiessen et al. (2010) Björk and Solomon (2012)
Open peer reviews	A procedure ' ...whereby the experts consulted on an article's worthiness submit their comments for publication along with the article, thus stimulating discussion in a way the article alone could not.' (p. 3)	Okerson and O'Donnell (1995)
Open access to data	A key tool to bring together people and ideas in a way that catalyzes science and innovation. It helps to maximize the research potential of new digital technologies and networks and provides greater returns from the public investment in research.	European Commission (2012) OECD (2007)
Negative results publications	Enabling later researchers to learn from earlier researchers' failures, so that resources (including time and money) would not be spent on repeating the same failures.	Goetz (2007) Kundoor and Mueen (2010)

(Continued)

Table 1. (Continued)

Open lab notebooks	(Virtual) lab notebooks containing information about all the components and processes related to a research project. Scientists report what they actually do. An open lab notebook includes all the information that any scientist needs to be able to understand and replicate the research.	Sanderson (2008)
Research social networks	Digital networks '...where scientists freely and easily share published work, experimental data, ideas and opinions and mutually benefit from the open and collaborative realm that is emerging in the digital age' (p. 342).	Rinaldi (2014)
Alternative reputation systems	Beyond traditional metrics based on citation analysis, '...scholarly impact would cover usage, captures, mentions and social media... Metrics should include mentions in blogs and other nontraditional formats, open review forums, electronic book downloads, library circulation counts, bookmarks, tweets and more. Such alternative metrics provide a more complete view of peer response to scholarly writings and better demonstrate the relative position of a research grant applicant and potential for influential work. (p. 35)	Buschman and Michalek (2013)
Big data analysis	Analysis of extremely large pools of structured or unstructured data that could not be processed using traditional analysis methods. A culture of data sharing and open access to big data sets can significantly accelerate the process of scientific research and breakthrough.	Choudhury et al. (2014)
Science blogs	Blogs published by scientists with a main focus on disseminating or commenting upon science. Through this way scientists share their research interests, thoughts, work in progress and research outcomes.	Wilkins (2008) Waldrop (2008)
Crowd-source science	Science based on crowd sourcing which facilitates research in a more effective (including cost-effective) and collaborative manner.	Franzoni and Sauermann, H. (2014)

networks can provide a way out of this impasse and extend the reach and accessibility of scientific publications. *Opening up the peer review process* would also guarantee the scientific rigour of ePublications (Harnad, 1994). This system could make the publishing industry in the field of scholarly publications practically redundant.[5] Okerson and O'Donnell, J. J. (1995) argued that whilst these new ideas are enticing, their slow uptake is due to the fact that the academic community is basically satisfied with the status quo of the scientific publishing process. In other words, academics are comfortable in operating within the limitations of the traditional process, even if it might defer or stop altogether the publication of their own research. The incentive system in place is such that the alternative publishing of ePublications, not at all favoured by promotion and tenure committees, altogether discourage this form of publication. The reaction to the perceived bias associated with the evaluation of research through metrics such as journal standings (measured by the journal impact factor) and research standing (measured by the number of citations) has spurred the debate on *alternative reputation systems* – at the time of writing one such example is Altmetric (altmetric.com). Buschman and Michalek (2013) explore the drawback of traditional evaluation metrics and propose a taxonomy based on 1) Usage of the article (downloads, views etc); 2) Capture (bookmarks, favourites readers etc.); 3) mentions (in blog posts in the news in comments and reviews; 4) social media (tweets, likes, ratings and shares); and 5) Citations (citation counts in indexing sites). These metrics, the authors argue, reflect more accurately the impact of research in an era of increased competition for research funding and tenure.

The importance of open access to scientific publications particularly around issues of dissemination and research impact has not gone unnoticed. The earlier work of Antelman (2004), McVeigh (2004), and Harnad and Brody (2004), investigated the research impact of open access publications. Antelman (2004) found that in a sample of some 2,000 articles in four disciplines with different rates of open access adoption – mathematics, electrical and electronic engineering, political science, and philosophy – open access publications had a greater research impact than traditional articles in terms of citations. McVeigh (2004), in a study for the publisher Thompson, assessed the impact factor and citation patterns of open access journals included in the ISI Citation Database. The study found that the open access journals were poorly represented in the ISI Databases and their impact factor was relatively low compared with that of traditional subscription journals, even though a handful of open access journals were classed in the top 10% in their category. Open access journals fared rather better in terms of Immediacy Index, suggesting that open access publications were accessed and cited more rapidly than papers in traditional subscription journals. Harnad and Brody (2004) argued that a more appropriate comparison between research impact of open access and traditionally published papers should focus on different citation patterns of open access papers and non-open access papers published in the same journal. The authors found that open access papers were cited between 2.5 and 5.8 times more than non-open access papers published in the same journals.

Studies on the diffusion of open access journals and publications, publishing models and attributes (Dallmeier-Tiessen et al., 2010), their comparative impact on research and the links between open access and citation counts (Björk & Solomon, 2012; Solomon et al., 2013 to name but a few) have been intensively studied in the last ten years. Gaulé and Maystre (2011) examined a dataset of over 4,000 papers published between 2004 and 2006 in one of the world's top scientific journals, the Proceedings of the National Academy of Sciences (PNAS) and found that the correlation between open access and citation is only marginal and not statistically significant when the quality of the paper and the status of the author within the research area are taken into account.

Access to data has recently been at the centre of attention. Data sharing is extremely important in science as replicability of studies, validation of results and extension of research can be enabled only through the re-use of data upon which original publications are based (Gorgolewki et al., 2013). It is also undeniable that open data is the first step towards data aggregation and *big data analysis*, a promising research strategy opening up possibilities of large-scale studies and sample-bias corrections (Choudhury et al., 2014). Data sharing also acts as a deterrent to fraud, encouraging the publication of high-quality research. In other words, data sharing plays a dual role in advancing knowledge creation and establishing best practices against fraudulent behaviours, however, raw data is of little or no value for researchers other than those who have collected them. This hardly justifies any form of protection. Nonetheless, when time and effort to systematise and appropriately document the information with the relevant metadata, their value becomes intrinsically high and adds to the burden of researchers who would likely prefer to be engaged in research rather than learn and practice data curation (Nature, 2011; Grand et al., 2014). Yet, when research data has been collected through public funded research grants, it is expected that it will be made openly available.

This concept, whilst pioneered by not-for profit research foundations such as the Wellcome Trust (2003) and the National Institute of Health in the US for grants over $500,000 in 2003, has progressively pervaded the policies of almost all public research funders in the US. In the UK the Research Councils have a policy regarding data-sharing for supported research and in the EU, the European Commission requires that funding bids are complete with a data management plan and the data have to comply with the standard adopted by the Commission Services. Within these frameworks it is not uncommon that a period of exclusive use of the research data is granted to the researcher(s) who have collected them.

The OECD (2007) has issued principles and guidelines for the access to research data obtained through publicly funded initiatives. The guidelines specify that research data should be made available to the research community in a timely, user-friendly format, preferably from the Internet and at the lowest possible cost. Moreover, the guidelines suggest that authors of scientific publications should make the data used in their work available. This 'suggestion' has been adopted by several journals (Pampel & Dallmeier-Tiessen, 2014) including those published by the high-profile publisher

Nature, which requires that materials, data and protocols used in experiments should be made promptly available to the reader upon request, preferably in a downloadable file from an institutional repository (OECD, 2007; Whyte & Pryor, 2011).

In theory, systems for the public access to research data collected in the course of publicly funded research are in place in most of the research active, Western countries; in practice, there are still many issues to be resolved. The costs of opening up research data comprise 1) Infrastructure and Administration, 2) Standardisation, 3) Human Resources and 4) Opportunity costs. These costs are not supported by grant agreements indefinitely and after the grant comes to an end, these are left with the researchers and their organisations (Wilhelm et al., 2014). Even when a public data infrastructure is available, it is still unclear how it should be funded. Berman and Cerf (2013) raised a sensible point when looking at the 'quantity' of data collected by federally funded R&D projects and noted that the variety of initiatives for data infrastructure sponsored by the US Government and the various agencies stated that

> *federal R&D agencies are unlikely to allocate enough resources to support all federally funded research data. The costs of infrastructure would absorb too great a proportion of a budget that must support both innovation and the infrastructure needed to drive innovation.* (p. 616)

There is one more aspect of research data sharing that needs consideration. Undeniably, research organisations might have institutional repositories and the costs for infrastructure, managing and maintaining them might be factored into budgets on a rolling basis from government funds or grants however, following the logic proposed by Berman and Cerf (2013), at one point the costs might become unsustainable. The involvement of the researchers in coding, documenting and curating the data that have been collected becomes strictly necessary prior to the integration in the repository. Yet, a reward system for research data work is non-existent. Two recent studies highlight very clearly the problem of sharing research data from the researchers' perspective. Haeussler et al. (2014) using a survey of over 1,000 bio-scientists based in Germany and in the UK found that researchers were more likely to share information if the gain derived from expected reciprocity outweighs the loss of competitive edge derived from sharing. Certainly, in research areas where competition is more fearsome, the incentive to share any information would be extremely low. Career stage also has an impact, an untenured researcher has very little incentive to share compared to a senior researcher. Andreoli-Versbach and Mueller-Langer (2014) analysed the data-sharing behaviour of some 500 empirical economists and management scholars, finding that their attitude to sharing data is often 'professed but seldom practised'. Interestingly they found that the likelihood that the researcher shares data increases predictably with 1) tenure, but also with 2) the standing of the researchers, 3) if data sharing is mandatory for the publications and, lastly, 4) if the scientists have a personal preference for open science.

A publication bias towards positive results has been evidenced since the 1960s. Smart (1964) highlighted that in psychological research there is a selection bias against the *publication of negative results* as only 9% of the papers in this discipline were reporting upon them. The reasons for this bias are attributable to the author selection – authors are less likely to decide to publish negative research results – and to greater editorial scrutiny. Fanelli (2012) highlights that, due to competition for research funding and citations, negative result publications are disappearing from most disciplines, even though they are particularly useful for the progress of science (Goetz, 2007; Hayes & Hunter, 2012; Foster & Putos, 2014). Several initiatives have been implemented in order to counteract this publication bias. These range from positive approach journals to negative results publications[6] (Wilcox, 2014) to the creation of journals where only negative experimental results are sought for publication (Kundoor & Mueen, 2010).

Information Technologies (IT) feature strongly in open science practice as an enabler. Practices such as open access to publication and open data rely strongly on the infrastructural capacity of IT. Other practices, using the IT infrastructure, are mostly a consequence of the behaviour of scientists towards said technologies. Amongst these practices are research social networks, open lab notebooks, science blogs and crowd sourcing.

Research social networks, from platforms such as ResearchGate to Twitter, are not intensively used as platforms to share published ongoing work, ideas, opinions or experimental data, all activities that may foster open collaboration and build a dialogue with the general public; instead they are increasingly becoming a means for public visibility of scientists, especially for the benefit of research funders, and a platform where constructive scientific debate takes place (Rinaldi, 2014). At one end of the spectrum activities addressed to the scientific community such as *open lab notebook* practices are employed by scientists to disseminate their findings as they are achieved. This practice is mainly used to claim priority on specific research endeavours and to stimulate the dialogue about the research undertaken. It has an interesting secondary effect of forcing a higher standard of record-keeping given that it is open to other scientists to peruse. The risks, however, are that data and/or methodologies can be employed by competing researchers, if, further down the line, the research outcome becomes of commercial value, it will not be patentable (due to non-originality) and, for the same reason, some journals will not publish results that have previously appeared in the public domain (Sanderson, 2008). On the other end of the spectrum, *science blogs* are a popular way to engage in science communication in a timely way and to relate to the public who otherwise would not have the skills to engage with traditional scientific publications (Wilkins, 2008). Crowd source science entails the participation of citizens and/or professional scientists to an open research endeavour. Many crowd science experiments have become very successful over the last decade including Galaxy Zoo, Fold it and Polymath. Nielsen (2011) and Franzoni and Sauermann (2014) highlight the point that crowd science projects are directed to professional scientists to exploit economies of scale in the scientific production and to citizen scientists in order to extend research capabilities in the collection of data or in non-technical labour intensive activities. These authors have highlighted that such ventures are heterogeneous and present many organisational challenges; thus, they also identify crowd science, as a new means of organising science that allows for 'significant experimentation' and considerable scope in the types of problems that can be addressed (Franzoni & Sauermann, 2014, p. 7).

In this chapter we focus our attention on the research professionals and the organisations within which they operate. Universities and research institute researchers in both the public and private sectors have a significant strategic role to play in the process of open science. The potential benefits of open science offered to researchers derive from the openness of the process and the opportunity to draw on a much wider and deeper range of expertise, including interdisciplinary expertise, than would otherwise be possible. Moreover, the public engagement of open science is likely to have wider impact and outreach as the research endeavour is open to scrutiny by the scientific community as well as by the public. This facilitates the research strategies of individual researchers, establishes an open system that mitigates misconduct and is an efficient use of resources across the science base.

METHODOLOGY: DEFINITIONS AND SURVEY

The methodology used in carrying out the analysis presented below consists of an e-survey conducted by the project partners led by Inno AG and a stakeholder workshop held at the European Commission, in Brussels, on the 4th of November, 2013. The survey and the workshop were part of the deliverables for a policy briefing prepared for the European Commission entitled *The Prospects of Science 2.0: policy implications*.

The survey was launched in October 2013 and was live and monitored for 4 weeks. The respondents were recruited through the professional networks of the research team. It attracted the interest of over 200 respondents. One hundred and eleven questionnaires returned were adequately completed and selected for analysis. Respondents were from 16 Countries, largely from Europe (n=89) and North America (n=11). Their occupations are Researchers (n=69), Research Project Managers (n=6), Research Support Staff (n=26) and Others (n=8), consisting of Research Communicators i.e., Journalists using research publications and findings in their work, University leaders and Research Practitioners.

The age of respondents has been classed according to three main classes: over 50 (n=22); between 34 and 49 (n=48) and younger than 33 (n=37). The majority of the respondents are employed by a University (n=57); by a public research organisation or a public body (n=27); by a private research organisation (n=7); by a company (over 250 employees, n=5; SME, n=7) or were free lancers (n=7).

The distribution of respondents by field of science, according to the Field Of Science (2007) is as follows: Natural Sciences (n=34); Engineering and technology (n=29); Medical and Health Sciences (n=7); Agricultural Sciences (n=4); Social Sciences (n=27) and Other (n=10).

The questionnaire comprised 6 main blocks of questions. The first block of questions explores the respondents' perceptions of open science. The second and third blocks investigate the use of Open Science practices and their perceived impact on conducting and disseminating research results. The fourth and fifth blocks of questions are intended for assessing the usefulness of publicly shared scientific outcomes and the propensity/willingness of the participants to openly share their research outcomes. The last group of questions focuses on the barriers to open science. All blocks of questions have an 'other, please specify' option where the respondents can enter open text to elucidate their answer. This option was used by the majority of the respondents.

The questions encompassing ranked responses have been assessed for consistency using Cronbach's-alpha.

The results of the survey were presented and discussed at the workshop. At the workshop other contextual issues were raised and highlights from the debate on the relationships between research performers and the organisations in which they work will be integrated in the discussion of the findings.

FINDINGS

The descriptive statistics from the survey reveal that the respondents have a good understanding of Open Science and what this concept entails, although their expectations towards its revolutionary potential are rather cautious. In the next table, we summarise the responses.

Table 2. Perception of open science (general)

OS statements	Mean score	Standard deviation	N
New modus operandi for science	1.77	0.735	111
Support better science and improve the quality	1.67	0.730	111
Reproducible science and uncover mistake	1.68	0.700	111
Current practices don't fit the needs	1.60	0.651	111
Lead to less inequality for researchers	2.14	0.830	111

Notes: 4 points Likert's scale (1= disagree, 4=totally agree); Reliability: Cronbach's alpha = 0.79

The only mean score above the median (2) relates to the statement that open science has the potential to level the playing field amongst researchers, especially in those areas of research where resources to produce new data or access a wider pool of knowledge are determinants in successfully completing research projects, namely, the Natural Sciences, Engineering and Technology and the Social Sciences to a lesser degree. Open science as a 'leveller' of opportunities in conducting science is seen positively by Public Research Organisations compared to Universities and by SMEs compared to Large Enterprises.

Two further questions were included in order to establish whether, in the pursuit of the open science disclosing process early results are seen favourably by those involved in research. Two statements were presented:

Table 3. Initial results and HQ peer-review

OS statements – disclosure and peer-review	Mean Score	Standard Deviation	N
Keeping some process and initial results private is necessary	2	0.751	111
Scientific publications should be restricted to high quality and peer reviewed work	2.25	0.919	111

Notes: 4 points Likert's scale (1=disagree, 4=totally agree)

The respondents were somewhat neutral in respect of the need to keep the research process and initial results concealed (mean score = median). However, older research professionals were proportionately more in favour of keeping some process and initial results private than their younger counterparts (Spearman's correlation of 0.27 with p value < 0.05). Greater emphasis was given to the importance of peer-review as the only acceptable means to ascertain scientific rigour.

The following two blocks of questions investigate the use and impact of open science practices. The items considered are those practices commonly associated with open science and the respondents were invited to rate their use on a $1 - 5$ Likert Scale where 1 = 'never heard of it' and 5 = 'regular use' and the potential impact the items have on science according to the scores 1= 'no impact' to 5 = 'very high'. Chi-square test for each item scored for 'Use' and 'impact' shows evidence of a significant relationship (at the $P < 0.01$ level).

The respondents declared that the main open science practices used in the course of their research activities related to Open Access to Publication, Science Blogs, Research Social Networks and Open Data/Linked Open Data whilst the main impact on their research is given by Open Access to publication and Open/Linked data.

Importantly, the mean scores for use and impact of 6 out of 10 items do not differ significantly accordingly to the t-stats test (p value > 0.5) indicating that their use somehow matches the impact these practices have on their research activities. Significant in this respect is the high mean score of Open Access publications and Open/Linked Data for both 'use' and 'impact' indicating that the respondents consider these two Open Science practices very highly in the advance of their research.

Table 4. Use and impact of open science practices

Open science practice	Use Mean Score	Impact mean score	Use Standard deviation	Impact Standard deviation	N
Open access publications	4.43	4.26	0.901	1.142	111
Negative results publications	2.95	3.09	1.052	1.671	111
Open data and linked open data	3.78	3.99	1.074	1.505	111
Open lab notebooks	2.75	2.51	1.202	1.747	111
Research social networks	3.87	3.07	1.010	1.469	111
Open reviews	3.19	2.91	1.195	1.703	111
Alternative reputation systems	2.81	2.57	1.411	1.910	111
Big data analysis	3.33	3.48	1.170	1.762	111
Science blogs	4.06	3.07	1.064	1.367	111
Crowd-source science	3.24	2.85	1.162	1.764	111

Notes: 5 points Likert's scale; Cronbach's alpha: Use = 0.852; Impact = 0.884

Conversely, the mean scores for use and impact of Research Social Networks, Open Reviews, Science Blogs and Crowd Sourcing are significantly different. Indicating that these open science practices are used more than their impacts justify their use. In other words, the hypothesis that we are here exploring is that an open science practice is used if its impact on own research justifies the effort of using it, i.e., if the mean scores of use and impact are not significantly different.

Table 5. Use/impact differences paired t test

Mean difference	(use-impact)	T-test	N
Research social networks	0.802	6.884***	111
Open reviews	0.279	2.118**	111
Science blogs	0.991	7.924***	111
Crowd-source science	0.396	2.976**	111

Sig. **P value < 0.05; *** = P value < 0.01

These results indicate that Research Social Networks, Open Reviews, Science Blogs and Crowd Science are used for reasons other than the impacts these practices might have on own research activities. These results are rather general as there is no significant difference depending on whether the respondent is active in a particular field of research, a type of organisation or her/his age.

The next block of questions is directed at assessing the usefulness of open science outcomes to progressing research activities and the propensity of research professionals to opening up, in the spirit of open science, the outcomes of their research to the public. The 'Usefulness' of shared outcomes has been assessed on a 4 point scale where 0 is 'not useful' and 4 is 'very useful'. The variable 'Willingness to share' assumes the value 1 if the respondent is willing to share the outcome of his research and 0 is she/he is not. In the case the item is 'not applicable' a 'missing value' is registered.

Table 6. Open access to research outcomes – Usefulness and propensity to share

Research outcomes	Usefulness Mean Score	Usefulness Standard deviation	Share Yes (1)	U*S	U*S Standard deviation	Adjusted Usefulness mean score	N
Bibliographies	2.05	0.888	0.98	2.00	0.924	2.02	104
Publications	2.75	0.579	0.98	2.72	0.643	2.75	105
Draft and incomplete papers	1.74	0.783	0.50	0.99	1.153	1.74	101
Negative Results	2.07	0.922	0.91	2.05	0.999	2.18	94
Datasets	2.53	0.772	0.86	2.29	1.112	2.60	98
Source code	2.16	1.005	0.86	2.23	1.113	2.45	80
Workflow (experiment log)	1.72	1.002	0.86	1.75	1.131	2.01	80
Figures, presentations and supporting material	2.21	0.799	0.95	2.15	0.896	2.22	105
Annotation and comments	1.98	0.963	0.79	2.00	1.202	2.00	103

Notes: Usefulness: 4 points Likert's scale; Cronbach's alpha: 'Useful' = 0.849;
'Willingness to Share': three variables: 'Not Applicable' (Missing Value),
'Yes' = 1, and 'No' = 0. The variable defined as U*S is the product of 'Usefulness'
times 'Willingness to Share'. The variable takes the value 0, whatever the rate of
usefulness, if the respondent is not willing to share and the value of attributed to
'Usefulness' if the respondent is willing to share. A Missing Value is reported in case
the outcome is 'Not Applicable'. Cronbach's alpha of U*S = 0.790.

The descriptives above show that items such as Publications, Datasets, Source Code, Negative results and Bibliographies are considered useful by the respondents; their willingness to share is also very high ranging from 50% of the respondents willing to share Drafts and Incomplete papers to 98% of the respondents who would willingly share their Publications and Bibliographies.

Direct comparison between the two variables is not possible as 'Usefulness' of research outcomes is assessed through a 4 point scale whilst the propensity to make available the outcome to the general public is a dichotomous variable. To overcome this impasse we have calculated a further variable (U*S) which also takes into account those respondents who declared that the particular outcome was not relevant in their research activities.

Table 7. Usefulness and sharing openly research outcomes: A comparison

Research outcomes	U-(U*S)	T-Test	N
Draft and incomplete papers	0.752	8.412***	101
Negative Results	0.128	2.413**	94
Datasets	0.316	3.708***	98
Source code	0.225	2.983***	80
Workflow (experiment log)	0.262	3.606***	80
Annotation and comments	0.291	4.091***	103

*Sig. **P value < 0.05; *** = P value < 0.01*

In this block of questions, the hypothesis we are testing here is whether there is a willingness to share a research outcome corresponding to its usefulness in conducting research activities or if the respondents find it useful for their own research process to consult or use material produced by other scientists but are less willing to share the intermediate outcomes of their research. Comparative analysis shows that Publications, Bibliographies and Figures, Presentations and other support material, are both useful in conducting research activities and are shared willingly by the respondents. This is unsurprising as those outcomes are increasingly part of the typical publication and dissemination process. These results only show the support of the respondents to open access to publications and dissemination.

T-tests evidence that drafts and incomplete papers, datasets and the other items highlighted in Table 7 are shared less willingly with other research professionals than they are considered useful for their own research.

Is the propensity to share different according to the various areas of research, the type of organisation the respondent works at or the age of the respondents?

'Useful therefore share' behaviours are particularly high in the Natural Sciences, Engineering and Technology and Social Sciences but only Publications, Datasets, Source code and Annotations and comments are statistically significant. There is no statistically significant difference in propensity to share between different types of organisations. The age of the respondent is slightly linked to the propensity to share research outcomes. In particular, respondents in the two age groups younger than 50 Years of Age share systematically and are more likely to share than respondents older than 50. In particular the relationship between age and willingness to share is particularly strong and statistically significant for Bibliographies, Draft and incomplete publications, Source code and Annotations and comments.

In the scoping study we have identified 4 operational barriers to open science; these concern 1) the difficulty of assessing the quality and the impact of research results when they are disseminated in their draft forms or through means other than peer-reviewed publications; 2) the time consumed by research professionals in contributing to open science initiatives and 3) the difficulty encountered in engaging the public in scientific projects in terms of time/resources needed and technological platforms involved and finally 4) research professionals may lack the skills to set up, deploy and maintain open science tools necessary to contribute to open science platforms, data repositories and dissemination fora.

The responses are collected through a binomial variable where 'yes' = 1 and 'no' = 0.

Table 8. Operational and institutional barriers

Operational Barriers	Mean	Standard deviation	N
Assessing quality and impact of the research results	0.51	0.502	111
Time consumed in participation in open Science	0.30	0.459	111
Public interest/involvement	0.15	0.362	111
Skills of the researchers in using the tools	0.34	0.477	111
Institutional Barriers	Mean	Standard deviation	N
Funding	48.6	0.502	111
Inertia of the science system	60.1	0.491	111

Assessing both quality and impact of the research results is the main operational barrier in the uptake of open science which was selected by 51% of the respondents whilst 34% of the respondents declared that the skills of researchers to using open science tools are a barrier. Thirty per cent of the respondents that they lack time to participate in open science practices.

Institutional barriers have been identified as 1) lack of funding to undertake open science initiatives and 2) inertia in the science system, which is still linked to the traditional organisation of science practices and hinders the uptake of open science by not providing incentives to research professionals to share publicly their research work.

Approximately half of the respondents agree that funding for open science is inadequate and that current funding practices, where only some of the open science practices can be written into proposals, might not be conducive to open science.

A very high and significant 60% of the respondents stated that the main institutional barrier to the uptake of open science is concerned with the inertia of the science system still steeped in Science 1.0 practices and not rewarding alternative modes of conducting or disseminating research.

The inertia of the science system element is particularly important and has been investigated further by looking at the attitudes towards open science of the research community in which the research professionals operate. In particular, the work environment of the respondents is at best neutral in respect of the involvement of research professionals in open science (in 37% of the cases) whereas in almost 20% of the cases, respondents stated that their peers or superiors would not appreciate their engagement in open science initiatives.

We have also investigated how barriers relate to the characteristics of the respondents (Field of Science, Type of Organisation, Country and Age of the respondent). Chi Square tests were carried out for this purpose. Fields of Science, Type of Organisations and Country of the respondent did not evidence any particular link with barriers however, Chi Square tests between Age and Barriers flagged a few significant connections. For the reason that age of the respondent might be taken as a proxy for career advancement, further investigation was conducted in order to ascertain the nature of this possible connection. Spearman's Rho correlations were calculated between the various barriers and the age of the respondent.

Table 9. Correlations between operational barriers and age of respondents

Operational Barriers vs Age of Respondent	Spearman's rho	N
Assessing the quality and the impact of the research results	0.290***	107
Time consumed in participation in Open Science	0.217**	107
Public interest/involvement	0.016	107
Skills of the researchers in using the tools	0.211**	107
Institutional Barriers vs. Age of Respondent		
Funding	-0.205**	107
Inertia of the science system	-0.084	107

Sig. (two-tails): ** = P value < 0.05; *** = P value < 0.01

The correlations show that operational barriers increase with the age of the respondent whilst institutional barriers, especially funding for open science activities, decrease with the age of the respondent.

Amongst the operational barriers, it is significant (p-value < 0.01) the correlation between 'assessing the quality and the impact of the research results' and age.

Concluding, thus far we have seen that open access to publication, dissemination activities and, importantly, access to open data are the key elements of open science both in terms of usage and of impact on the research activities. Other open science practices and research outcomes are also used widely by research professionals, although their impact on the advancement of science is not considered as determinant as other practices and outcomes. Moreover, researchers and research professionals reported that they found it useful to access the work of other researchers and research professionals, which has been made available openly but are often reluctant to share the outcomes of their own research openly for others to use. The uptake of open science practices or the diffusion of some research outcome openly varies also according to the field of science the research professionals are working in, the type of organisation they work at and their age/career status. Nonetheless, barriers to a wider diffusion of open science, both operational and institutional, affect the diffusion of open science. In particular the inertia of the research system to embrace open science practices is seen as a hindrance by the largest majority of the research professionals that have responded to our questionnaire.

DISCUSSION AND CONCLUSIONS

This research presented highlights the great complexity of the science system and the relations amongst the components of such a system, especially during the current period of transformation in the process of the practice of science. A degree of this complexity is due to the relationships between research professionals and the research organisations within which they work. Several factors are at play, some are related to the attitudes and preferences of the research professionals and some are institutional.

From the literature review and the workshop we found that in many circumstances research professionals and their employers have aligned interests in open science, especially when it concerns the final outcome: publications. However, open science has demonstrated it has much more to offer to researcher professionals, from project conception to pooling of data archives, public engagement, alternative funding methods (crowd funding) and dissemination of research findings. The range of opportunities for outreaching and collaboration activities is virtually limited only by the imagination of the researchers. Yet these opportunities are often weighted against the benefits involved in following traditional practices. This usually means maintaining research progress as confidential until a claim to priority of discovery over the research findings can be made. Our analysis suggests this behaviour is customary in almost all organisations and is a consequence of the rewards system in place which is a contract between the research professional and her/his employer that does not reward full disclosure of the scientific process.

The incentive system in place is shown to be firmly linked to the traditional process of knowledge creation and dissemination based on peer-reviewed publications in high-ranking journals. In the words of Nielsen: *[this] is perhaps the most open system for the transmission of knowledge that could be built with seventeenth-century media* (Nielsen, 2011, p. 183). With such a precise definition of the objectives in place, the remit of the researcher is constrained between their organisation's 'visions' and 'mission statements' which encourage collaborations and openness[7] and the incentive to exert caution in disclosing research findings until these are certified by a certain type of publication. Perhaps for this reason, the respondents' opinions of the open science movement are much more timid that we expected albeit there are marginally greater expectations that open science can act as an 'opportunity leveller' between poorly resourced research organisations (public and private) and their more richly endowed counterparts. The cautious approach to open science is also supported by the views of the respondents that high-quality peer-reviewed publications should be sought as a primary aim of the scientist and in order to achieve this goal, a certain degree of confidentiality at the initial phase of the research process is necessary. In particular, the avenue of publication – high-quality peer-reviewed journals – when seen together with the operational barriers, reinforces a narrative that privileges traditional publications as a guarantee of scientific legitimacy.

Nonetheless, open science practices are used by respondents and such use is matched by the impact that these might have in driving further the quest for new knowledge creation and dissemination. This aspect has been acknowledged by all respondents but the analysis of the correspondence between the use of some aspects of open science and the impact these have on research leads us to think that the interests of research professionals in some open science practices such as blogs, research social networks, reviews or crowd-sourced initiatives might be motivated by reasons other than impact. These might be in the realm of professional curiosity or sense of belonging to the science community.

We also investigated the usefulness of some of the common outcomes of the scientific process involving most of the steps of knowledge creation and dissemination and the propensity of the respondents to share these outcomes publicly (see Tables 6 and 7 – Usefulness and Sharing). In this case we found that the outcomes leading directly to the process of publication and of dissemination of research findings mirrors the process in the traditional idea of science where publications, bibliographies, figures, presentations and support material are considered very useful and the willingness to share of the respondents is also correspondingly high. Conversely, research outcomes that might either affect the research professional's reputation, their claim to priority or that might jeopardise further exploitation of their research effort, are considered very useful but are shared less willingly. The first examples encompass drafts and incomplete publications and negative results whilst the last includes datasets, research logs and annotations and comments. We have highlighted some difference in the sharing behaviours present in the various disciplines: in the natural sciences, engineering and technology and the social sciences, respondents were keener to share than professionals in the medical and health sciences and agriculture.[8] Some differences in the propensity to share research outcomes are also significant between groups of respondents, for example, respondents older than 50 although considering publicly available research findings useful for their own research activities do share consistently less often than younger researchers. This factor can possibly be explained either by the constraints on the time available to share own resources or by the lack of the necessary skills to use newer networking tools.[9] Certainly, access to funding does not constitute an explanation for the poor sharing behaviour of senior academics and research professionals because from the analysis of barriers, we found that funding constraints decrease with seniority.

As mentioned earlier we also explored barriers to the uptake of open science. Operational barriers, the barriers hindering the practical application of open science initiatives have some effect on the uptake of open science but these are limited in terms of scope and extent. The most significant barrier concerns the assessment of the quality and the impact of research results when these are not published in the traditional form. The narrative emerging from the study of operation barriers is that the burden of 'assessing the quality and the impact of research output' is somehow outsourced (or surrendered) to traditional peer-review journals. The reason for this may either be that researchers have little time to dedicate to the verification of the scientific claims made in open science outcomes or that they are not familiar with the tools of open science. It is also noteworthy that this attitude toward open science increases with the age (and career progression) of researchers. In other words, older respondents, either because they lack the time to verify the claims presented in perceived lesser journals or the skills to trawl through open science outcomes, rely on high-quality journals (either open access or traditional subscription journals) for their rigorous process of peer review – either real or perceived – as a guarantee against misconduct and scientific fraud.

Institutional barriers, those linked to the governing of the research process within universities and other research organisations play a determinant role in the uptake of open science. These types of barriers operate at the organisation-researcher level and are caused by the misalignment of interests between the parties affecting the system of incentives, especially when it comes to promotion and career advancement of academic and research professionals.

Our findings are in line with the emerging literature on open science and have indeed brought to the fore the point that scientific effort is organised in a system of interconnected stakeholders whose practices are definitely changing. Contextually, we can see that although the effort to adopt open science practices by researchers and by research organisations is driven more by enthusiasm than a strategic approach to opening up of the scientific process, the relationships between universities and other research organisations and their academic and research professional employees is still governed by the policies of traditional science. Research organisations are still extremely slow in integrating open science within their routines except for those open science practices which are 1) in line with the traditional science policies which are currently in force within the institution and 2) there is a funding line for their implementation.

LIMITATIONS OF THE STUDY AND FINAL REMARKS

We wish to remind the reader that this study is exploratory, as the sample, though drawing from a community of research professionals with some knowledge of open science both as users and contributors, is limited in terms of number of respondents and concentrates uniquely on the relationships between use/impact, drivers and barriers to open science. Moreover, the sample is geographically skewed in favour of European respondents hence, although it does not emerge from the analysis, it may reproduce a Europe-centric view of open science with marginal inputs from other parts of the world.

Nonetheless, this exploration has demonstrated valuable insights into particular aspects of the relationships between research professionals and research organisations and has identified promising perceptions for a roadmap for further research.

With regard to this last observation, empirical and conceptual research on the theme of open science is therefore encouraged. Fruitful lines of research will necessarily involve a deeper understanding of the scientific process and its evolution by means of the introduction and diffusion of more web-rich technologies in carrying out research. This, as highlighted in the present study, alters the balance of interests between the parties. This paper took into consideration only the relationship between research professionals and research performing organisations uncovering that research professionals freely engage in open science practices even if the participation cost outweighs the return on their work in terms of career progression. The study has also shown that the usefulness of openly shared, scientific outcomes is considered positively yet, research professionals have little or no incentives to publicly share the results of their unpublished research.

The reasons for this behaviour can be explained by the operational barriers to open science. More importantly, such behaviour seems to be informed predominantly by institutional inertia and in particular by the organisations that are failing to recognise the contribution of research professionals to the creation and diffusion of knowledge, when this is provided in modes other than the research papers published in highly rated peer-reviewed journals.

Issues relating to funding of open science initiatives have also been found to be a determinant barrier to the uptake of open science. Consequently, as modes of public funding for scientific research are changing in order to accommodate new open science practices there is an identified need for further investigation of resourcing. This point is particularly important as open science has great potential in the advancement of knowledge and its wider and faster dissemination, whilst constraints on public budgets and debates on the orientation of the scientific effort towards societal challenges are at the centre of the policy makers' agendas.

ACKNOWLEDGEMENTS

Financial support from the European Commission, Directorate General of Research and Innovation, contract 30-CE-0496945/00-23 is gratefully acknowledged. The authors are grateful for the work undertaken by the Commission services, INNO group and SQW for the organisation of the workshop and the contributions of the participants. The opinions herein expressed are not necessarily those of the sponsor or the participants, the authors are solely responsible for the content of the paper and usual caveats apply.

NOTES

[1]   This essay does not enter into the debate on the terminology: Science 2.0, Open Science, eScience or New Science. In the study, we opted for Open Science as Science 2.0 is linked to the Information and Communication Technological Platform upon which the new scientific process is being increasingly undertaken, the Web 2.0. Yet, the Web 2.0 is increasingly morphing into 'the Internet of Things' whereby semantic technologies are systematically introduced and used in rich-web contents, consequently the next wave of Web 3.0 is seamlessly taking shape.

[2]   Influential work on the nature of science, the scientific revolution and the instituted rules of science are: Ziman, (1968); Kuhn (1962); Cournand (1977) amongst others.

[3]   The tension between openness and secrecy is rather more complex than we stated above (David, 2004, p. 577, 578). It sees juxtaposed the interests of the public in supporting open science for its objectives are the maximisation of the rate of growth of the stock of knowledge versus the private interests to secrecy, in view of the exclusive acquisition and the application of knowledge for the appropriation of the rent or personal gain. The resulting system of science, organised accordingly to the principles of open science is therefore the result of a long evolutionary process that entailed institutional change amidst the resolution of the agency problems between research performers and funding agencies rather than a "solution-by-design" implemented for the goodness of science.

[4]   See http://doaj.org/ for the Directory of Open Access Journals (DOAJ).

[5]   This, coupled with the observation that the price per subscription of scholarly publications rose at a rate much above the Consumer Price Index (CPI), constituted the precondition for the demise of the traditional scholarly publishing industry in the mind of many practitioners. Panitch and Michalak (2005) estimated that members of the Association of Research Libraries in 2004 were paying 215% more per each subscription than they were paying in 1986 against a CPI increase of only 68% during the same period. Considering also that the number of subscriptions also increased the greater outlay for research libraries had become highly onerous. Van Noorden (2013) provides an interesting update on revenues and costs of publications.

[6]   The Journal of Young Pharmacists describes itself as the first open access source for research concerning negative results. Journal of Negative Results in BioMedicine is an open access, peer-reviewed, online journal that provides a platform for the publication and discussion of unexpected, controversial, provocative and/or negative results in the context of current tenets.

[7]   Some responders have highlighted that there is a generalised enthusiasm within their organisation and amongst their peers even though there is little understanding of what opening the scientific process entails. The discussion held at the workshop informed that usually open science initiatives within the organisations are taken only in accordance with contractual terms: if the grant or funding contract

allows or demands that publications are placed ir open access repositories (either golden or green) and/or if the grant agreement involves also the curation and the publication of data. Moreover, open science practices are encouraged within the limit that they do not affect the organisation's interests. Other than this, open science is practised at the expenses/advantages of the research professionals in their personal capacity.

[8] The level of aggregation used in exploring this factor is the 1 digit of the Field of Science (FOS, 2007) classification. It is however legitimate to expect that significant variation might be present within sub-field of science. This level of granularity could not be investigated given the nature of our sample.

[9] Age can be seen as a proxy for career advancement, in this case it is consistent to think that career academics and research professional might have time constraints, moreover, the literature agrees that baby boomers – those born before 1964 – find relatively more cumbersome the use of Web 2.0 technologies compared to people of the "X-generation" – those born between 1965 and 1980 – the digital natives – those born after 1980.

REFERENCES

Andreoli-Versbach, P., & Mueller-Langer, F. (2014). Open access to data: An ideal professed but not practised. *Research Policy, 43*(9), 1621–1633.

Antelman, K. (2004). Do open-access articles have a greater research impact? *College & Research Libraries, 65*(5), 372–382.

Bartling, S., & Friesike, S. (2014). Towards another scientific revolution. In S. Bartling & S. Friesike (Eds.), *Opening science: The evolving guide on how the internet is changing* (pp. 3–15). Heidelberg, Germany: Springer International Publishing.

Berman, F., & Cerf, V. (2013). Who will pay for public access to research data? *Science, 341*(6146), 616–617.

Björk, B.-C., & Solomon. D. (2012). Open access versus subscription journals: A comparison of scientific impact. *BMC Medicine, 10*(73). doi:10.1186/1741-7015-10-73

Burgelman, J.-C., Osimo, D., & Bogdanowicz, M. (2010). Science 2.0 (change will happen…). *First Monday, 15*(7).

Buschman, M., & Michalek, A. (2013). Are alternative metrics still alternative? *Bulletin of the American Society for Information Science and Technology, 39*(4), 35–39.

Carayannis, E. G., & Campbell, D. F. J. (2006). In E. G. Carayannis & D. F. J. Campbell (Eds.), *Knowledge creation, diffusion, and use in innovation networks and knowledge clusters: A comparative systems approach across the United States, Europe and Asia* (pp. 1–25). Westport, CT: Praeger.

Choudhury, S., Fishman, J. R., McGowan, M. L., & Juengst, E. T. (2014). Big data, open science and the brain: Lessons learned from genomics. *Frontiers in Human Neuroscience, 8*, 239.

Cournand, A. (1977). The code of the scientist and its relationship to ethics. *Science, 198*(4318), 699–705.

Dallmeier-Tiessen, S., Goerner, B., Darby, R., Hyppoelae, J., Igo-Kemenes, P., Kahn, D., … van der Stelt, W. (2010). *Open access publishing – models and attributes.* Max Planck Digital Library/ Informationsversorgung.

David, P. A. (2004). Understanding the emergence of 'open science' institutions: Functionalist economics in historical context. *Industrial and Corporate Change, 13*(4), 571–589.

David, P. A. (2005). From keeping 'nature's secrets' to the institutionalization of 'open science'. In R. A. Ghosh (Ed.), *Collaborative ownership and the digital economy* (CODE). Cambridge, MA: MIT Press.

Eamon, W. (1985). From the secrets of nature to public knowledge: The origins of the concept of openness in science. *Minerva, 23*(3), 321–347.

European Commission. (2012). *Towards better access to scientific information: Boosting the benefits of public investments in research.* Brussels, Europe: Communication from the Commission to the European Parliament, the Council, the European Economic and Social Committee and the Committee of the Regions.

Fanelli, D. (2012) Negative results are disappearing from most disciplines and countries. *Scientometrics, 90*, 891–904.

Fecher, B., & Friesike, S. (2014). Open science: One term, five schools of thought. *Opening science* (pp. 17–47). New York, NY: Springer International Publishing.

Field of Science (FOS). (2007). *Revised field of science and technology (FOS) classification in the Frascati manual.* The Organisation for Economic Co-operation and Development (OECD). Retrieved from http://www.oecd.org/science/inno/38235147.pdf (Accessed online April 18, 2015)

Foster, W. S., & Putos, S. M. (2014). Neglecting the null: The pitfalls of under reporting negative results in preclinical research. *UOJM, 4*(1), 31–34.

Franzoni, C., & Sauermann, H. (2014). Crowd science: The organization of scientific research in open collaborative projects. *Research Policy, 43*(1), 1–20.

Gaulé, P., & Maystre, N. (2011). Getting cited: Does open access help? *Research Policy, 40*(10), 1332–1338.

Gibbons, M., Limoges, C., Nowotny, H., Schwartzman, S., Scott, P., & Trow, M. (1994). *The new production of knowledge: The dynamics of science and research in contemporary societies.* London, UK: Sage Publications Ltd.

Goetz, T. (2007). Freeing the dark data of failed scientific experiments. *Wired Magazine, 15*(10), 15–10.

Gorgolewski, K. J., Margulies, D. S., & Milham, M. P. (2013). Making data sharing count: A publication-based solution. *Frontiers in Neuroscience, 7*(9).

Grand, A., Wilkinson, C., Bultitude, K., & Winfield, A. F. T. (2014, April 25). Mapping the Hinterland: Data issues in open science. *Public Understanding of Science, 1–17.* doi:10.1177/0963662514530374

Haeussler, C., Jiang, L., Thursby, J., & Thursby, M. (2014). Specific and general information sharing among competing academic researchers. *Research Policy, 43*(3), 465–475.

Harnad, S. (1994). Publicly retrievable FTP archives for esoteric science and scholarship: A subversive proposal. *Scholarly Journals at the Crossroads: A Subversive Proposal for Electronic Publishing.*

Harnad, S., & Brody, T. (2004). Comparing the impact of open access (OA) vs. non-OA articles in the same journals. *D-lib Magazine, 10*(6).

Hayes, A., & Hunter, J. (2012). Why is publication of negative clinical trial data important? *British Journal of Pharmacology, 167*(7), 1395–1397.

Kuhn, T. S. (1962). *The structure of scientific revolutions.* Chicago, IL: University of Chicago Press.

Kundoor, V., & Mueen, A. K. (2010). Uncovering negative results: Introducing an open access journal "Journal of Pharmaceutical Negative Results". *Journal of young pharmacists: JYP, 2*(4), 339.

McVeigh, M. E. (2004). *Open access journals in the ISI citation databases: Analysis of impact factors and citation patterns: A citation study from Thomson Scientific.* Retrieved from http://science.thomsonreuters.com/m/pdfs/openaccesscitations2.pdf

Merton, R. K. (1942/1973). The normative structure of science. In R. K. Merton (Ed.), *The Sociology of science* (pp. 267–278). Chicago, IL: University of Chicago Press.

Merton, R. K. (1973). *The sociology of science: Theoretical and empirical investigations.* Chicago, IL: University of Chicago press.

Nature. (2011). A little knowledge. *Nature, 472,* 135.

Nielsen, M. (2011). *Reinventing discovery: The new era of networked science.* New Jersey, NJ: Princeton University Press.

Nowotny, H., Scott, P., & Gibbons, M. (2001). *Re-thinking science: Knowledge and the public in an age of uncertainty.* Cambridge, MA: Polity Press.

OECD. (2007). *OECD principles and guidelines for access to research data from public funding.* Retrieved from http://www.oecd.org/science/sci-tech/38500813.pdf

Okerson, A., & O'Donnell, J. J. (1995). *Scholarly journals at the crossroads: A subversive proposal for electronic publishing.* Association of Research Libraries.

Pampel, H., & Dallmeier-Tiessen, S. (2014). Open research data: From vision to practice. *Opening science* (pp. 213–224). Dordrecht, The Netherlands: Springer International Publishing.

Panitch, J. M., & Michalak, S. (2005). *The serials crisis: A white paper for the UNC-Chapel Hill scholarly communications convocation.* Chapel Hill, NC: University of North Carolina. (Accessed March 17, 2006)

Peters, M. A. (2010). Openness, web 2.0 technology, and open science. *Policy Futures in England, 8*(5), 567–574.

Peters, M. A., & Roberts, P. (2011). *The virtues of openness*. Boulder, CO: Paradigm Publishers.

Polanyi, M. (1962). The republic of science: Its political and economic theory. *Minerva, 1*(1), 54–73. (Re-issue *Minerva*, 2000, *38*(1), 1–21).

Popper, K. R. (1935). *The logic of scientific discovery*. (First English edition published 1959).

Priem, J., Taraborelli, D., Groth, P., & Neylon, C. (2010). *Altmetrics: A manifesto*. Retrieved from http://altmetrics.org/manifesto/

Rinaldi, A. (2014). Spinning the web of open science *EMBO Reports, 15*(4), 342–346.

Sanderson, K. (2008, September 18). Data on display – Two researchers explain why they're posting their experimental results online. *Nature, 455*(7211), 273. doi:10.1038/455273a

Smart, R. G. (1964). The importance of negative results in psychological research. *Canadian Psychologist/ Psychologie Canadienne, 5*(4), 225.

Solomon, D. J., Laakso, M., & Björk, B.-C. (2013). A longitudinal comparison of citation rates and growth among open access journals. *Journal of Informetrics, 7*(3), 642–650.

Van Noorden, R. (2013). The true cost of science publishing. *Nature, 495*(7442), 426–429.

Wagner, C. S. (2008). *The new invisible college*. Washington, DC: Brookings Press.

Waldrop, M. M. (2008). Science 2.0. *Scientific American, 298*(5), 68–73.

Wellcome Trust. (2003). *Sharing data from large-scale biological research projects: A system of tripartite responsibility*. Report of a meeting organized by the Wellcome Trust and held on 14–15 January, 2003, The Wellcome Trust at Fort Lauderdale, USA.

Whyte, A., & Pryor, G. (2011). Open science in practice: Researcher perspectives and participation. *International Journal of Digital Curation, 6*(1), 199–213.

Wilcox, A. J. (2014) A positive approach to negative results. *Epidemiology, 25*(2), 165.

Wilhelm, E. E., Oster, E., & Shoulson, I. (2014). Approaches and costs for sharing clinical research data. *Journal of the American Medical Association, 311*(12), 1201–1202.

Wilkins, J. S. (2008). The roles, reasons and restrictions of science blogs. *Trends in Ecology & Evolution, 23*(8), 411–413.

Ziman, J. M. (1968). *Public knowledge: An essay concerning the social dimension of science* (Vol. 519). Cambridge, England: CUP Archive.

Dimitri Gagliardi
Manchester Institute of Innovation Research, Manchester Business School
The University of Manchester

Deborah Cox
Manchester Institute of Innovation Research, Manchester Business School
The University of Manchester

Yanchao Li
Manchester Institute of Innovation Research, Manchester Business School
The University of Manchester

SECTION 2

MOVING BEYOND SECTORAL AND DISCIPLINARY BOUNDARIES IN HIGHER EDUCATION

ROSEMARY DEEM, SALLY BARNES AND GILL CLARKE

5. SOCIAL SCIENCE DOCTORAL TRAINING POLICIES AND INSTITUTIONAL RESPONSES

Three Narrative Perspectives on Recent Developments in and Consequences of the UK Transition to Collaborative Doctoral Training

INTRODUCTION

The paper explores the history of recent doctoral training policies in UK social sciences, how universities have responded to these and some of the positive and negative unintended consequences of the policies, principally but not exclusively in the period 1992 to 2014, as the gradual move first to specification of discipline-specific training requirements and department-specific accreditation, then to delegation of the selection of candidates for Economic and Social Research Council (ESRC) doctoral studentships to universities rather than a national competition and finally to institution-wide or inter-institutional arrangements for doctoral education began.

After a brief introduction and discussion of the theoretical framework for the paper, three collective auto-ethnographic narratives are presented, based on observations from the three authors, each with significant roles in UK doctoral education over a long period and first-hard knowledge of current ESRC Doctoral Training Centres (DTCs). The paper then pulls together the main themes of the narratives and summarises the major changes that have taken place in UK social science doctoral education between 1992 and the present time, as well as examining a number of areas where some of the more negative unintended consequences of DTCs on universities and students are most evident (challenges of inter-institutional collaboration, effects on university autonomy, what constitutes doctoral training leadership and the effects of ESRC policies on unfunded students in relation to diversity and inclusion). Theoretically the paper draws on concepts of unintended consequences of 'purposive social action' in the guise of national policies (Merton, 1936; Krücken, 2014), as well as on theories about collaboration, university autonomy and leadership.

UK social science research doctoral training has moved in two and a half decades from national recognition of individual departments for their training and supervision (often focused on Masters programmes) and a national competition for all ESRC funded studentships to the current system of twenty-one national Doctoral Training Centres initiated in 2011 and funded by the UK wide social science research funding

E. Reale & E. Primeri (Eds.), The Transformation of University Institutional and Organizational Boundaries, 137–162.

body, each running their own studentship competition. The new DTCs (which are also sometimes called Doctoral Training Partnerships) are both multi- and inter-disciplinary and nine of them involve more than one institution. Instead of disciplines in separate departments being approved to provide doctoral training, institutions had to make a single bid setting out a number of pathways, single disciplines and interdisciplinary, with the expectation that one leader and administration would run the whole Centre. Institutions were also able to bid with in collaboration with other institutions. However, compared with the more common European model of doctoral programmes which have developed following the Bologna process (CHEPS, 2011), DTCS do not necessarily have Doctoral programmes per se (Brox & Werner, 2011; Clarke & Lunt, 2014) but rather menus of training which different subject constituencies tap into, mostly at Masters level, except for specialised advanced training workshops, the latter partly funded by ESRC.

Though the DTCs each received a 6-year allocation of fully-funded PhD studentships from 2011–12 onwards, ESRC is also encouraging part-ESRC funded studentships combined with other funding (under the banner of 'collaboration') found by the Centres from their own institutional resources and from external bodies. The system of collaborative CASE studentships with outside organisations is not new to UK research councils but whilst currently such co-funding is not thriving in DTCs (Bartholomew Report, 2015), the use of institutional funding is. We would want to argue that the emphasis on the latter is changing the relationship between ESRC and institutions. The context in which DTCs operate (the other 6 UK research funding councils are all following somewhat similar paths to ESRC in respect of doctoral training) is that there is something of a crisis in the funding of UK-domiciled postgraduate students (Higher Education Commission, 2012). This is important because in the UK, unlike in much of Western Europe, doctoral candidates are still much more likely to be students than employees.

THEORETICAL FRAMEWORK

The paper looks both backwards and forwards, appraising what some of the official and unofficial rationales for the various policy twists and turns in UK social science research training have been and, using the narratives, how institutions have responded. Both the intended and unintended consequences of current policies are explored (Margetts et al., 2010) and following Krücken (2014) and Merton's (1936) work on the unintended consequences of what he termed purposive social action is adapted for this purpose. As Krücken observes, Merton was referring to social actors not organisations but as with Krücken's own analysis of changing policies on higher education in Germany, this needs to be refocused to take account of organisational actions, since policy decisions are rarely taken by individual actors and certainly not implemented in this way. Hence, the focus here is placed on what in Krücken's terms is the 'idea of a discursive field in which remarkable change processes take place'

(2014, p. 1440). Merton talks in his (1936) paper mainly of isolated purposive acts but here the emphasis is on a series of relatively coherent acts and policy statements. Merton (1936) suggested five causes of unintended consequences, namely error, ignorance, immediate interest, basic values and self-defeating prophecy. Of these the first three seem the most plausible in relation to social science doctoral training, that is: possible extra consequences weren't considered or modelled (error), that ESRC was unaware of the effects some of its policies would have on institutions (ignorance) or that they only considered the immediate short-term consequences of the policy (immediate interest). The question of whether there have been unintended consequences is applied both in the narratives and at the end of the paper, in analysing some of the institutional policy consequences of ESRC DTCs, particularly in respect of collaboration, university autonomy and Centre leadership and for the majority of UK-based social science research students who are not ESRC funded, many of whom are international or part-time students.

There is a literature specifically on UK social science doctoral training (Burgess, 1994; Acker et al., 1996a, 1996b), some of it funded in the 1990s by ESRC itself, looking at how supervisors, academic departments and students viewed the changes to more streamlined and more prescribed doctoral training in the social sciences and to the 'training' model of a doctoral thesis rather than a 'knowledge' thesis (Winfield, 1987). This literature reveals some of the possible sources of resistance to the training model and particularly, a critique of the need for part-time self-funding students to undertake research training alongside funded full-time students (Collinson & Hockey, 1997). Others pointed out on the basis of detailed ethnographic study that academics across a range of disciplines were not necessarily that enthusiastic about formal time tabled research training and used a variety of other means to enculturate doctoral students into the methods and mores of their disciplines (Delamont et al., 2000). The controversial idea of critical mass in research training was also critiqued by the same writers (Delamont et al., 1997a, 1997b). Questions began to be asked about how ESRC funded and other home students and international students respectively experienced immersion into their departments' research cultures (Deem & Brehony, 2000). Detailed policy analysis (Becher, Henkel, & Kogan, 1994) showed that UK postgraduate policy was largely based on a science model that did not take account of the different characteristics of areas like social science research. More recent work on doctoral education has explored student and supervisor perspectives on research training and many other issues relevant to a variety of doctoral candidates, from early career researchers to part time mature students (Boud & Lee, 2009; Turner & McAlpine, 2011; Overall et al., 2011) as research training has become more commonplace and as academic employment for those obtaining a PhD has become much more rare.

Though the paper focuses on UK social science research training initiatives, there are implications for other disciplines and for doctoral training policies in other countries. It has been argued that DTCs and other similar policies of UK research councils are widely admired by other countries (Clarke & Lunt, 2014) but it is possible that this is based on a rather sketchy understanding of what actually happens.

CONTINUITY & CHANGE IN DOCTORAL EDUCATION SOCIAL SCIENCE RESEARCH TRAINING: ROSEMARY DEEM

Beginnings

In the early 1970s I was an MPhil student in the Sociology Department at Leicester University on a 2 year award from the Economics and Social Science Research Council's predecessor, the Social Science Research Council.[1] The short length of this studentship, in addition to my Department's belief that a PhD was a magnum opus that could take 15+ years to complete, led me to leave Leicester with an MPhil. It was 18 years later before I finally got a PhD from the Open University. Only one of my fellow students at Leicester left with a PhD and several did not complete their MPhil. This was not unusual in UK universities then, since there were many academic jobs due to expansion of the HE system and it was not essential for an early career academic to have a completed doctorate. Even by the mid 1980s, less than 20% of all ESRC funded PhDs were completed at all and most of those were not submitted within four years (Burgess et al., 1994).

Lancaster University – Shifting to Multi Disciplinary Training

My earliest involvement with ESRC itself in terms of doctoral training rather than as a research grant or studentship holder was when I moved from the Open University (OU) to Lancaster University in 1991 to take up a chair in Educational Research. At the OU I had been an associate dean for research and postgraduates in the School of Education and had organised various training events for research students and their supervisors. I had also worked on a distance-learning Research Methods Masters programme. Soon after I arrived in Lancaster, the ESRC began a new recognition exercise for doctoral training, with the emphasis on departments developing Masters degrees in research methods based on an ESRC curriculum for each discipline. One unintended consequence of this was that with a lot of social science research students *not* funded by ESRC, such Masters were never going to have many recruits. The emphasis on research training followed the Winfield Report (1987), which investigated the various schemes for funding masters and research studentships and gathered evidence from institutions, students and other stakeholders. Winfield recommended that there be two future models for PhD theses, one focused on research training and one based on knowledge-creation, alongside a greater degree of supervisor training. In the event only the former survived.

In 1991–2 as a new member and subsequently Head of the Educational Research Department I was involved in putting together Lancaster's submission to the ESRC for the doctoral training recognition exercise for doctoral training and supervision, which involved both cross-university research training (Faculty of Social Sciences and School of Management) in qualitative and quantitative methods and specialized subject-specific training for each Department, with the discipline-specific Masters degrees in research methods formed of a combination of both components. This exercise was not greeted with enthusiasm by many social science academics, most of whom had not experienced much training in their own PhD and felt it was a distraction from writing a thesis. This resistance to training was an unintended consequence of the new policy. There was, however, a small group of committed individuals at Lancaster who began planning what we would do when (and if) we got recognition for our departments. This group were subsequently involved in running training courses when most of the departments submitted to the recognition exercise were recognised by ESRC. In 1996 I became a member of a national ESRC recognition panel for doctoral training in Education Departments, a role I did again in 2000, this time as panel chair. It was never entirely clear just how much training helped to improve submission rates, as it now took up much of year one for full-time students, though it certainly helped ensure students had a better grasp of the methods they were using and gave them valuable skills for subsequent employment. But during the 1990s, some UK institutions changed their PhD regulations to specify that a doctorate *could* be completed in four years full-time study, which included research training.

We had a site visit by the ESRC in the mid 1990s to see our doctoral training but they did not like our large student multi-disciplinary cohort across all disciplines taking one introductory qualitative methods course. Ironically the way that unit was taught, with readings and other triggers given to participants well in advance and notes of the sessions written up by the course convenors within a week, would now be seen as innovatory as an example of a so-called 'flipped lecture' technique. We also prepared distance-learning units for part-time students unable to come into the sessions on campus and Lancaster was one of the first in the UK to do so outside the Open University, a specialist distance learning institution. As Collinson and Hockey (1998) have noted, part-time and/or mature doctoral students are often the most sceptical about research training and the least likely to easily access it. In 1998–9 I set up Lancaster's university-wide Graduate School as its founding director and one of our first tasks was to explore the extent of research student training across the university, not just in the social sciences. This task was helped by the work already undertaken in the social sciences on doctoral education, another but positive unintended consequence.

The Move to Bristol and ERSC Quota Studentships

At the end of 2000, I left Lancaster for a chair in Education at the University of Bristol and quickly got involved in doctoral training, becoming Graduate Dean for

Social Sciences and Law in 2004. Soon after, ESRC decided to move to quotas for recognized Departments, thus ending the all-comers national studentship competitions that had been in place for some considerable time, though a smaller cross-disciplinary competition remained for institutions without quotas. The pressure to enhance research training, the focus on the need for full-time students to submit within four years and high research metrics (successful research grants, high Research Assessment Exercise grades) and a critical mass of academics and students remained in place in that new exercise. The latter is even though Delamont et al. (1997a, 1997b) had already questioned, based on ESRC funded ethnographic fieldwork, the relevance of the critical mass hypothesis.

Following the mid-2000s changes, decisions on awarding studentships were now handled at department level, not by ESRC and new structures had to be set up to deal with this, as aggrieved non-recipients of awards were in much closer proximity to those who had refused them an award than when decisions were made by members of national awarding panels. At Bristol, the continued pressure of the 5 yearly recognition exercises and the challenges of motivating the many non-ESRC funded social science research students to take research training seriously, eventually led to another (unintended) consequence, the institution of a postgraduate diploma in research methods, awarded separately from the doctorate, an initiative which I began as Graduate Dean in 2005–6.

Royal Holloway and the Formation of the SE DTC

In February 2009 I left Bristol University to become Dean of the Faculty of History and Social Sciences at Royal Holloway, part of the University of London. On arrival, I got involved in seeking partners for a possible collaboration in the next phase of ESRC's doctoral training via new doctoral training centres. The original brief for this exercise also included the possibility of smaller Doctoral Training Units without the resources to do full-scale training but in the aftermath of the Lib-Dem Comprehensive Spending Review following the May 2010 election and the 2008 global financial crisis, DTUs were hurriedly dropped. Interestingly, the University of London colleges, with over a century of collaboration, showed no interest in a single collaborative bid for DTC status. Royal Holloway went into a consortium with Kent, Surrey and Reading universities. Final bids had to be submitted to ESRC in spring 2010 but the outcomes of the process were delayed until early in 2011 awaiting a government Comprehensive Spending Review, by which time it was rumoured that the prospect of RCUK expenditure cuts had necessitated a reassessment of the DTC bids beyond the initial assessment. My new institution did not have the same track record of social science research training as my two previous institutions but I was able to draw on that experience and a failed early-1990s bid for Higher Education Funding Council for England (HEFCE) funding for a collaborative UK virtual graduate school between UK universities whilst I was at Bristol.

When the results of the DTC exercise were announced in early 2011, the South East DTC was established and I remain a Management Group member. It has not been easy melding together four very different institutions, with variations in regulations, VLEs, cultures, traditions and structures as well as varying reputations and sizes of social science departments. One institution has tended to dominate the studentships awarded since the very first year (it is not the lead institution) and at times this has caused tensions between the partners. We have nine disciplinary pathways: Anthropology, Economics, Geography, Management, Politics, Psychology, Socio-legal, Social policy, Sociology and one interdisciplinary one: Environment, Energy and Resilience. It has not been straightforward to get different departments even in the same discipline to work together. Academic jealousy or (assumed) superiority can be a big challenge to institutional collaboration. There is now some cross-institutional supervision, an annual student conference, an annual public engagement event and a growing number of collaborative awards with outside organisations. Nationally it took ESRC a while to set up a DTC directors network. It was Pam Denicolo and myself who ran the first national event for DTCs under the auspices of the Society for Research into Higher Education in summer 2012.

When the ESRC visited the South East DTC in February 2014 as part of its institutional visits, we were surprised at the emphasis the panel placed on DTC distinctiveness, what staff research collaborations had come out of the DTC and what progress we had made in merging our research and education strategies across the partner institutions (which given all four universities have different partners for other RCUK DTPs, might be extremely challenging) rather than on the achievements of our students which it was accepted were high. In addition, some SE DTC partners are struggling to find the resources for internal co-funding of studentships (currently this is set at 20%) and this is often at the expense of international students getting access to institutional studentships. This is one of the many challenges to student diversity posed by ESRC DTCs. Others include the hurdles to be jumped to obtain part-time ESRC funding, somewhat out of proportion to the benefits received and that EU students funded by ESRC get only fees and no maintenance awards.

The Future

As almost all the UK research funding councils are now moving or have moved into doctoral partnerships and centres, questions are beginning to be asked about the consequences of these initiatives and the increasingly required matched funding and administrative costs (UUK, 2014). Meanwhile, a more widespread major crisis in postgraduate funding in England in particular has emerged, which recent policies have not yet solved (Higher Education Commission, 2013; Deem, 2014; Delamont & Atkinson, 2014).

CHANGING NOTIONS OF DOCTORAL EDUCATION: SALLY BARNES

Up to the mid-1990s a British Social Science PhD involved an individual student, working on their own with one supervisor to develop an original piece of research. This work typically took anywhere from 3–8 years to complete, there were very few regulations concerning time, length, quality or supervision. The work was assessed through a *viva voce* examination by two examiners, one internal to the candidate's department and one from a different university. Prestigious ESRC studentships were available through an annual open competition. I arrived in Bristol in 1979 to work on a research project funded by the precursor to the ESRC, the SSRC. I came with no academic qualifications bar an American high school diploma. I learned about the Open University and much to my surprise they offered me the opportunity of doing a research degree with them, given my research experience in the US and Bristol. In 1984, I completed my MPhil, having no desire to upgrade. I did regret that decision for many years! In 1984, I was asked to teach Introductory Statistics to cover a colleague's study leave. I then went on to teach Statistics for 25 years. From the start my plan was to allow students, of any sort, from anywhere in the University, to take Statistics for credit or as audits. I soon realized that many of the people I was teaching had no knowledge of research methods (nor methodologies) and so as well as Statistics, by early 1985, Sandra Acker and I had developed a suite of units covering research methods, questionnaire design, qualitative interviewing. These were, I believe, some of the first methods courses offered to doctoral students. Over the years, these units grew and expanded into other areas but always with a mix of assessed and non-assessed participants. Through this period I worked to complete my PhD, as a member of staff. Staff did not have named supervisors because it was felt they didn't need them. I had asked for a named person so that I wouldn't feel too guilty asking for advice and support. It was only on achieving my PhD that I then formally began supervising doctoral students.

In the mid-1990s the Harris Review of Postgraduate Education (1996) was published. This dramatically changed the nature of PhD studies. To ensure that government funded doctorates were value for money and meeting the needs of the academy, the ESRC had already introduced an element of research training for all ESRC-funded PhD students following the 1987 Winfield Report. Every department wishing to receive ESRC accreditation and ESRC sponsored students applied to the ESRC, detailing the research training required of students. In addition, the department had to submit evidence of PhD completion rates, academic research activity and resources available to doctoral students.

In 2001 the ESRC extended the need for research training by publishing very detailed research training requirements for each discipline. Disciplines applied for accreditation from the ESRC, based on their revised Research Training Programmes. Successful disciplines were accredited with (or at times without) a quota of studentships funded on an annual basis. My role as PGR Director, in 2002 was to implement the now accredited ESRC research training program in Education. In 2005 disciplines went through a further re-accreditation process and new quotas for the award of ESRC-funded studentships were allocated. I wrote the Education re-accreditation bid with Rosemary Deem and others in the Faculty of Social Sciences and Law.

RCUK and ESRC Initiatives

In 2009 the ESRC, in line with changes in other research councils, set forth its plans to substantially change the way doctoral students were funded. The Science and Engineering research councils had implemented DTCs for very small groups of highly specialized niche areas. In this way they developed a critical mass of doctoral students working within established research teams. ESRC proposed something, slightly different, concentrating their resources into a much smaller group of Institutions who would bid to deliver a new-style doctoral programmes rather than individual disciplines. In 2009 I became Graduate Dean for Social Sciences and Law and therefore took on a key role of developing research training for the Southwest DTC bid. There was a further complication in that the ESRC was allowing institutions to apply for, what they called, Doctoral Training Units (DTUs) which would allow institutions to compete for studentships through an open competition but those students would receive some of the doctoral training through a nearby DTC.

Resulting ESRC DTC Structures

While the ESRC encouraged some institutions to develop collaborative bids, they didn't clarify what they meant by collaboration and it was left to institutions to develop their own vision of and criteria for what collaboration meant and the pros and cons of what institutions could bring to a partnership.

The ESRC received a total of 84 applications for institutions to be either DTC or DTUs. In the end, only 21 DTC applications were successful. Of these 11 were single institution bids and 9 were collaborative with multiple institutions. The vision for developing DTUs was dropped. The collaborative DTCs are each distinctive in their own way. The Scottish DTC and Welsh DTC cover whole countries, whereas the Bloomsbury DTC covers a few square miles in London. Each DTC created its own vision of doctoral education and this varies in terms of the strengths of each of the institutions as well as their combined strength. The Southwest Doctoral Training Centre (SWDTC) is based on three universities, Bristol, Bath and Exeter. The three institutions began working on the bid in the spring of 2009, a full year before the bid was submitted. In that time we developed a governance structure to manage developing the overall bid and to develop the research training programmes we would offer:

The SWDTC builds on established, collective disciplinary research and training strengths by offering *twelve pathways in ESRC Disciplines: Area and Development Studies; Economic and Social History; Economics; Education; Human Geography; Management and Business Studies; Political Science and International Studies; Psychology; Social Policy; Social Work; Socio-legal Studies* and *Sociology* ... In addition, we will make a major contribution to national skills development through a *new interdisciplinary pathway* in *Advanced Quantitative Methods in Social Science and Health* that will reduce supply side research capacity deficits. We will also collaborate on *four new interdisciplinary pathways* that address ESRC Strategic Research Challenges set out in the Strategic Plan 2009–14: *Environment, Energy and Resilience; Global Economic Performance, Policy and Management; Health and Wellbeing; Security, Conflict and Justice.* (Case p. 3)

The Vision

The ESRC DTC initiative is important in its own right. It has encouraged institutions to consider quite carefully the strengths and weaknesses of their disciplinary breadth, the strength of its staff and its size. But developing a collaborative DTC is also an opportunity to test our understanding of how organizations change and thrive; how our beliefs about learning can be incorporated into new structures. One of the underlying drivers for going into a regional DTC was the belief that we could achieve a critical mass in more disciplinary areas than any one partner could do on its own. There was also the belief that each institution has its own culture and identity and bringing these different cultures together would force staff and students to reflect and consider their own beliefs.

The SWDTC presents an effective and future-focused research strategy that will catalyse the forging of deeper academic relationships at the regional level and foster further interdisciplinary research both within and beyond the social sciences. SWDTC academics will work more closely with each other, government, employers and other stakeholders to shape research and training for a new generation of researchers. These interdisciplinary, inter-institutional and cross-sectoral engagements will allow us to address global research challenges in joined-up ways that have broad economic and societal impact. (page 1 Case for support)

Reading through the vision and structures we have developed makes it sound simple and straightforward. In fact, the writing of the bid took a year and the implementation of our programmes is still a work in progress. To align three universities structures to offer joint degrees is incredibly difficult. We discovered early on that one of our institutions had moved to ECTs as their credit structure while the others worked with 180 UK 180 Masters-level credits. We also discovered that we had different pass marks and slightly different regulations covering the examination ratification processes. All of these issues needed to be aligned.

Collaborative Working

The key to the success of any collaborative partnership has to be based on the development of strong working relationships. This doesn't happen overnight. We anticipated this within the SWDTC from the first meeting between the three institutions. We developed a two-tier management structure. The Shadow Management Board (SMB) initially had responsibility for determining the criteria for determining which disciplines were to be included, or not, from each institution. This board would sort out the division of studentships between institutions, should our bid be successful. We also set up a Shadow Academic Advisory Board (SAAB) which developed the detailed research training programmes and the alignment of institutional policies and procedures needed for the interdisciplinary pathways we envisaged. There were long discussions about every decision SMB and SAAB made. Each board had to develop ways of working with each other and for negotiating the different needs of each institution. Developing and awaiting the outcome of the bid, we learned our individual strengths and weaknesses, who to go to for what, and to trust each other that we really did all believe in the SWDTC as a good way forward.

Developing Different Structures

Each institution already had ESRC recognition for many of their Masters in Research programmes (MRes) for a range of disciplines. The Academic Advisory Board looked at all of the existing MRes programmes and considered how best to reconfigure them so that they would have similar structures. This would, for example, allow students to follow units of their choice at any of the three institutions. By extension we also developed MRes degrees for each of the new interdisciplinary pathways.

For all our MRes programmes (disciplinary and interdisciplinary), the taught component is made up of 3 compulsory units (a quantitative unit, qualitative unit and a unit on philosophy and research design) and three other units which tend to be a mix of disciplinary specific and optional and a dissertation. A longer term goal is for these core units to be team-taught by staff across disciplines within or across institutions (the latter is a given for the interdisciplinary pathways). In this way different disciplinary perspectives are integrated into the learning materials. More importantly, academic staff are encouraged to work outside their own academic silos which could in the longer term, result in joint research activities.

For the interdisciplinary MRes programmes, we devised a supervisory structure which requires each student to have supervisors based in different institutions AND in different disciplines. This team works with the student through the MRes and on through the PhD. The three optional units which students take can be taken from any of the three institutions. The dissertation is supervised by the supervisory team but is submitted to the student's home institution.

Partnership Agreement

The details of our working arrangements and the agreements we had about how to manage the interdisciplinary MRes and PhD students were formalised in the Educational Partnership. Many collaborative DTCs have a research contract formalizing their relationships. We felt that given the educational programmes we developed specifically for the SWDTC and all the associated student- facing procedures, an Educational Partnership was a better fit for our purposes.

REFLECTING ON RECENT DOCTORAL EDUCATION DEVELOPMENTS:
GILL CLARKE

As a comparative newcomer to the personal doctoral experience (I am currently a part-time PhD candidate at Oxford) my observations for this paper draw mainly on my professional experiences:

i) In a senior university role spanning administrative and academic practices in managing postgraduate education, including collaborative partnerships (e.g., from the Southwest Doctoral Training Centre and similar partnerships in other disciplines, to joint-supervisory arrangements for individual PhD students through Erasmus partnerships).

ii) During a secondment to a national body (the UK Quality Assurance Agency), developing policy for quality assurance and enhancement of postgraduate (particularly research) degrees in consultation with universities and other organisations, including the research councils, VITAE (an organisation concerned with researcher development, particularly of contract researchers) and others.

iii) Internationally, contributing to policy development with respect to the Bologna Declaration, in particular the third cycle.

iv) As a consultant contracted to evaluate a multi-partner ESRC doctoral training partnership.

My contribution to this paper is to highlight some of the critical issues I have observed in social sciences research education, mainly through professional practice but also as a result of my personal experiences.

The Role of ESRC and the Research Councils

The UK research councils have a co-ordinating body, Research Councils UK (RCUK); each council is an equal partner in RCUK whose Executive Group is made up of the chief executives of the individual research councils. The research councils also work with other funders of UK research which helps to optimise the funding available and increase the impact of research outputs. One of the strengths of the UK system is that, because the individual research councils retain their own identity and have developed specialised knowledge of their disciplines, they are better able to support the group of subjects that sit within their funding remit. A disadvantage of having separate research council, despite some harmonisation, is that each council has individual requirements, for example, with respect to thesis submission times and how student awards may be used.

The introduction of doctoral training partnerships and centres for doctoral training beginning in 2003, with the terminology clarified in 2013 (RCUK, 2013b), was an innovative development by the UK research councils. It put the UK in a primary position globally for doctoral training through encouraging critical mass and supporting the development of professional skills, in parallel with release of Roberts Funding (Roberts, 2002; RCUK, 2010) for generic skills training to universities with research council funded students for five years in the first decade of the 21st century. The new model, encouraging interdisciplinarity and formal collaborations and partnerships between institutions, was a way of restructuring resource distribution at a time of decreasing government financial support and designed to achieve a new doctoral education paradigm somewhat different to the rest of Europe. Criticisms of this model, however, included the difficulties for universities not in receipt of research council funding in creating similar doctoral education models and the perception that the changes could lead to a two-tier system of education for doctoral candidates, to the potential detriment of non-research council funded students.

Leadership Qualities

Having been involved in the early stages of a collaborative bid for a regional doctoral training centre I became aware of the importance of strong and positive leadership by senior staff to overcome any hesitation and nervousness among subject groups to enter into such a partnership. One occasion is particularly memorable: a meeting of social sciences subject groups including representatives from all the partner institutions where negativity as well as excitement was apparent. The senior member of staff from the potential lead partner chaired the day-long event and inspired participants to focus on the benefits of the prospect of participating in a DTC rather than to worry about some of the potential difficulties, such as structural differences, regulatory inconsistencies and geographical constraints. This leadership was critical, not just in the initial stages but in seeing the bid through to submission, requiring a wide range of interpersonal skills to reassure and enthuse staff, attention to detail in developing the inter-university agreement (supported by academic and professional services colleagues), and securing buy-in from the senior management team in each university, who needed to be persuaded to underwrite the enterprise. The high stakes involved in the whole process, the uncertainty about whether or not the partner universities would be awarded the DTC and the many difficult stages of development required strong, flexible and committed leadership. Similarly, the leadership of this particular partnership, once established, has been key to its success, with high levels of personal commitment and sound, thoughtful decision-making by the centre's management teams and directorate.

Avoiding Over-Bureaucratic Management While Establishing a Sound Regulatory Framework

This topic is relevant to any doctoral training partnership, especially one that involves several institutions. UK universities' quality assurance arrangements are mature and established, with most institutions being able to rely on comparators having in place similar procedures, e.g., external examining, annual programme review and good practice guidelines for teaching, learning and assessment. But the existence of similar yet different arrangements at partner institutions can potentially be a barrier to creating a partnership agreement. If any of the partners choose to be over-prescriptive about regulations, potentially significant delays can occur and potentially put the partnership at risk. Trust and flexibility among the partners, in particular those who are leading the bidding process within the institutions, is essential for a cohesive and credible submission, as well as development and implementation of a successful partnership agreement.

Within an institution, those leading the establishment of an interdisciplinary DTC also have complexities to negotiate, including inconsistent school or faculty practices arising from disciplinary conventions or structural differences (e.g., faculty or school-level graduate schools). Navigating these difficulties requires similar qualities to those at inter-institutional level, possibly the most important being flexibility and the ability to see the bigger picture, together with a commitment to make the enterprise work.

As with any exercise of this kind, there are benefits in all areas as a result of writing an analytical account of practice, in this case the management and delivery of doctoral education. Simply going through the process of putting a bid together involves a large amount of learning and increased self-awareness, which can only add value to the eventual partnership.

Figure 1 attempts to summarise some of the complicated relationships and lines of responsibility that can exist between and within institutions, especially those with multiple DTC/DTP affiliations.

The Importance of Organic Development

In any research collaboration, including doctoral training partnerships, one effective approach is to build on research synergies at a detailed level and, if possible, existing relationships between academic staff and research areas. This is equally true for single-discipline and interdisciplinary research. In the regional partnership I am most familiar with, the strongest groupings were those where staff at the various institutions were already working together or had a deep knowledge of one

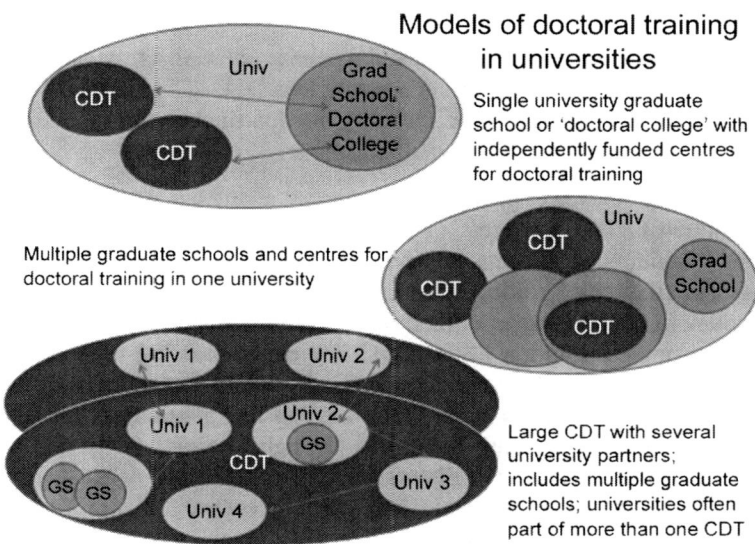

Figure 1. Different modes of organising doctoral education in a university
Source: Clarke (2014)

another's research specialisms. In these areas, the content of the student pathways was decided upon more quickly and the level of trust among the partners was strongest. An early survey of students on an interdisciplinary pathway in a regional doctoral training partnership appeared to show that overall they were finding the pathway broadening, rewarding and challenging – the pathways were certainly challenging for the staff responsible for developing them yet creating something completely new led to the discovery of more synergies and closer links between the disciplines involved.

The Student Experience and Perspective

It may be difficult to envisage how a DCT will affect the students it is designed for, but this is a critical part of creating the doctoral education environment. How will the student's experience be affected? – positively and negatively – is a question that needs to be considered from the first day of planning if the centre is to be successful. In the survey mentioned above, some of the factors of most importance to students were:

• Existence of a critical mass of students, either within the DTC itself or in the immediate environment of the subject or school
• Clarity of regulatory information and advice about progress and completion
• Flexibility in institutional requirements for completing structured modules

151

Positive features related to being part of a [regional] DTC included:

- Access to a wide range of resources at the partner universities
- The cachet attached to being part of a prestigious DTC
- Disciplinary heterogeneity of the student group (particularly for interdisciplinary pathway students)

As mentioned above, residual concerns exist about the extent to which the implementation of DTCs is creating a 'two-tier' system that disadvantages non-research-council funded students. Some universities with DTPs and DTCs are trying to ensure that all doctoral students they recruit experience similar training and have opportunities to attend generic skills development programmes. As a self-funding student in a single-institution ESRC DTC, my experience has been no different from research council-funded candidates in this regard. However, this may not be so everywhere and universities without DTCs have to find alternatives for delivering a parallel experience; some are doing this through inter-university and regional partnerships, including non-academic partners.

The UK HE sector appears to have only partially accepted that this new way of organising doctoral training through a DTC or DTP model, whether or not research council-funded, is the optimum structure for all students but more empirical evidence is required, such as is beginning to emerge (Lunt et al., 2013; Bartholomew, 2015) so that the model can be properly evaluated.

COMMON THEMES IN THE NARRATIVES

The first message which is evident from the three narratives is that people and leadership do make a difference to research training and collaborations as well as staff mobility between institutions or opportunities to contribute to national policy allowing 'policy borrowing' and learning from earlier implementations and experiments, as well as from the research literature on doctoral training. The significance of individual institutional histories of social science research training is also demonstrated by the three narratives. The narratives also show that interpretation of ESRC policies has varied by institution and academic department over the period covered by the paper, leading to uneven implementation of policies in different locations. The contextualisation of doctoral training at local level is where implementation gaps and unintended consequences often first become visible. Collaboration between disciplines and institutions in social sciences has gradually emerged since 1992 but has taken different forms in different local contexts, so where Lancaster had reached in the early 1990s with cross-university training modules, Oxford only reached after the DTC initiative in 2011. Collaboration partners for doctoral training are sometimes strategic (SW DTC) but may be related to geography (SE DTC), senior team networks or not considered because of institutional prestige (Oxford). Two of the accounts, Deem and Barnes, note the considerable resistance to training by both students and supervisors in the early years of the period. Clarke's account of different departmental and institutional structures for doctoral education shows the organisational complexity of current arrangements where institutions' own structures do not always sit easily with what the UK Research Funding Councils have been doing. Divisions between ESRC funded students (Home and EU) and part-time and international students are long standing but have been exacerbated by the increased emphasis on collaborative training which may take place in locations inaccessible to the latter. The accounts also tell of innovation sparked off by ESRC policies such as recent staff research collaboration across institutions in the South West DTC, the growth of interdisciplinarity, the introduction of the Bristol PG Diploma in the late 2000s, and the Lancaster distance learning units on research methods.

Clarke raises the issue of what critical mass actually means in relation to social science doctoral training; this is a long standing concern which was extensively researched in several disciplines by Delamont et al. (1997a, b) in the 1990s. Research culture integration of research students has perhaps been the least successful element of UK social science doctoral training but this goes well beyond the social sciences in the UK as the 2013 results from the Higher Education Academy's National Postgraduate Research Student Experience Survey show only 64% of students in 122 institutions responding positively to comments about research culture, varying from departmental seminars (which got a higher positive response) to opportunities to discuss their research with others or become involved in the wider research community beyond their department. The other theme emerging from the narratives is about the gradual erosion of institutional autonomy in return for studentships, with many administrative costs being absorbed by universities that were previously covered by ESRC staff and the permeation of all aspects of research by DTC policy including who academics collaborate with and the wording of institutional strategies.

MAJOR CHANGES IN DOCTORAL TRAINING OVER THE PERIOD 1987–2014

First and foremost of these is a seemingly irrevocable shift to the 'training' PhD model of a thesis rather than the 'knowledge' model that the 1987 Winfield Report suggested was a parallel model for research theses in the social sciences. Secondly, it has gradually become almost impossible for ESRC students to escape research training in both qualitative and quantitative skills but this has notably been done without introducing the highly structured doctoral Programmes that many Western European countries have adopted as a consequence of the Bologna process and the third cycle of higher degree study (e.g., Sweden, Portugal, Germany) and which some other UK research councils (e.g., EPSRC) have introduced. Thirdly, there is now more emphasis on quality assessment. Although the DTCs are subject to evaluation and there are periodic centre visits to host institutions, for multi-site collaborations this is insufficient. Also, it is not an international peer evaluation as takes place in some countries and the curriculum is assumed to be that prescribed by ESRC for different disciplines without much investigation. Clarke was a major national player in the setting out by the UK Quality Assurance Agency of a code of practice for research degrees in 2004, which has now been adapted and was incorporated into a broader UK Quality Code in 2012. But this is tested only in periodic institutional reviews to universities (every 6 years or so) and only in a fairly general way, which is again different to what happens in much of Europe (e.g., in Portugal, AE3S, their HE quality assurance agency and their research funding council Fundação para a Ciência e a Tecnologia (FCT) are responsible for accrediting and evaluating doctoral programmes).

Fourthly, there has been a striking shift of almost all administrative responsibilities and many of the associated costs of social science doctoral training to UK host institutions since the mid-2000s and especially since 2011, whilst ESRC retains a considerable degree of control over what is done, going well beyond the confines of training of ESRC-funded students and including what should happen to non-ESRC funded students, intervening in with whom academics can or should do research and even wanting to influence the wording of institutional research and teaching strategies.[2] Whilst some of this might be reasonable in a context where ESRC was paying significant amounts of money to institutions for the administration of DTCS, this is far from the situation, as in the main, only studentships are funded.

Fifthly, a greater emphasis on a variety of forms of collaboration has been evident since 2011, ranging from cross-disciplinary and cross-institutional Doctoral training, to cross institutional supervision, external sponsorship of studentships and offering of work placements by outside organisations, emphasis on user engagement in research and encouragement of students to consider the non-academic 'impact' of research findings and how this might be advanced during their studies. This is not specific to ESRC but has been a feature of other RCUK schemes for doctoral education too and the 2014 UK Research Excellence Framework also placed a high emphasis on non-academic impact of research.

Sixthly, there has been a major shift over the period considered in this paper from national competitions for ESRC studentships to locally organised competitions whose standards may or may not be as rigorous and which are harder to make consistent. This change took place in the mid-2000s. Seventhly, where once the ESRC had a single date for all studentship applications, now these vary by DTC and this creates an (assumedly) unintentional market between the collaborative DTCS and the single institution DTCs as the latter are less complex to organise and generally take place earlier.

An eighth point is an enhanced focus on advanced research training mainly but not exclusively through the ESRC funded National Centre for Research Methods based at the universities of Edinburgh, Southampton and Manchester but with an emphasis largely on quantitative skills. DTCs are restricted in how many advanced research training units they may have funded each year (this funding provides for non-DTC students to attend for a small sum) and qualitative proposals are often rejected. The definition of 'advanced' training is a contested one, as 'advanced' in one discipline may be someone else's basic training.

Ninth, a greater focus on generic skills training is another new feature during the period, initially through the Research Councils UK Roberts initiative money in the early 2000s (Roberts, 2002) and now unfunded but continuing in most universities as institution-wide programmes. The focus and content of Generic skills training is now based on the UK-wide Researcher Development Framework initiated by VITAE, a body which focuses on the training and careers of research students and postdocs and which was once RCUK funded but is now a membership-based organisation. This scheme has been seen by other countries as a good one (Clarke & Lunt, 2014), though this will depend on the number of postgraduate research students in universities and the state of the employment market they are entering.

Tenthly, there is a continued emphasis on prompt thesis submission and completion rates which in England are now monitored by HEFCE as well as by ESRC. Finally, there is a greater focus on internationalisation, both through allowing (at considerable institutional expense as ESRC studentships only cover Home/EU fees) recruitment of international (non-EU) students to ESRC awards in certain subject areas, a pilot ESRC scheme which fosters international collaboration via doctoral candidates and also encouraging international institutional visits by ESRC funded students, albeit with very modest sums of money. This slow recognition of the importance of internationalisation to the future excellence of social science is in sharp contrast to the more extensive way that many European doctoral programmes have already incorporated this, by emphasising how to publish in international journals and collaborate with international peers and academics.

UNINTENDED CONSEQUENCES OF DTCS FOR UNIVERSITIES AND STUDENTS

In this concluding section some of the unintended consequences of the shift to DTCs by ESRC are considered. Policies always have unintended consequences (Margetts et al., 2010; Krücken, 2014) and some of these for DTCs are still emerging. Using Merton's 1936 categories, we can see that some of these come about accidentally (error), unknowingly (ignorance) or because of immediate rather than long-term focus. The history of social science doctoral training and broader postgraduate education policy is littered with such consequences (Burgess et al., 1994; Becher et al., 1994, Delamont & Atkinson, 2014). The focus here for both reasons of significance and space is on four themes where such consequences are visible: collaboration, university autonomy, leadership and student diversity and inclusion, though there are certainly other possible themes. What is also interesting is that whilst during the 1990s, ESRC actively commissioned research (as contrasted with evaluation) on its initiatives in respect of doctoral training (e.g., Burgess et al., 1994; Acker et al., 1994a, 1994b; Delamont et al., 2000), it has not sought to do so this time.

Collaboration

The shift to inter-institutional collaboration by ESRC in relation to the DTCs initiative demands more interrogation than it has sometimes received. Lunt et al. (2013) suggest that it was part of the logic of the 2009–10 exercise but it is not clear if this was actually the case or whether collaboration (beyond institutional level) was an afterthought. Certainly at the 2009 autumn ESRC 'town meeting' at LSE questions about collaboration were met by puzzlement. Collaboration is quite possibly an unintended consequence of both the minimum numbers of studentships it was suggested might be required for a DTC plus, more importantly, the actions of the Welsh Assembly and Scottish government in encouraging their universities to submit single national collaborative applications for DTC recognition.

The concept of collaboration is quite a loose one and it can be applied to a variety of relationships between different organisations. At best it may be a relationship of equals, at worst, a connection in which one partner is very dominant. Collaborations and institutional mergers can also be thought of as being on the same continuum (Harman & Harman, 2003), as Harman (2002) notes:

> mergers can take any number of different forms, from loose affiliations at one end of the spectrum to tightly integrated models at the other. In turn, the particular form of a merger is likely to have a major influence on the merger process, the kinds of difficulties likely to be experienced in bringing different types of institutions together, the kind of structures likely to emerge and the degree of success of efforts to integrate the partner institutions. (ibid, p. 2)

Furthermore, mergers are not necessarily beneficial for all involved, or for education, as Ursin et al. (2010) note in relation to HE mergers in Finland. Collaborative DTCS, whilst ostensibly freely chosen, were the product of a situation in 2009–10 that forced institutions with smaller social science departments to seek partners wherever they could get one. A couple built on existing collaborations (South West, White Rose) but others did not and so some could be seen as at least partially involuntary. Furthermore, whilst an ordinary research collaboration can seek out academic excellence *per se*, in a DTC collaboration there may be considerable variation in the standard and focus of research in different disciplines in the same or partner institutions. DTCs *can* stimulate extra research collaboration, strive for the merging of institutional research strategies and the development of elite cohorts of students but all of this is in a context where UK HEIs are encouraged to compete with each other and the former Competition and Markets Authority has been criticising collaboration and collusion between 'public' HEIs on the grounds that the new home EU fees for undergraduates meant that universities which worked together ran the risk of being seen as anti-competitive. Furthermore, successful research collaboration of any kind may depend on the quality of the underlying research, the discipline, the focus and many other factors (Brew et al., 2013, Lewis et al., 2012). Forced partnerships may not facilitate research collaboration nor make any other positive contribution to the health of social science outside of doctoral education. Interestingly, the 2015 evaluation of ESRC DTCS suggests the case for all DTCS being collaborative has not yet been made (Bartholomew, 2015).

University Autonomy

The table explores the effect of DTCs on university autonomy, using Estermann et al. (2011) four categories of such autoromy: organisational, financial, staffing and academic. The table below suggests that all four forms are threatened by the ESRC DTC policy, though this is much less evident and apparent for single institution DTCs than collaborative ones. UK 'public' universities have considerable autonomy on paper compared to some other European countries in respect of organisational, staffing and academic autonomy but their financial autonomy is heavy regulated by the state despite rapidly declining public funding for teaching in particular.

Table 1. ESRC doctoral training centres and university autonomy

	Positive	Negative
Organisational Autonomy	Allowed to choose collaborating partners, subject to mutual agreement	'Encouraged' to align all doctoral education objectives and training. Under pressure to align research strategies and possibly education strategies too. High degree of ESRC micro- management of DTCs compared with other UK Research Funding Councils
Financial Autonomy	Access to ESRC studentships; Some control over different modes of studentship funding.	Must increasingly contribute own funds towards studentships, Nc DTC administrative costs paid for except Wales and Scotland.[3] In collaborative DTCS all funding handled by lead institution
Staffing Autonomy	Yes in single institution DTCs	Pressure for cross- institutional supervision, though resources rarely follow this. Collaborative DTC leaders must manage people they don't employ.
Academic autonomy	Help select successful students	Increasingly expected to choose new research collaborators for ESRC grants from those in DTC partners' institutions.

Other Research Council DTCs/DTPs vary in the extent to which they threaten university autonomy, with the recent Arts and Humanities Research Council DTPs coming the closest to ESRC in this respect but as these have only just admitted any students, it will be some time before the full extent of the consequences for autonomy become apparent. Whether or not the pressures on DTCs/DTPs will lead in time to both coercive and mimetic isomorphism (DiMaggio & Powell, 1983) in UK universities is not yet clear but it is entirely possible.

Leadership of DTCs

Lunt et al. (2013) in their study of the initial DTC phase, focused mainly on interviewing directors and other key actors but in collaborative DTCs directors must manage a 'management group', institutional DTC 'leads', administrator(s) and supervisors, many of whom are not employed by the lead organisation. This in itself is challenging but also some DTC directors are doing it as part of a standard academic job and are not always easily able to negotiate with senior management in their university, which given the resource and other requirements required can be problematic. It is also something for which no dedicated support is provided, apart from the ESRC DTC Directors' meetings. So although it may seem as though some form of distributed leadership (Gronn, 2000) is appropriate, the cross-institutional nature of nearly half of the DTCS makes this complex and draws on forms of leadership which are very different from running a research group or teaching programme. It is also rare for UK leadership programmes to tackle such specialist forms of leadership and management as collaborative endeavours. There are also problems of succession planning, as those who led the original ESRC DTC bids move onto other things, which is not dissimilar to the situation with the UK HEFCE's Centres of Excellence in Learning and Teaching initiated in the mid-2000s (Gosling & Turner, 2012), whereby towards the end of the initiative, quite a few of the original CETL leaders had left their institutions or moved onto other things.

Consequences for Non-ESRC Funded Students: Diversity or Exclusion?

ESRC (and previously SSRC) studentships for doctorates have been around for several decades but there are many fewer of them than in the past and we now know much more about how social class, ethnicity and gender, to name but three, shape access to postgraduate study in the UK (Wakeling, 2009, 2013). ESRC, despite dealing with the social sciences, has adopted what Becher (1994) terms the science model, that is it expects that research students will be young, straight from a first degree or masters and with a first in one and a distinction in the other and will generally want to study full-time. But in the social sciences, unlike in STEM subjects, most research students tend to be part-time (HESA) and many come back to study some time after their first degree, perhaps fired up by aspects of their work or other experiences. Though it is possible to study part-time and get ESRC funding, it is time-consuming and quite burdensome to do so for the amount of money involved. Furthermore, a good many full-time social science research students are international (as are many undergraduates too, see UUK, 2012) and with the exception of Economics, international students are not eligible for ESRC funding unless departments subsidise it. European Union-domiciled students are eligible for ESRC awards but only get programme fees without any maintenance element. In theory, all research students (ESRC or not) in the relevant disciplines in DTC institutions get access to DTC training schemes but no travel money is provided for non-ESRC funded students and in practice it is probably an unrealistic proposition for training is available in multi-locations since travel costs for can be high (a few DTCs have experimented with using VLEs or other e-technology but different licences make this challenging). As ESRC funding for research training in the social sciences becomes ever more selective, large numbers of social science students are being excluded, perhaps because they lack the money or time to benefit from ESRC training, are nowhere near a DTC and cannot move (related to jobs or dependant care) or because their original degree class is not good enough and nothing they have done since is allowed to compensate. ESRC DTCS are thus potentially divisive and exclusionary and who is to say that the end product of ESRC funded doctoral students is always going to be better than that of non-ESRC funded students?

IN SUMMARY

The paper has used personal narratives as a means to understanding some of the recent twists and turns in UK social science doctoral training, culminating in the DTCs policy and the early years of its implementation. The tales also incorporate many of the key policy decisions of ESRC from 1992 to the present and a number of the unintended as well as intended consequences, using Merton's framework, are discussed in some detail. The story is far from over but there are important lessons to be learnt from the DTC story, especially for other countries that are considering making such a move to collaborative training. The issues about university autonomy and student diversity and inclusion are not amongst those that UK HE policy makers have fully considered but they are some of the most disturbing consequences of the drive towards the social science 'training' PhD that was first envisaged by the 1987 Winfield Report.

ACKNOWLEDGEMENTS

An earlier version of the paper was presented at the 2014 Conference of Higher Education Researchers, Rome, September 8–10th and the 2014 Society for Research into Higher Education Conference at Celtic Manor, Newport, Wales, December 10th–12th. We are grateful to the editors for their helpful comments on an earlier draft and participants at both conferences for lively discussions about our paper. Special thanks are due to George Krücken for drawing our attention to his recent paper on the unintended consequences of German higher education policy and Carlinda Leite for pointing out the similarities and differences between recent doctoral training policies in the UK and Portugal.

NOTES

[1]   The name was changed in the early 1980s by Sir Keith Joseph, a Conservative politician who felt that social science except for Economics was not scientific
[2]   All of these points were raised at the SE ESRC DTC institutional visit in February 2014.
[3]   I am grateful to Sara Delamont for pointing this out.

REFERENCES

Acker, S., Black, E., & Hill, T. (1994a). Research students and their supervisors in education and psychology. In R. G. Burgess (Ed.), *Postgraduate education and training in the social sciences* (pp. 53–74). London, UK: Jessica Kingsley.

Acker, S., Transken, S., Hill, T., & Black, E. (1994b). Research students in education and psychology: Diversity and empowerment. *International Studies in Sociology of Education, 4*(2), 229–251.

Bartholomew, R., Disney, R., Eyerman, J., Mason, J., Newstead, S., Torrance, H., & Widdowfield, R. (2015). Review of the ESRC doctoral training centres network (the Bartholomew report). Swindon, England: Economic and Social Research Council Swindon. Retrieved from http:\\DTC-final-report-tcm8-33469.pdf

Becher, T., Henkel, M., & Kogan, M. (1994). *Graduate education in Britain*. London, UK: Jessica Kingsley.

Brew, A., Boud, D., Lucas, L., & Crawford, K. (2013). Reflexive deliberation in international research collaboration: Minimising risk and maximizing opportunity. *Higher Education, 66*, 93–104.

Boud, D., & Lee, A. (Eds.). (2009). *Changing practices of doctoral education*. London, UK: Routledge.

Burgess, R. G. (Ed.). (1994). *Postgraduate education and training in the social sciences*. London, UK: Jessica Kingsley.

Centre for Higher Education Policy Studies (CHEPS). (2011). *Exploration of the implementation of the principles for innovative doctoral training in Europe*. Final Report to the European Commission DG RTD, University of Twente, Enschede, The Netherlands.

Collinson, J., & Hockey, J. (1997). The social science training-model doctorate: Student choice? *Journal of Further and Higher Education, 21*(3), 373–381.

Clarke, G. (2014, April). *Evolution of the doctorate: A UK perspective on an international qualification.* Paper given to Quality in Postgraduate Research Conference, Adelaide, Australia.

Deem, R. (2014). Current UK postgraduate policies and developments. *British Educational Research Association: Research Intelligence, 124*, 10–11.

Deem, R., & Brehony, K. J. (2000). Doctoral students' access to research cultures: Are some more equal than others? *Studies in Higher Education, 25*(2), 149–165.

Delamont, S., & Atkinson, P. (2014, May 6). *Putting social science methods on the research agenda.* Paper presented to Symposium in honour of the academic work of Professor Robert Burgess, College Court, University of Leicester.

Delamont, S., Atkinson, P., & Parry, O. (1997a). Critical mass and doctoral research: Reflections on the Harris report. *Studies in Higher Education, 22*(3), 319–332.

Delamont, S., Parry, O., & Atkinson, P. (1997b). Critical mass and pedagogic continuity: Studies in academic habitus. *British Journal of Sociology of Education, 18*(4), 533–549.

Delamont, S., Atkinson, P., & Parry, O. (2000). *The doctoral experience*. London, UK: Falmer Press.

DiMaggio, P. J., & Powell, W. W. (1983). The iron cage revisited: Institutional isomorphism and collective rationality in organizational fields. *American Sociological Review, 48*(2), 147–160.

Gosling, D., & Turner, R. (2012). Rewarding excellent teaching: The translation of a policy initiative in the United Kingdom. *Higher Education Quarterly, 66*(4), 415–430.

Gronn, P. (2000). Distributed properties: A new architecture for leadership. *Educational Management and Administration, 28*, 317–338.

Harman, G., & Harman, K. (2003). Institutional mergers in higher education: Lessons from international experience. *Tertiary Education and Management, 9*(1), 29–44.

Harman, K. M., & Meek, V. L. (2002). Introduction to special issue: Merger revisited: International perspectives on mergers in higher education. *Higher Education, 44*(1), 1–4.

Harris, M. (1996). *The Harris review of postgraduate education.* Bristol, England: Higher Education Funding Council for England.

Higher Education Commission. (2012). Postgraduate education – An independent enquiry (the Spittle report). London, UK: Policy Connect.

Higher Education Policy Institute, and British Library. (2010). *Postgraduate education in the United Kingdom.* London, UK: Ginevra House.

Krücken, G. (2014). Higher education reforms and unintended consequences: A research agenda. *Studies in Higher Education, 39*(8), 1439–1450.

Lewis, J. M., Ross, S., & Holden, T. (2012). The how and why of academic collaboration: Disciplinary differences and policy implications. *Higher Education, 64*, 693–708.

Lunt, I., McAlpine, L., & Mills, D. (2013). Lively bureaucracy? The ESRC's doctoral training centres and UK universities. *Oxford Review of Education, 40*(2), 151–169.

Margetts, H., Perri 6, & Hood, C. (Eds.). (2010). *Paradoxes of modernization: Unintended consequences of public policy reform.* Oxford, England: Oxford University Press.

Merton, R. K. (1936). The unanticipated consequences of purposive social action. *American Sociological Review, 1*(6), 894–904.

Overall, N. C., Deane, K. L., & Peterson, E. R. (2011). Promoting doctoral students research self-efficacy: Combining academic guidance with autonomy support. *Higher Education Research and Development, 30*(6), 791–806.

Research Councils UK. (2010). *Review of progress in implementing the recommendations of Sir Gareth Roberts, regarding employability and career development of PhD students and research staff.* Swindon, England: Research Councils UK.

Research Councils UK. (2013a). *Statement of expectations for doctoral training: Joint vision for collaborative training.* Swindon, England: Research Councils UK, Research Councils UK. Retrieved from http://www.rcuk.ac.uk/RCUK-prod/assets/documents/skills/RCUKDoctoralTrainingLetter.pdf (Accessed June 2014)

Research Councils UK. (2013b). *Research council common terminology for postgraduate training.* Retrieved from http://www.rcuk.ac.uk/RCUK-prod/assets/documents/skills/RCUKCommonTerminologyforPostgraduateTraining2013.pdf (Accessed June 2014)

Roberts, G. (2002). *SET for success: A review.* Retrieved October, 2011, from http://webarchive.nationalarchives.gov.uk http://www.hm-treasury.gov.uk/ent_res_roberts.htm

Turner, G., & McAlpine, L. (2011). Doctoral experience as researcher preparation: Activities, passion, status. *International Journal for Researcher Development, 2*(1), 46–60.

Universities UK. (2012). *Patterns and trends in UK higher education.* London, UK: Universities UK. Retrieved from http://www.universitiesuk.ac.uk/highereducation/Documents/2012/PatternsAndTrendsinUKHigherEducation2012.pdf

Universities UK. (2014). *The funding environment for universities 2014: Research and postgraduate research training.* London, UK: Universities UK.

Ursin, J., Aittolaa, H., Henderson, C., & Välimaaa, J. (2010). Is education getting lost in university mergers? *Tertiary Education and Management, 16*(4), 327–340.

Wakeling, P. (2005). La noblesse d'état anglaise? Social class and progression to postgraduate study *British Journal of Sociology of Education, 26*(4), 505–522.

Wakeling, P. (2009). Are ethnic minorities underrepresented in UK postgraduate study? *Higher Education Quarterly, 63*(1), 86–111.

Wakeling, P. (2010). Inequalities in postgraduate education: A comparative review. In G. Goastellec (Ed.), *Understanding inequalities in, through and by higher education* (Vol. 21, pp. 61–74). Rotterdam, The Netherlands: Sense Publishers.

Winfield, G. (1987). *The social science Ph.D: The economic and social research council enquiry on submission rates.* Swindon, England: Economic and Social Research Council (The Winfield Report).

Professor Rosemary Deem
Principal's Office and School of Management
Royal Holloway & Bedford New College

Professor Sally Barnes
Graduate School of Education
University of Bristol

Gill Clarke
Department of Education
University of Oxford

SOFIA BRUCKMANN

6. SHIFTING BOUNDARIES IN UNIVERSITIES' GOVERNANCE MODELS

The Case of External Stakeholders

Higher Education reform trends hit Portugal in 2007, with law 62/2007 (RJIES) defining a new institutional framework and imposing major changes to higher education institutions (HEIs). These were given the chance to choose between two institutional models and required to restructure their governance model. One of the visible outcomes of this reform is a blurring of boundaries between HEIs and society. Academics now have to share a space that was traditional theirs with people coming from outside academia.

The present study results from an analysis of the changes occurred in six Portuguese universities after implementation of the RJIES, considering the context of broad public administration reform embedded in a managerialist framework. Changes to the governance model were analyzed focusing on the presence of external stakeholders in top governing bodies. The perceptions of both academics and external stakeholders were analyzed in order to assess to what extent the presence of external stakeholders is perceived as a necessary and effective change. Furthermore, this study also intends to shed some light to the following question: how do academics and external stakeholders perceive the presence of external stakeholders, at HEIs' top governing bodies?

INTRODUCTION

Higher Education (HE) has changed more in the last 30 years than it ever did before. From the 1970s and 1980s onwards, European HE systems were faced with the consequences of a rise in neo-liberal ideologies, implementation of new public management (NPM) based reforms, consequent attempts of marketisation of HE and adoption of quasi-market principles (Amaral & Magalhães, 2007; Reed, 2002). In parallel, higher education institutions (HEIs) also faced an increased demand for HE, with HE systems in general moving away from elite type systems to mass HE systems (Trow, 1974), which came to place 'further burdens on already stretched resources' (Taylor, 2013: 82).

Changes driven by NPM and managerialism principles produced effect also on governance models. Governance reforms in HEIs reflect some of the

E. Reale & E. Primeri (Eds.), The Transformation of University Institutional and Organizational Boundaries, 163–184.

main characteristics of a NPM reform, such as governing bodies structured in a corporate-like manner, with leadership roles reinforced and traditional collegial structures replaced by stakeholder boards (Carvalho & Bruckmann, 2014; Carvalho & Santiago, 2010). The political discourse conveys the need for such reforms by claiming that more efficacy, efficiency and accountability are needed in public sector institutions. By assuming that private sector management practices are more efficient than the traditional bureaucratic governance model of public administration, and that therefore the public sector should adopt the management techniques typical of the private sector (Ferlie et al., 1996), NPM reform may be seen as an attempt to question and to change the Weberian bureaucratic administrative pillar (Carvalho & Bruckmann, 2014).

In Portugal, HE reform trends became effective in 2007, with a new law (known by its acronym RJIES) defining a new institutional framework and imposing major changes to higher education institutions. For the first time in the history of the Portuguese HE system, HEIs were given the chance to choose between two institutional models: they could either remain a public institute or become a foundation.[1] They were also required to restructure their governance model in a manner that was new to them. Some of the major elements of this reorganisation can be here shortly accounted for: a reduction in size of university governing bodies and in the number of governing bodies; mandatory participation of external stakeholders in top governing bodies; selection modes of members of governing bodies have changed and include now appointment and co-option, besides the traditional election; candidates to Rector may come from other institutions and countries; among others.

One of the visible outcomes of this reform is a blurring of boundaries between HEIs and society. Academics now have to share a space that was traditional theirs with people coming from other professional backgrounds outside academia. Following an international trend, academics in management positions are now more accountable to the State and to society, as HEI's governing bodies include external stakeholders, some of them co-opted by the HEI, others appointed by the government following a proposal from the HEI. In fact, the increased presence of external stakeholders in top-level bodies is a worldwide trend. Several European countries have undergone reforms that resulted, inter alia, in an increased presence of external stakeholders in important decision-making university boards, even if in different degrees and roles (Boer & File, 2009). The door to the 'ivory tower' is open.

The inclusion of external stakeholders in university governance results in a shift in balance on traditional decision-making roles. For a long time decisions on matters concerning the university were taken by a large majority of academics, in highly represented and collegial boards, where external stakeholders were mostly nonexistent. Nowadays, the presence of external stakeholders at governance level became a rule and academics have seen their presence diminished in important decision-making boards. As the CAP survey results show "the faculty's role in decision-making has shrunk somewhat" (Locke, Cummings, & Fisher, 2011: 4). This came to change the governance paradigm in force, with a new shared governance paradigm being legitimised.

As the study aims to analyse the way internal and external stakeholders perceive the presence of external stakeholders at top governing bodies, the theoretical perspective will also consider the idea of 'shared governance' (Shattock, 2002, 2006; Stensaker & Vabø, 2013). Shared governance refers to a governance model that values decision-making processes participated by a great diversity of actors, including both internal actors (academics, non-academic staff and students) and external actors (members of the society and the entrepreneurial world not related to academia).

Thus, the theoretical framework seeks to articulate NPM and managerialism concepts with the idea of shared governance and the shift in university's stakeholders' role, the first helping to understand what triggered reform and discuss how the mandatory presence of external stakeholders in top governing bodies fit into this reform movement, the latter to help discuss whether these external stakeholders are perceived as having an effective role in university governance.

This chapter is organised in five main sections. It starts with a brief reflexion over the context of higher education reform in Portugal, followed by a presentation of the chosen framework for analysis, and the methodological approach adopted for this study. Section 5 presents and discusses the empirical findings and the final section presents the conclusions, summing up the main findings and their implications for the future of the university's governance model.

CONTEXT OF REFORM IN PORTUGAL

Portugal had a somewhat later development of its HE system due to the dictatorial regime in place for great part of the 20th century. Most of the Portuguese HE system remained almost unchanged until the 1970s. At the early 1970s, Minister Veiga Simão created a binary system made of universities and polytechnic institutions, and made it possible for new HEIs to emerge (Bruckmann & Carvalho, 2014), thus expanding the system both in terms of the offer as well as the demand for HE. The 1974 revolution made it possible to democratise the Portuguese HE system, and the governance model in place was a reflection of the new democratic period the country was experiencing: extensively participated collegial governing bodies (by all academic groups), whom the rector hat to consult and follow the majority's decision.

Whereas in other developed countries NPM reforms were in place since the 1970s and the 1980s, in Portugal it is during the 1990s that NPM discourse starts to be present at the political discourse level. Actual reform becomes a reality in the early 2000s with the publication of a set of new legislation that followed recommendations from international organisations such as the OECD. From this set of new legislation, law 62/2007 is of great significance to Portuguese HE as it imposed a major reform to the Portuguese HE landscape.

The key elements of the reform brought by the RJIES include the possibility given to HEIs to choose between two different institutional models, which is new to Portuguese institutions: HEIs can now choose to remain public institutions or to become a foundation. Foundation universities were until then non-existent in the Portuguese HE system: they are considered to be public foundations operating under private law. The hybridism suggested by this term, mixing public and private realm, has a reflection on the institutions themselves: they are still public and must abide by the terms imposed by the government, but at the same time they have a greater autonomy, namely on financial issues and do not have to abide by the general rules applying to other public administration institutions; they may have staff careers of their own which gives them more flexibility in terms of recruitment and personnel management; financing is based on multi-annual contracts with the state and on funding they get from other (private) sources. This is mainly what differentiates HEIs that chose to become a foundation from those that opted to remain public institutes.

At the governance level, the main difference lies on the fact that foundations have an extra mandatory body when compared to public institutes: the board of trustees. Otherwise they share the main governing bodies at central level: the rector, the general council and the management board.

Another new aspect brought by the RJIES in terms of the governance reform it implies was the introduction of external members in top governing bodies of HEIs, at an important decision-making level. Their presence is mandatory in the general council and the board of trustees. Selection of external members is not done through election. Instead general council external members are co-opted by the internal members. The government at suggestion of the HEI appoints external members to the board of trustees.

Besides these more striking aspects of reform, RJIES also implied: a reduction of governing bodies and of the number of members that constitute them; power concentration in one-person bodies, such as the rector and the directors of organisational unit; greater accountability requirements; increased professionalization of management; among others.

SHIFTS IN UNIVERSITY GOVERNANCE MODELS: A THEORETICAL APPROACH

Governance shifts in HE must be set in a context of broader public administration reform and increased relevance of market-oriented perspectives, claiming for the need for more efficiency and efficacy on behalf of public sector organisations. Claims for low levels of efficiency and efficacy in public organisations, present in policy makers' discourses, have been used as the driver for reforms associated to a rise in managerialism ideology. The environment of economic crisis, experienced by countries implementing NPM reforms, gave governments the legitimacy they needed to implement such reforms and to gather general approval and acceptance of the idea that more efficiency is needed in public sector organisations and that this is achieved by the adoption of private sector management practices (Larbi, 1999). Such claims are part of a broader trend in public administration reform known as new public management (NPM) (Barzelay, 2001; Clarke & Newman, 1997; Ferlie et al., 1996; Hood, 1991; Kirkpatrick, Ackroyd, & Walker, 2005; McLaughlin, Osborne, & Ferlie, 2002; Pollitt, 2002). This reform trend, based on managerialism ideology, can be said to be a generalised tendency to reform the public sector by incorporating private sector management practices (Bruckmann & Carvalho, 2014; Lodge & Hood, 2012).

The rise of a managerialist ideology cannot be dissociated from an increased influence from neoliberalism and resulting questioning of the bureaucratic State model and the Welfare State itself (Larbi, 1999). The idea that the State has failed in several areas, that public sector organisations lack transparency and accountability to society, the widespread criticism to bureaucracy and the generalised idea that the private sector is far more efficient than the public sector (Simonet, 2011), conveyed by interested stakeholders, is indeed a neoliberal type of discourse and it managed to attract support from the general population. Public sector reforms associated to NPM are the result from a shift in the role the State is expected to play in modern societies (Carvalho, 2009; Henkel, 2000; Neave & Vught, 1994; Vught, 1994). Pressure to reform the public sector is also enforced by international organisations such as the OECD, IFM, and the World Bank (Larbi, 1999) that besides the need for an increased efficiency of public organisations, also claim the need to improve (i.e., decrease) public expenditure.

Briefly put, these reforms aimed at changing the public management paradigm in force from the traditional bureaucratic model to a more managerial one, based on private sector practices (Bruckmann & Carvalho, 2014; Mongkol, 2011). The 'NPM menu', as Mongkol (2011: 35) puts it, is composed of various items, not all of them being present in every reform: decentralization of management processes, marketisation of public services with increased competition within public services and between public and private services providers, contracting-out and outsourcing, use of market-like mechanisms, emphasis on performance and on results (Bruckmann & Carvalho, 2014; Larbi, 1999; Mongkol, 2011). These are some of the key elements of this NPM menu.

NPM in the HE context becomes visible through a number of changes that have implemented new practices typical of a more managerial model for public institutions, from which we can highlight: government-HEI contracts, focus on targets and outputs and on performance indicators; strengthening of management and leadership positions; stronger client and market orientation reflected by a focus on quality issues and on marketing; concern with value for money issues.

Whether NPM represents a new paradigm in public sector management remains to be fully asserted. Some authors believe it does (Eakin et al., 2011; Kirkpatrick, Ackroyd, & Walker, 2005; Larbi, 1999; Liguori, 2012). What is certainly true is that NPM represents a dominant set of ideas about public administration, within a given timeframe, responsible for important changes occurred in public sector institutions, among which we find HEIs.

Governance Shift in Higher Education

In HE, NPM reform is specifically visible at governance and management levels (Stensaker & Vabø, 2013). In what concerns the university, there is not one single governance model, as there is not one single model of university either. Although universities worldwide have a common root and share therefore a common heritage, they are also single institutions as they have developed according to the environment around them, which differs geographically and socially, having to adapt to it (Altbach, 1991: 190). Differences among institutions worldwide are also visible at governance level, with institutions showing different governing structures in their organisation.

University governance has traditionally been characterised by a model based on the principle of 'shared governance' (Shattock, 2002, 2006; Stensaker & Vabø, 2013). Although there is still much discussion about the definition of 'shared governance' specifically in the context of higher education, it can be briefly described as a governance model in which decision-making is a process participated by the organisation's actors. As Shattock puts it '[...] university governance is defined as the constitutional forms and processes through which universities govern their affairs' (Shattock, 2006: 1). In HE, the actors involved are above all academics, but also students and non-academic staff, whose presence in HEI's governing bodies is part of the university tradition, although with different degrees of participation. The supremacy of the academic staff role in decision-making bodies of HEIs has always been and still is a major characteristic of the governance model of HEIs (Stensaker & Vabø, 2013).

Traditionally, the university governance model was also defined by collegiality and was constituted by highly represented governance bodies, i.e., not only were all internal academic groups represented, as they were represented in large numbers. The reforms that followed NPM principles questioned this traditional governance model, imposing not only a reduction of governance bodies' size, as well as the introduction of external members in top decision-making bodies of HEIs. The concept of shared governance is thus extended and came to include a group that had for a long time been out of the traditional university governance model: members from the society that were external to HEIs, the stakeholders Amaral and Magalhães define as 'the representative of interests of the organisations' surrounding environment' (2000: 16).

We recall here four changes considered by Peter Eckel and Adrianna Kezar (2006) to be factors that might 'reshape' the decision-making model of HEIs as indeed they are major elements that contributed to a shift in governance in HE: the relationship between the State and public institutions has changed, with the latter being subject to more scrutiny and accountability measures; increased influence from the marketplace, as public institutions get less financial support from the State and must therefore look for other sources of financing; globalization puts HEIs in a much larger context, requiring interaction and competition at an international level; significant changes to the academic workforce, claimed to have an important and direct implication for governance (Eckel & Kezar, 2006: 6). Some of these factors are already a result from NPM based reforms, some have sustained them and some are simply contextual factors that cannot be dissociated from the rest.

As part of this reform of the traditional university governance model of managerialist influence, some authors even consider that a new form of university governance has emerged, introducing the notion of corporate governance (Kezar, 2004), with a clear decline of academic participation in decision-making, considered to be too self-interested, and an increase of external participation.

Higher Education Stakeholders' Role

The reforms addressed in this study reflect, as we have seen, a shift of the traditional relationship of higher education institutions and the State. Whereas traditionally this relationship was characterised by a State control model, neo-liberal ideology's discourse conveyed the idea that the State should withdraw from what was considered to be excessive regulation of public organisations, thus giving rise to a model of State supervision (Neave & Vught, 1994; Vught, 1994). The argument was mostly based on the idea that public sector organisations were ineffective, over bureaucratised, unproductive and wasting too much State money. The shift from the State control model to the State supervision model resulted in higher education policies enhancing autonomy, accountability and quality assessment, considered as requirements for more effective and efficient higher education institutions and thus became the cornerstones of the reforms that followed (Magalhães & Santiago, 2011). The State thus leaves up to higher education institutions to define their strategy and to adapt to the environment they are in, assuming that this will enhance their efficiency, capacity to innovate and accountability (Magalhães, 2001: 127). However, the State does not entirely retreat from controlling higher education institutions. It shifted the control that was traditionally done upfront to a control based on results, visible in the widespread performance assessment instruments set up across European higher education institutions (Veiga, Magalhães, Sousa, Ribeiro, & Amaral, 2014). Guy Neave names this model of State based on regular assessment of the performance of institutions, through agencies and committees set up for the purpose, the Evaluative State (Neave, 2012).

The shift in the relationship between State and higher education institutions and the subsequent concerns with autonomy, accountability and quality assessment had a direct impact on the role of both internal and external stakeholders, redefining it (Leisyte, Westerheijden, Epping, Faber, & Weert, 2013). Considering that a stakeholder is anyone or any entity having a share of interest in higher education

(Amaral & Magalhães, 2002), it is possible to identify a group of internal stakeholders, composed of members of the academia (academics, non-academic staff and students), and a group of external stakeholders, who represent, in the institution, the interests of society in higher education (members of society at large, the State and some international organisations). External stakeholders' presence in governance boards of higher education institutions is a way of bringing into institutions the interests of society and to make institutions be more accountable to society (Veiga et al., 2014). It also came to change internal dynamics and the role of internal actors, as they have seen their presence reduced in governance matters, by being imposed a shared governance model where the presence of external stakeholders became mandatory. Internal actors, traditionally used to collegially decide on important and strategic matters concerning their institution, now have to share discussion and decision-making with people from outside academia. This leads us to a 'new stakeholder model' with boards of trustees being introduced, composed by external members who very often come from the business world; with rectors being elected by smaller boards integrating external stakeholders; with senates being decreased of their decision-making power and the Rector having a redefined and more empowered role (Sporn, 2003).

The balance between internal and external stakeholders has shifted, with roles being redefined. However, in spite of the greater prominence external stakeholders have been assuming in higher education institutions' governance models, internal stakeholders, namely academic actors, still keep a leading role on governance matters.

METHODOLOGICAL APPROACH

The present study is based on empirical data gathered through semi-structured interviews to key actors from six Portuguese HEIs, as well as content analysis of legal documents defining the new governance structures (statutes, regulations and website information). The focus being on governance changes that occurred after implementation of the RJIES, the study could not leave aside the fact that 3 Portuguese HEIs decided to adopt the foundational status. Thus, it became interesting to consider perceptions on governance changes, namely on the increased participation of external members in top governing boards, from both public institute universities and foundation universities' actors. The three existent foundation universities integrate the study: Aveiro, Porto and ISCTE. In order to have a comparable set of institutions on the public institute side, 3 universities were chosen according to criteria of age, size and internal structure: Minho, Coimbra, Nova de Lisboa. The study integrates 2 organisational units (OUs) per HEI, as the law foresees the possibility to integrate external stakeholders also at this governance level. Table 1 presents the study sample.

Table 1. Sample description

Universities Foundational model	Organisational Units[2]	
University of Aveiro (UA)	Civil Engineering Department	Social, Political and Territorial Sciences Department
University of Porto (UP)	Faculty of Arts	Faculty of Pharmacy
ISCTE-IUL (ISCTE)	School of Social Sciences and Humanities	School of Technology and Architecture
Public institute model		
University Nova de Lisboa (UNL)	Faculty of Sciences and Technology	Faculty of Social Sciences and Humanities
University of Coimbra (UC)	Faculty of Arts	Faculty of Sciences and Technology
University of Minho (UM)	Law School	School of Engineering

Although the Portuguese HE system[3] comprises both a public and a private sub-system, for the purpose of this study only public HEIs have been considered. In the same line, in spite of the fact that the Portuguese HE system is binary, composed both by universities and polytechnic institutes, only universities were considered for this study.

The analysis to the statutes and regulations of these institutions made it possible to identify the governance boards integrating external stakeholders, both at central and unit level. Information made available on the institutions' website enabled to gather data on the professional background of external members of the general council, which is the top governing board of the HEI.

Semi-structured interviews were conducted to key actors of the 6 universities: Rectors, Presidents of the general council, Administrators, and Directors of organisational units. Interviewees are identified according to the type of institution they belong to: *UF* for foundation universities and *UIP* for public institute universities; and the post they held at the institution: *r* for Rectors, *p* for Presidents of general council, *a* for Administrators, and *d* for Directors of organisational units. The numbers are assigned in a random way, e.g., the Rector of a university foundation is identified as follows: *1UFr*.

Interviews took place between November 2013 and June 2014.

Both interviews and documents were subject to content analysis, the latter to establish facts about how HEIs reorganised themselves to implement the new governance structures according to the RJIES, the former to have key actors' insight

171

Table 2. Interviewees' map

	Rector	President of general council	Administrator	Director of OU	Total
Foundations	3	2	2	5	12
Public institutes	3	2	3	5	13
Total					25

specifically on the presence of external stakeholders in top governing boards of the institution, and the strengths and weaknesses of a governance model including external members. Interviews were subject to thematic content analysis (Bardin, 2009), based on 4 major themes:

- The end of the 'ivory tower'? – to discuss the interviewees' perception on the need of opening the university to society. The use of the 'ivory tower' metaphor has long been used to refer to universities as institutions closed in on themselves. As Rüegg tells us: "Since the late nineteenth century the universities have been compared to 'ivory towers' to symbolize their arrogant distancing from the world." (Rüegg, 2011: 16).
- External stakeholders: a fresh look into the university – to get the perceptions of both internal and external stakeholders on the benefits of having someone from the outside world involved in the university's governance.
- Higher education: moving closer to the business world? – to analyse and discuss whether internal and external stakeholders perceive the presence of external members in top governing boards as a move towards a more managerial model of university governance.
- Internal vs. external stakeholders: who is in charge? – to discuss the perceptions of internal and external stakeholders about their role in governance.

EXTERNAL STAKEHOLDERS IN GOVERNANCE BOARDS: STRENGTHS AND WEAKNESSES

The RJIES brought no doubt a major change to HEIs' governance model. Part of that change has to do with the introduction of external members in important governance boards of the institutions. Their presence is mandatory at the top central boards of HEIs, such as the general council, where external members account for at least 30% of members, and at the board of trustees (in foundation universities), constituted solely by external members to the HEIs. It is left to HEIs to choose to include external members in other governance boards, both at central level and at organisational unit[4] level. Analysis of the statutes of the six universities that integrate this study made it possible to map the presence of external members in these HEIs' governance boards, as shown in Table 3.

Table 3 Presence of external members in governance boards

HEI	General council			Other governing boards with ext. members		External members at organisational unit level	
	Board of trustees	Nr. Ext. members	Total nr. members	Nr. of gov. boards	Nr. of ext. members	Nr. of ext. memb.	Selection mode
UA	5	5	19	2	Not defined	–	–
UP	5	6	23	–	–	1	Co-opted
ISCTE	5	10	33	–	–		
School of Social Science						All	Appointed by Director
School of Technology and Architecture						3	Appointed by Director
UC	–	10	35	–	–	–	–
UM	–	6	23	1	≤ 10	–	–
UNL	–	7	21	–	–		
Faculty of Sciences and Technology						5	Appointed by Rector
Faculty of Social Sciences						4	Appointed by Rector

The roles assigned to these external members vary according to the board they belong to. The general council has to be presided by an external member, giving this external member a very important role within this board and the institution. The other external members of the general council have the same power as all other members, except for the choice of external members themselves, which is exclusively up to internal members to decide through co-option. Among the duties of the general council we find the election of the Rector, to which every single member gets to vote for in equal shares. According to Law 62/2007, the general council gathers its members four times per year, which might mean that external members only have to physically be at their higher education institution at the four meetings established by law. A greater involvement of external members in the life of the institution might depend on the relationship established between them and the Rector, as became apparent from some interviews. A greater involvement might mean a closer relationship and the development of an informal role of external members, which goes beyond the formal role established by law.

The government, upon suggestion of the institution, appoints external members to the board of trustees, in the case of foundation universities. This is a supervisor and monitoring board to the general council's decisions. Its members cannot have any work relation to the institution, so as to assure a certain distancing between them and the institution. If this was the case of first choice members, further boards of trustees sometimes include former rectors or members of the institution, which might mitigate the law's expectations.

A shared governance model is, thus, present in the general council, where internal actors (academics, students and non academic staff) and external stakeholders share decision-making powers on the same matters. It is absent in the case of the board of trustees, as this board is constituted solely by external members.

Analysis of the statutes shows that four out of the six universities of this study chose to expand the inclusion of external members beyond law requirements, which might indicate the acceptance of the discourse claiming for the need to change the traditional university governance model, where the academia was run by academics, to a new governance model, in which the society has also a word to say about how a university should be governed, and also claiming for more accountability. The fact that the University of Coimbra chose not to include external members in governing boards other than those required by law might be connected to the weight tradition and history still have in this university, the oldest in the country, the foundation of which dates back to the 13th century. The same cannot be said of the University of Minho, created only in the 1970s. It might however be related to the fact that this university made the choice of remaining a public institute and not become a foundation university, clinging to a more traditional model of university.

Subsequent interviews done to key actors of the six universities in question made it possible to better understand what might have been beneath these choices, on one hand, and on the other hand to have an insight on how the presence of external members is perceived, giving us a better idea of the actors' perceptions on the strengths and weaknesses of a governance model including external members.

The End of the 'Ivory Tower'?

Analysis of the interviews to both internal and external actors shows that the presence of external stakeholders in top governing bodies of HEIs is generally perceived to be very positive. Most interviewees refer the need for universities to open themselves to society and the outside environment in general, and most claim that having external members as part of top governing boards is a way to do it. When asked to give their opinion on the subject, interviewees rate the presence of external members very positively:

> I rate it [external stakeholders' presence] as very, very positive. It promotes a greater openness of the university to the outside, and also a higher level of discussion and agenda at the highest governing body of the university. (1UIPr)

[...] I think that this was a very positive measure only because universities were completely closed: the academics, their careers were what determined it all. (2UIPa)

Not only do most interviewees perceive the presence of external stakeholders as promoting a necessary openness of universities to society, as they also consider that the university was too closed in upon itself, which is perceived negatively. Most actors, irrespective whether they come from foundation universities or public institute universities, share these opinions. There seems to be no significant difference to notice when comparing opinions from actors from foundation universities and public institute universities.

I think that institutions must increasingly open to the outside [...]. If the university is an ivory tower it dies. (1UIPd)
It basically means to extend the link to society, if you wish. (1UFr)

This is also the view of external stakeholders, themselves. They consider that the university should open to the outside and letting in external members is considered as a means of doing so.

I think that the RJIES has ideas that are very worthwhile ideas, intending to make universities stop living in their own closed system, by introducing general councils and external members. (1UIPp)

The university seems to be moving beyond the 'ivory tower' it used to be. By perceiving as positive and accepting the participation of external members in important decision-making boards, academics are accepting the idea that discussion of and decision on university affairs benefit from an external insight, thus opening the door of the 'ivory tower', which was traditionally shut. Although foundation universities have an extra board composed solely by external members, this does not seem to have an impact on stakeholders' perceptions when compared to those of public institute stakeholders, as both seem to share the same opinions regardless of the institutional model chosen by their university.

External Stakeholders: A Fresh Look into the University

This idea shared by most interviewees that the university was too closed in upon itself and needed to open to society at large might explain the reason why the introduction of external members in important governing boards seems to be so widely accepted and considered as a positive measure brought by the RJIES. Most interviewees perceive external stakeholders as having brought to universities a new look and a new way of running the institution, which is rated as positive by internal actors.

I think they [external members] have brought a new way of looking at things and even of managing things, which I rate as good. (1UFd)

> I think it is always good to have a look from outside, from someone who is
> an outsider [...]. I think they have brought a different way of seeing things, of
> looking at things, and even of managing things that I rate as good. (1UFd)

> I think it is always good to have people from the outside, not least to ask: why
> is this like this? (5UFd)

The traditional model of university shared governance is changed by the RJIES
that extends it to another group (society members) who comes to have a word on
university matters, where they used to have none before. It is curious to notice that
it is furthermore unquestioned and unchallenged by academics who, traditionally,
were the main decision-makers in matters relating to their institution and themselves
as professionals. This supports the idea that the NPM discourse widespread by
international organisations, national governments and ultimately accepted by society
at large, also found careful listeners at the institutions aimed by the reform, where it
seems to have come to be institutionalised.

The presence of external members in HEIs is also perceived as a two way thing
by some members of academia: not only can HEIs benefit from an external look, but
also external members can get a better idea of how HEIs actually work, the problems
they face, and take this knowledge to the outside. This is seen as a positive aspect of
the inclusion of external stakeholders in top governing boards.

> First, it requires us to consider different looks, it brings along different looks
> and requires from us to reflect about those looks; the external members
> themselves change their own looks when they are, say, influenced by the
> institutional experience [...] (3UFr)

> [...] there is a positive aspect I am noticing about those external elements.
> [...] there used to be that dominant discourse saying that universities should
> adapt themselves to the market world, etc., and this, I think, is being put in
> perspective because some external representatives are being confronted with
> the universities' own reality. [...] And they are themselves taking initiatives to
> resolve that issue. And that is interesting because there is a certain awareness
> that goes a bit against what was previously said. (2UFd)

Once more these results seem to support the idea that the University is no longer
seen as an organisation that should remain closed in itself. Academics seem to be
willing to let in ideas and insights from the outside and see this as beneficial for the
discussion of university matters and consequently for decision-making on matters
concerning the academia.

Higher Education: Moving Closer to the Business World?

One of the key characteristics associated to NPM is to value the private sector
management techniques to the detriment of those of the public sector. This results
in bringing the public sector closer to the private sector in various ways. In HE, the

inclusion of external stakeholders in top governing boards can be seen as a way of doing this. The analysis of the composition of the general council and the board of trustees' members – where most external members are – shows us that there is a considerable number of external members coming from the business world. This might indicate that HEIs consider it as an added value to have among their members, known figures from the business world. Table 4 shows the percentage of external members with a business background in both general council and board of trustees.

Table 4. Percentage of external members with business background

HEIs	General council (1st mandate)	General council (2nd mandate)	Board of trustees
UA	60%	60%	60%
UP	50%	16,7%	60%
ISCTE		∠0%	40%
UC	50%	20%	–
UM	33,3%	33,3%	–
UNL	14,3%	42,9%	–

It is of interest to notice that there are some differences in the percentage of external members with business background between first and second general council mandates. There is a significant decrease in the universities of Porto and Coimbra, which might indicate that the inclusion of business people was not considered to have been as positive or valuable as expected. On the contrary, the University Nova de Lisboa increased the number of members with a business profile in the 2nd mandate, which might be considered to be in line with the decision of becoming a foundation university.

Some interviewees consider that the reform could have gone even further in terms of the ratio of external members and the way they are selected, specifically in the general council, where their presence should be, by law, of at least 30% of the members.

[...] we could still have more elements in a higher percentage of external elements in the general council [...] (3UFr)

Selection of external members is done by co-option by the internal actors and therefore I think that we should consider the possibility of part of the external members be co-opted by the external members and not only by the internal members. I think it is necessary to find other ways of selecting external stakeholders. (1UIPp)

This goes in line with what has already been said: external stakeholders seem to be widely accepted in HEIs and some even consider that their presence should be increased. When asked about whether they considered that the new governance model imposed by the RJIES had contributed to move public sector governance models closer to those of the private sector, some interviewees claim it has and make a direct relation with the presence of external stakeholders. At organisational unit level, scientific area seems to matter in terms of how important is the presence of external members perceived to be.

> A little, though not totally. And I think that the inclusion of external members in decision-making bodies has a bit to do with that. It is the university moving closer to the business world. Of course that also depends much on the faculties and on the scientific areas, it is not the same in a faculty of economics or of engineering, or a faculty of arts. And the external members are not equally important in all faculties because the link of faculties to the business world is not the same, it depends much on the scientific areas that are lectured. (3UFd)

The acceptance of the idea conveyed by NPM discourse that the private sector is more efficient than the public sector (Larbi, 1999; Pollitt, 2002) and that the public sector might benefit from public sector management techniques is present in answers such as the two below:

> [...] the perception we have is that [external members] really bring a different vision and therefore place different levels of ambition than those we were used to. On the other side, they are facilitators of the relationship with the community, namely the business world, and that I think is a very considerable gain for a university, even in what concerns the degree of rigour they place on accountability [...]. We have here a slightly superior level of demand than the one we were used to. And that is good, bringing experiences from the private world. (1Ufa)

> [...] there is an entrance of external elements in the general council, which I rate as positive as it brings a new look and it contributes to the presence of external elements... and they come from more rigorous governments, more experienced and more strategically determined. (3UFr)

Although the presence of external members in HEIs seems to be widely accepted, some interviewees refer a few aspects they perceive as of concern. One interviewee notes that the initial trend to choose external members coming from the business world might bring along the tendency to implement in public HEIs management practices typical of the private sector, perceived as not applying to the reality of a university.

> The first temptation of the universities was to pick up representatives of the business world. [...] namely the Presidents of the general councils bring along a logic of hard management to the general councils and to the university, which is not necessarily... I hold nothing against management but this cannot work like it was a supermarket... (2UFd)

Others perceive the number of external representatives in top governing boards of HEIs as too high and question whether that number should be as high as it is, although still not opposing to their presence.

[...] as a matter of principle, I think it might be interesting to include members from the civil society; but what I can ask is whether the percentage should be that high. (3UFd)

These answers show that among academics there is still opposing voices to the idea conveyed by NPM supporters that private sector management practices should be applied to the public sector because they are considered to be better and able to solve public sector management problems.

Internal vs. External Stakeholders: Who is in Charge?

The analysis to the legal documents of the six universities, namely the statutes that define the new governance model according to the RJIES, shows that, except for the board of trustees (where external members account for 100% of the seats), the academics still hold the majority of seats in most governing bodies. The RJIES itself establishes that academics should hold more than 50% of seats in the general council, giving them the majority and the most important word to say on the matters discussed at general council level. The presence of external members in other governing bodies is not significant, as already mentioned, and happens mostly in consultative boards. So, clearly academics still are in charge of their institutions. But how is this perceived by members of academia and also by external members? How do academics perceive this share of governance with members from outside academia? And specifically in the case of the board of trustees, how is their presence perceived in terms of their duties towards the institution?

Internal interviewees perceive that in spite of the fact that university governance is now shared with external members, the traditional internal balances have not changed: the top governing board is still composed by a majority of academics, and non-academic staff and students are still present.

Actually, the general council is still composed of a majority of academics. There is a representative from the non-academic staff and then the external personalities, and those yes, they do bring a new dynamics, but internally the balances did not change substantially. (1Ufa)

When questioned about the board of trustees some interviewees reveal a lack of knowledge of what this board actually does and speak of it as a 'symbolic board', though recognising it as a means of supervision by the State of the HEI's activities, as all members are appointed by the government.

I think it was, on one hand, ... when institutions chose to become a foundation, it was the assurance that the State still kept controlling foundations through the board of trustees, because they are appointed by the government. Now, what I think is that it is more of a symbolic board, at this point, than actually a board with strong powers, isn't it. (2UFd)

For me it is a non-existent board... I don't know what it does... I have the feeling it is inoperative. (1UFd)

The answers above transcribed come from directors of organisational units, who might feel a bit more distant from central governing boards, whereas rectors have a greater interaction and articulation with them. To the same question, one rector from a foundation university answered:

The board of trustees is very important [...]. They used to say that this was to governmentalise the institution: I prefer to have five members that I get to choose and propose to the government, than one minister I didn't vote for. [...] A good part of the functions of the ministry have been delegated. Therefore, I have a much greater intervention on the names I propose to the government because it cannot nominate them until I have proposed them, and I also accept that the government, since it delegated on the board of trustees patrimonial responsibilities, have a word to say on the nomination. (1UFr)

Some interviewees perceive that external members have a too great decision power on matters concerning the university. Others make the distinction between issues that should exclusively fall within the competence of academics and that are not to be decided by external members – such is the case of scientific and pedagogical matters – and issues that can fall within the competence of external members.

It seems to me that it is a bit exaggerate that they [external members] should have such a decision-making power, specially if they are not familiar with the university's life. (3UFd)

It depends on the competences of the board because, for instance, if that board has scientific and pedagogical competences I totally disagree, it makes no sense. If the board has economic, financial and administrative competences, if it is not the decision-making board just of control, so to say, then it is not as preoccupying because I think that the academics are important specially on those matters where they have a word to say, which is the most important of all: the academic issues, especially on scientific and pedagogic issues, especially in those. [...] Now, is it essential for academics to have an opinion on financial or administrative issues? I have some doubts about that, lots of doubts, I even have doubts whether university management has to be done exclusively by academics. I have doubts. (4UIPd)

Interviewees also refer as positive the fact that the presence of external stakeholders changes the kind of discussions that used to happen in some university boards, more of an internal and corporative nature:

The presence of external members was very reduced, the meeting was presided by the Rector, and easily those boards were lost in internal discussions of more or less corporative nature, or of corporative interest [...]. The qualitative leap there is huge. (1UIPr)

Perceptions of academics on who is in charge or ought to be in charge show that 'tribes and territories' are still part of the academic culture. Academics perceive positively the presence of external stakeholders in top governing boards but still see themselves as the rightful decision-makers on academic and scientific matters.

CONCLUSIONS

Analysis of the interviews seems to indicate that both academic actors and external stakeholders perceive change brought by the RJIES, regarding the mandatory presence of external members in top governing bodies, such as the general council and the board of trustees, as a positive change of the governance model of universities. They seem to consider that the traditional way of running a university was lacking insight from outside and is, therefore, benefitting from the outside view brought by these members. This wide acceptance of external members seems to be unquestioned by academics, which is curious to notice since they are traditionally the main decision-makers in university matters and those who may have felt they had more to loose with the inclusion of external members in important decision-making boards. Nevertheless, they seem to accept this new model and even consider it positive. This fact might indicate that there is wide acceptance of the idea conveyed by NPM-based discourse about the need for more efficiency in university governance and the benefits of getting the public sector closer to the private sector in terms of their governance and management model. However, this cannot be dissociated from the fact that all academics that have been interviewed hold government and management positions within their institutions, which means they deal directly with external stakeholders.

A study by Magalhães and Amaral, published in 2007 – year of the publication of RJIES – shows that academic actors' perceptions were already mostly favourable to a shift from the traditional model of governance of HEIs to a more managerialist one. It also shows that the perceptions of some actors were then already in a 'hybrid position', gathering elements from both the 'collegial-bureaucratic rationale' and the 'managerialist rationale' (Magalhães & Amaral, 2007: 322).

Several interviewees refer to the fact that they see the benefits of the presence of external members as a two-way opportunity: HEIs benefit from a new view on the institutions, but external members also get to know how a university really works, the problems they face and take that knowledge out, which is perceived as very positive by academics.

In spite of the fact that the university governance model now includes external members, the shared governance model in place continues to have a majority of members coming from academia. Academics still perceive they have and should continue to have a word to say on university matters, especially on scientific and pedagogical issues. This seems to indicate that the NPM reform discourse is generally perceived as a positive change, but still members of the academia are not willing to give up the majority of seats they hold in university governance.

In spite of the wide acceptance of external members in top governing boards, some internal actors warn about the danger of bringing to universities a governance model characteristic of the private sector, as they do not apply to the reality of a university.

The university has moved away from the 'ivory tower' it was considered to be; boundaries are shifting and the governance model seems to be drifting away from the traditional bureaucratic archetype towards a managerialist paradigm of running a HEI.

ACKNOWLEDGEMENTS

This work was supported by the Portuguese Foundation for Science and Technology (FCT) under Grant number SFRH / BD / 71581 / 2010, funded by POPH / FSE.

The author would like to thank to Teresa Carvalho and Rui Santiago for their valuable insights on the topic.

NOTES

1   As defined by Law 62/2007 (RJIES), foundations are public institutions operating under private law.
2   The number of organisational units per university is as follows: University of Aveiro 16 departments, University of Porto 14 faculties / institutes, ISCTE 4 schools, University of Coimbra 8 faculties, University of Minho 11 schools / institutes, University Nova de Lisboa 9 faculties /schools / institutes.
3   The Portuguese public higher education system is composed of 14 universities, 32 polytechnic institutes and 4 military and police academies. The private sub-system is composed of 29 institutions within the university sub-system and 42 polytechnic institutions.
4   By 'organisational unit' is meant the units that constitute HEIs such as schools, faculties and departments.

REFERENCES

Altbach, P. G. (1991). Patterns in higher education development: Towards the year 2000. *Prospects, 21*(2), 189–203.
Amaral, A., & Magalhães, A. (2000). O conceito de stakeholder e o novo pradigma do ensino superior. *Revista Portuguesa de Educação, 13*(2), 7–28.
Amaral, A., & Magalhães, A. (2002). The emergent role of external stakeholders in European higher education governance. In A. Amaral, G. A. Jones, & B. Karseth (Eds.), *Governing higher education: National perspectives on institutional governance* (Vol. 2, pp. 1–21). Dordrecht, The Netherlands: Kluwer Academic Publishers.
Amaral, A., & Magalhães, A. (2007). Higher education research perspectives. In P. B. Richards (Ed.), *Global issues in higher education* (pp. 173–193). Hauppauge, NY: Nova Science Publishers.
Bardin, L. (2009). *Análise de conteúdo*. Lisboa, Portugal: Edições 70.
Barzelay, M. (2001). *The new public management: Improving research and policy dialogue*. Berkeley, CA: University of California Press.

Becker, T., & Trowler, P. (2001). *Tribes and territories.* London, UK: The Society for Research into Higher Education & Open University Press.

Boer, H. D., & File, J. (2009). *Higher education governance reforms across Europe.* Brussels, Belgium, Europe: ESMU–European Centre for Stategic Management of Universities.

Bruckmann, S., & Carvalho, T. (2014). The reform process of Portuguese higher education institutions: From collegial to managerial governance. *Tertiary Education and Management, 20*(3), 193–206.

Carvalho, T. (2009). *Nova gestão pública e reformas da saúde: o profissionalismo numa encruzilhada.* Lisboa, Portugal: Edições Sílabo.

Carvalho, T., & Bruckmann, S. (2014). Reforming the Portuguese public sector: A route from health to higher education. In C. Musselin & P. Teixeira (Eds.), *Reforming higher education: Public policy design and implementation* (pp. 83–102). Dordrecht, The Netherlands: Springer.

Carvalho, T., & Santiago, R. (2010). Still academics after all. *Higher Education Policy, 23*, 397–411.

Clarke, J., & Newman, J. (1997). *The managerial state.* London, UK: SAGE.

Eakin, H., Eriksen, S., Eikeland, P.-O., & Øyen, C. (2011). Public sector reform and governance for adaptation: Implications of new public management for adaptive capacity in Mexico and Norway. *Environmental Management, 47*(3), 338–351.

Eckel, P. D., & Kezar, A. (2006). The challenge facing academic decision making: Contemporary issues and steadfast structures. In P. D. Eckel (Ed.), *The shifting frontiers of academic decision making: Responding to new priorities, following new pathways.* Washington, DC: ACE/Praeger Book Series.

Ferlie, E., Ashburner, L., Fitzgerald, L., & Pettigrew, A. (1996). *The new public management in action.* Oxford, England: Oxford University Press.

Henkel, M. (2000). *Academic identities and policy change in higher education.* London, UK: Jessica Kingsley Publishers.

Hood, C. (1991). A public management for all seasons? *Public Administration, 69*(1), 3–19.

Kezar, A. (2004). Obtaining integrity? Reviewing and examining the charter between higher education and society. *The Review of Higher Education, 27*(4), 429–459.

Kirkpatrick, I., Ackroyd, S., & Walker, R. (2005). *The new managerialism and public service professions.* London, UK: Palgrave-MacMillan.

Larbi, G. A. (1999). *The new public management approach and crisis states.* Geneva, Switzerland: United Nations Research Institute for Social Development.

Lazzeretti, L., & Tavoletti, E. (2006). Governance shifts in higher education: A cross-national comparison. *European Educational Research Journal, 5*(1), 18–37.

Leisyte, L., Westerheijden, D. F., Epping, E., Faber, M., & de Weert, E. (2013). *Stakeholders and quality assurance in higher education.* Paper presented at the 26th Annual CHER Conference, Lausanne, Switzerland.

Liguori, M. (2012). Radical change, accounting and public sector reforms: A comparison of Italian and Canadian municipalities. *Financial Accountability & Management, 28*(4), 437–463.

Locke, W., Cummings, W. K., & Fisher, D. (2011). *Changing governance and management in higher education: The perspectives of the academy.* Dordrecht, The Netherlands: Springer.

Lockwood, G. (2011). Management and resources. *A history of the university in Europe* (Vol. 4, pp. 124–161). Cambridge, England: Cambridge University Press.

Lodge, M., & Hood, C. (2012). Into an age of multiple austerities? Public management and public service bargains across OECD countries. *Governance: An International Journal of Policy, Administration, and Institutions, 25*(1), 79–101.

Magalhães, A. (2001). A transformação do modo de regulação estatal e os sistemas de ensino: A autonomia como instrumento. *Revista Crítica de Ciências Sociais, 59*, 125–143.

Magalhães, A., & Amaral, A. (2007). Changing values and norms in Portuguese higher education. *Higher Education Policy, 20*(3), 315–338.

Magalhães, A., & Santiago, R. (2011). Public management, new governance models and changing environments in Portuguese higher education. In P. Teixeira & D. D. Dill (Eds.), *Public vices, private virtues? Assessing the effects of marketization in higher education* (Vol. 2, pp. 177–192). Rotterdam, The Netherlands: Sense Publishers.

McLaughlin, K., Osborne, S., & Ferlie, E. (2002). *New public management: Current trends and future prospects*. New York, NY: Routledge.

Mongkol, K. (2011). The critical review of new public management model and its criticisms. *Research Journal of Business Management, 5*(1), 35–43.

Neave, G. (2012). *The evaluative state, institutional autonomy and re-engineering higher education in Western Europe: The prince and his pleasure*. New York, NY: Palgrave Macmillan.

Neave, G., & Vught, F. V. (1994). *Government and higher education relationships across three continents: The winds of change*. Oxford, England: Pergamon Press.

Pollitt, C. (2002). The new public management in international perspective: An analysis of impacts and effects. In K. McLaughlin, S. P. Osborne, & E. Ferlie (Eds.), *New public management: Current trends and future prospects* (pp. 274–292). Oxon, England: Routledge.

Pollitt, C., & Bouckaert, G. (2004). *Public management reform: A comparative analysis*. Oxford, England: Oxford University Press.

Reed, M. I. (2002). New managerialism, professional power and organisational governance in UK universities: A review and assessment. In A. Amaral, G. A. Jones, & B. Karseth (Eds.), *Governing higher education: National perspectives on institutional governance* (Vol. 2). Dordrecht, The Netherlands: Kluwer Academic Publishers.

Rüegg, W. (2011). *A history of the university in Europe: Universities since 1945* (Vol. 4). Cambridge, England: Cambridge University Press.

Shattock, M. (2002). Re-balancing modern concepts of university governance. *Higher Education Quarterly, 56*(3), 235–244.

Shattock, M. (2006). *Managing good governance in higher education*. Berkshire, Shire county: Open University Press.

Simonet, D. (2011). The new public management theory and the reform of European health care systems: An international comparative perspective. *International Journal of Public Administration, 34*(12), 815–826.

Sporn, B. (2003). Management in higher education: Current trends and future perspectives in European colleges and universities In R. Begg (Ed.), *The dialogue between higher education research and practice*. The Netherlands: Kluwer Academic Publishers.

Stensaker, B., & Vabo, A. (2013). Re-inventing shared governance: Implications for organisational culture and institutional leadership. *Higher Education Quarterly, 67*(3), 256–274.

Taylor, M. (2013). Shared governance in the modern university. *Higher Education Quarterly, 67*(1), 80–94.

Trow, M. (1974). Problems in the transition from elite to mass higher education. *Policies for higher education*. Paris, France: OECD.

van Vught, F. (1994). Autonomy and accountability in government/university relationships. In J. Salmi & A. M. Verspoor (Eds.), *Revitalizing higher education*. Oxford, England: IAU Press.

Veiga, A., Magalhães, A., Sousa, S., Ribeiro, F., & Amaral, A. (2014). A reconfiguração da gestão universitária em Portugal. *Educação Sociedade & Culturas, 41*, 7–23.

Sofia Bruckmann
University of Aveiro and CIPES
(Centre for Research in Higher Education Policies)

SECTION 3

BLURRING BOUNDARIES IN ACADEMIC PROFESSIONS

JOAKIM CASPERSEN AND NICOLINE FRØLICH

7. MANAGING LEARNING OUTCOMES

Leadership Practices and Old Modes of
New Governance in Higher Education

INTRODUCTION

It is probably uncontroversial to say that the last few decades have witnessed an increasing interest in leadership in higher education. The interest has been spurn by policy changes in higher education and public administration in general that have changed higher education governance profoundly. The general observation is that leadership in higher education has shifted from old modes of leadership based in academic and collegial values to new modes of governance increasingly based in social responsibleness and managerialism (consult for example Bleiklie, 2005; Shattock, 2002). For the last decades higher education has been characterized through labels such as new governance and new public management (Amaral, Meek, & Larsen, 2003; Bleiklie, Høstaker, & Vabø, 2000; Frølich, 2005).

Nevertheless, due to the multi-institutional character of universities there are similar good reasons to expect that currently leadership in higher education draws on more than one leadership template. Recent articles pin-point some of the contested and interpretative character we assume contemporary leadership in higher education imply (Blackmore, 2007; Johnson, 2002; Juntrasook, 2014; Uusiautti, Syväjärvi, Stenvall, Perttula, & Määttä, 2012). Furthermore, policy reforms can been seen as carriers of templates for governance and leadership, but also as carriers of solutions to problems that has yet to be defined (Frø ich & Sahlin, 2013).

In this paper we apply the introduction of qualification frameworks and learning outcomes in higher education (HELOs) as a case to investigate contemporary leadership in higher education. HELOs can be seen as a device for teaching, learning and assessment, but also as a tool linked to governance and management, in the sense that the introduction of HELOs entails a move to a results orientation. The underlying assumption is that accountabi ity in higher education will improve as leaders in higher education are assigned the responsibility for meeting set targets, according to measurable indicators (Frølich, 2011). Due to new obligations related to the importance of leadership and management of higher education introduced the last decades (Bleiklie, Enders, Lepori, & Musselin, 2011), the formal, top-down leaderships structures in higher education has been strengthened (Bleiklie, Ringkjøb, & Østergren, 2006; Stensaker et al., 2013).

E. Reale & E. Primeri (Eds.), The Transformation of University Institutional and
Organizational Boundaries, 187–202.

However, when trying to understand recent attempts at improving accountability and transparency in higher education, it is also important to recognise that higher education has been used, and is still used, as a means for development and status attainment for professional groups. This process of recognition has developed in tension between the state as a counterpart and as a collaborator, the balance being different in different countries and professions, and has been described by many (e.g., Burrage, 1993). As Abbott argues (1988), professions work to obtain and retain jurisdictions through claims of abstract knowledge (among other claims). Universities serve as legitimators for this knowledge, and through universities this knowledge is promoted and advanced. Universities are also an arena for interprofessional competition. Seen together this implies that new policies (such as learning outcomes), will be taken in, translated and adapted differently.

In our investigation of leadership practices in higher education we take four modes of academic leadership as our starting point (Bleiklie, 2005). Based on the modes of academic leadership, we explore the extent to which these modes of leadership are spelled out in the daily practices of academic leadership. We seek to answer the following questions: How do academic leaders conceive HELOs as a tool? How are different modes of leadership played out in relation to the introduction of HELOs?

We depart from findings that have been established in previous research, and that can be seen as "common ground" for all studies of higher education. First, this means that the historical context of each program and how the tension between profession and state has played out in different cases, is of importance for interpreting changes and development in higher education (see e.g., Muller (2009) for a discussion of how resistance to change can be linked to academic identities developed differently in disciplines and professions). This means that old divisions and tensions, e.g., between discipline orientation and practical orientation, or professional and governmental control, are revitalized when new changes are introduced.

Previous studies on the introduction and implementation of HELOs indicate that the process vary greatly between study programmes (Caspersen & Frølich, 2014): Some leaders use the introduction in order to pursue their own agendas, while elsewhere the introduction is stacked upon other educational reforms. In the former, leaders are eager to implement the reform at all levels, meaning that they use them as managerial tools, providing guidelines for employees and feeds result information back to the leaders. In the latter, the implementation is seen as an imposition, and use and control of the HELOs are mostly symbolic administration.

THE MULTI-INSTITUTIONAL CHARACTER OF ACADEMIC LEADERSHIP

Several researchers have underlined the multi-institutional character of university governance (Frølich & Sahlin, 2013) which put weight on the fact that different constituencies address different expectations towards the university, what it is good for and how it should be managed (Krücken, Kosmützky, & Torka, 2007; Olsen, 1987). Looking more closely at studies dealing with higher education leadership, the multi-institutional complexity of academic leadership are described. Bryman (2007) discusses how policy-changes in the last decades have made new demands on leadership, and searches for indications of effective leadership. Bolden et al. (2008) explore tensions in higher education leadership and tease apart the multilevel nature at individual, group and organizational levels. Jameson (2012) takes as point of departure that the multiple uncertainties of higher education may lead to a decrease of trust in the values, collegial ethos and civic role of universities. The study indicates that it was necessary to challenge managerial cultures, which restrict the self-organizing egalitarian, collegial scholarship. Moreover, that the implication of skillful leadership and being able to listen and reflect may contribute to maintain trust in the purpose of universities. Durand and Pujadas (2004) argue that universities must establish new leadership paths and practices in order to establish community building and value-oriented behaviour. This implies the stimulation and development of a non-utilitarian culture and behaviour at the institution. Stensaker & Vabø (2013) analyze how a sample of Nordic universities perceive the place and role of governance in their strategic development. They find that most universities emphasize leadership and leadership development as a key instrument to strengthen their governance capacity. Nevertheless, the cultural and symbolic aspects of governance, internal legitimacy and trust seems at stake. In line with these arguments, there are reasons to assume that different conceptualisations of academic leadership can be at work at the same time (Bleiklie & Frølich, 2014).

In the following, we spell out Bleiklie's four leadership templates (2005: 194) which are constituted by expectations modern university leaders face. The templates originate partly in different tasks of the university, partly in different normative or ideological conceptualisations of the tasks and their relative importance. The four templates are the academic authority, the collegial coordinator, the socially responsible leader and the business executive. The templates were originally developed to analyse changes in leadership over time or across different higher education institutions. However, they are also a useful tool for studying leadership practices that are played out when academic leaders are confronted with higher education policy reforms such as the introduction of HELOs.

The academic authority template draws its legitimacy from academic quality (Bleiklie, 2005: 195). The expectation is that high disciplinary competence forms the basis for legitimate leadership. Expectations of academic quality form the power basis for legitimate leadership, but the academic authority template does not provide any guidance regarding what leaders are expected to do nor regarding style of leadership. Hence academic authority is a kind of earned leadership ideal. Based on outstanding academic merits, one becomes qualified for leadership.

The collegial coordinator template claims authority based on the leader's capacity as a member of an egalitarian and autonomous academic disciplinary community (Bleiklie, 2005: 196). The collegial leader of a disciplinary community draws his authority from his capacity to represent the community and act as a politician rather than disciplinary authority. The collegial coordinator's power basis rests in his capacity to protect the academic community, provide protective working arrangements and to some extent to secure the flow of resources into the community. The socially responsible leader draws his power basis from the extent to which he acts in line with expectations directed at a civil servant who loyally follows the social obligations defined by public authorities. The socially responsible leader template is also based on community service as ideal. The university is considered legitimate to the extent to which it provides society with educated elites or contributes to effective exploitation of human capital (Bleiklie, 2005: 197). As representatives of public institutions, academic leaders are expected to assume and interpret their social responsibilities within the framework of national policies and programmes.

The business executive is expected to produce useful services efficiently in the form of research and candidates to a number of users and stakeholders. The administrative element of university governance is expected to be strengthened to ensure controllable handling of the growing burden of teaching and research. The tasks of formulating goals and mobilising resources and support becomes crucial tasks within this leadership template, and suppresses the development of academic quality (Bleiklie, 2005: 198).

The academic authority is first and foremost concerned with the academic quality, and therefore responds to the demands from the academic community. The collegial coordinator, however, must balance and negotiate between the academic community and the state, in order to promote the interests of the academic community. The social responsible leader is perhaps the most difficult role, as it on the one hand answers to demands of loyalty to the national policies and implementation of these, while it on the other hand also holds social responsibilities to the market and society at large. The understanding of the leader as a business executive, means first and foremost that the leader has to answer to demands for relevance to the market, and that quality of content is understood by its measurable output.

ACADEMIC LEADERSHIP IN THE CONTEXT OF INTRODUCING HELOS

As the different leadership templates in varying degree respond to different demands, it seems reasonable to assume that the introduction of HELOs will be interpreted differently depending on which of the templates the leadership practices align with. When market and relevance, is emphasised, HELOs can be seen as possibilities for sharpening the relevance of the educational programs. When academic quality is emphasised the introduction can be seen as an imposition of bureaucracy into the academic fields. In the former, learning outcomes can be perceived as useful tools for developing the program further. In the latter, the implementation might take form of an administrative ritual activity, or as political symbols with no real content. Examining how such "pure forms" of use of HELOs are played out provides an opportunity to discuss the complexity of academic leadership.

This way of reasoning is in line with an institutional theory perspective on organizational change (DiMaggio & Powell, 1983; Meyer & Rowan, 1977). Leaders in higher education have to balance the external requirements and claims directed at universities and higher education institutions with the internal functioning of the organisation. One way of doing this is to decouple the external claims from the internal dynamics. In this perspective, HELOs as managerial tools can be managed in a political-symbolist way and administrative management of HELOs may take on a ritual character not closely related to improving the quality of the learning processes. A second way of managing interrelationship between external claims and the internal functioning of the organization is by adhering to external claims that matches the normative foundation of the internal functioning (e.g., academic standards), while rejecting those that conflict with this normative foundation (Selznick, 1957). Yet a third way of combining external conflicting claims, is to adjust and translate the claims so that they match the internal functioning of the organisation in a softer and more adjusted way (Sahlin & Wedlin. 2008). Taken together we apply these expectations to explore how academic leaders conceive HELOs as a tool and how different modes of leadership are played out in relation to the introduction of HELOs. We are interested in, how, where and why the introduction of HELOs are legitimized in line with the academic authority template, the collegial coordinator template, the public interest template and/or the business executive template.

METHODS AND DATA

The chapter is based on qualitative interviews with 15 academic and administrative leaders in 7 study programmes in three fields of science: two programs in the humanities and social sciences (teacher education and linguistics), three programs in natural sciences and technology (master and bachelor in engineering plus leaders from the faculty of mathematics and natural sciences) and three programs in medicine and health (nursing and medicine), during spring 2013.

The different programs were chosen in order to ensure variation within and between different academic and professional fields and disciplines. The shorter professional programs, such as teacher education (four year bachelor program), bachelor in engineering (three years) and nursing (three year bachelor program), have different relations with the state, at least in Norway. Teacher education has been described as politically governed (Heggen. 2010) with rapid reforms aligning with current debate on education. Nursing education has been described as developed under the auspices of the profession, although the development of nursing's role and place in the formal education structure has happened through the general expansion of the public education system.

Engineering has developed as part of the general development of the industrial economy, and the rebuilding period after WWII, and thus had a clear applied focus from the beginning. The division between a bachelor programme with a general, applied orientation and a master program with an academic and applied orientation has been part of the education system for a long time in Norway, and graduated students find work in both public and private sector. Thus, engineering in Norwegian higher education has been catering for the need of a growing economy, but the supply of qualified graduates has been controlled through the public governance system (see also Caspersen, Frølich, Karlsen, & Aamodt, 2014).

As for medicine, the profession itself has played a profound role in developing the programs, which can be described as elite programs in a Norwegian context. Elite in this sense refers a high ranking in the educational system, and where a large proportion of the students achieve economic and cultural high-status positions (Kingston & Lewis, 1990). It also means that the profession has had a strong position in negotiating and influencing the role of medical training in the higher education system, for instance controlling the entrance demands and content for the specialization programs in medicine, and also playing an important role in the development of the graduate study programs.

Finally, the linguistics program holds a somewhat different position, being a more traditional university master degree, with few direct ties to the labour market. Thus, they are subject to general study reforms from the state, but the problem of relevance is not as clearly framed there, although the general (and global) "crisis of the humanities", which might have escalated in the past decade (see e.g., Nussbaum, 2012) have long traditions (see e.g., Rosenhaupt, 1940).

Together, the programs chosen stand in different tensions between the professional, state and market system (Clark, 1983), which gives different challenges for the leaders. Thus, by interviewing leaders from a broad array of programs, the complexity of the leader role in higher education is covered as good as possible.

The interviews lasted about one hour and notes were taken and shared across the different members of the research team. Two broad questions from the interviews are the starting point for our analysis: What is the perceived purpose of HELOs? How are HELOs used? During the interviews, the leaders were probed as to whether HELOs were seen as political symbols, administrative ritual activity or as useful tools for improving learning activities and outcomes and quality of learning processes.

As this paper aims to explore how HELOs are used as tools by leaders in higher education, the data from the interviews are used as empirical examples from the different cases. In the following section, different uses and approaches to HELOs as tools for higher education leaders will be presented.

FOR WHAT PURPOSES ARE HELOS INTRODUCED

In medicine and nursing the introduction of HELOs was perceived differently. In medicine, it was seen more as a shift in language and descriptions, while in nursing it was welcomed as an opportunity for change, and even described as a "revolution" by one of the leaders. A similar reception was found among the technologists, where the introduction was seen as an opportunity to emphasise relevance and to organize the study in a more multidisciplinary way than before.

In medicine, learning goals similar to learning outcome formulations had been introduced in the early nineties, replacing the traditional curriculum. In their studies, students have only the definition of learning outcomes to guide after, not a list of curriculum texts. The introduction of HELOs was seen as a continuation of the study organisation introduced in the nineties, as part of a broad curriculum reform. A variation of problem based learning (PBL) was then introduced, and this process entailed orientation towards international trends and pedagogical knowledge, and learning goals was the guiding principle. The introduction of learning outcomes was by and large seen as a continuation of this reform, although some adjustments had to be made. At this particular university, introduction of learning outcomes and the transfer from a "traditional" curriculum organization was also undertaken as a top-initiated project, with pedagogical support offered for all institutes, and in-house courses in writing learning outcomes descriptions in accordance with the qualification framework template. This indicates that the top administration and leaders at the university wanted the process of introduction of HELOs to run as smooth as possible, and it might also indicate a positive orientation towards HELOs as a tool.

In nursing the leaders emphasised that relevance, understood as orientation towards actual work in the health sector, was much easier to emphasise after the introduction of learning outcomes. Being oriented towards learning outcomes means being oriented towards the end goal of studies, the leaders in nursing argued, and during their work in revising local curricula they had found the national qualification framework useful for clarifying the connection between goals and assessment.

If the introduction of HELOs was seen as an opportunity for re-orientating the study programs in health and technology, or, as in the case of medicine, just a continuation of something they were already doing right, the purpose was seen as far more unclear and even threatening in the humanities. In teaching, the introduction of HELOs was seen as an externally forced change, which was introduced together with a new government-initiated reform of the study program. The Norwegian teacher education has been the subject to a row of consecutive reforms over the last decades, and in 2010 a binary model for the primary and secondary school teachers was introduced. HELOs was introduced as a part of this, and the leaders interviewed said that they "drowned" in the new model, giving little time for working with HELOs as a tool. They questioned directly the purpose of introducing HELOs as a "package" together with other changes, and found it hard to separate "the silent reform" of learning outcomes and qualification frameworks from the simultaneously introduced teacher education reform. Teacher education was among the first programs to implement the reform:

> The reform was presented in April/May, and we were to implement from the fall semester. In the middle of exams. This kind of organisation is provoking us. The reform was conceived on the basis of an evaluation from 2006, and the ministry had years to follow up, and they gave us a few months only.

The humanities program at the university had a similar experience to the leaders from medicine. The introduction was seen as less of a change than previous reforms, and especially the so called Quality Reform in Norwegian Higher Education, implemented in 2003. However, the reception was still more ambiguous than among the teachers. It was on the one hand seen as a continuation of previous work with study quality, on the other hand it was seen as an opportunity to improve the relevance and raise awareness about the quality and purpose of the humanities at the university, which had been questioned in graduate surveys and public debate.

All in all, the purpose of HELOs was differently interpreted in the different fields and study programs, ranging from "what's new" to "why something new, again?", and from providing an opportunity for change and attention to relevance to an unwanted disturbance. As will be illustrated in the next section, these differences in understanding also meant that the use of HELOs as tools also varied greatly.

HOW ARE HELOS USED

In medicine, the use of HELOs varied between the two institutions included, although both programs had been reformed in the nineties and was more or less aligned with the learning outcome thinking at an early stage. At one institution, HELOs as a leadership tool was questioned, with the argument that HELOs provided "an information overload". The massive amount of information included in the outcome descriptions of the courses in medicine, written up in loose-leaf files, was described as hard to navigate in. The lack of a traditional curriculum for the students, only recommended readings were suggested for students so that they could reach the described learning outcomes, also made it unclear what they really were supposed to learn. The fact that learning goals were already a major part of the old PBL-reform meant that the introduction of HELOs was seen as a smaller, and also partly unnecessary, change. This was said to lead to some resistance and hesitation towards the introduction of HELOs, and the use of HELOs was more or less an administrative change.

At the second medicine program, HELOs were used as a tool for change in how the courses were organised and seen as an opportunity for promoting constructive alignment in courses. The associate dean had lead a process where all teachers with coordinator responsibilities from all semesters were invited in order to promote a discussion on the academic quality and design of the study program. Although they had a discussion over this in the nineties, with the old reform of the program, the leader argued that a discussion on quality and outcome needs to be revitalised at regular intervals. However, keeping up the quality of teaching was perceived as hard, as research gives more merit for the individual teacher, and a tension between the academic meritocracy and teaching quality is noted. It was also commented that the students perceive a tension between the level of detail in exams and the relevance of this in an integrated study-model. To some extent, this can also be interpreted as a tension between academic standards and relevance.

194

The need for ongoing discussions about the quality of teaching was also emphasised in nursing, and the introduction was perceived as an opportunity to shake things up:

We need to redesign the courses in a totally new way, and we have to ask whether this is the emperors' new clothes, or something genuinely new. This might imply turning everybody's previous contributions upside-down.

The leader interviewed saw this process as a positive development.

In the technological field, the leader from the faculty of mathematics and natural sciences also had experienced the tension between academic orientation and the autonomy of the individual researcher/teacher. The "old" model provided more room for each teacher to design his or hers "private" course, whereas in the new model each course had to be designed to fit in with the overall learning outcomes for the program, and specify how they contributed to this. This made the responsibility less individualised and required more of a collective effort and orientation, and it was described as a "de-privatisation" of courses, and opened up new possibilities for creating core-modules for several programs. The introduction of HELOs provided an opportunity for creating cross-disciplinary courses, which was seen as essential for an efficient organization of the faculty. Courses were also designed in order to be used across levels (bachelor, master, PhD), although with somewhat different content at different levels. The introduction sparked administrative changes with academic implications.

Also within engineering, the introduction of HELOs was seen as a positive opportunity for restructuring and sharpening the cross-disciplinary profile, and emphasising relevance for "users", meaning employers of graduates. To sharpen this perspective even more, representatives from relevant business and industry took part in an evaluation of the program at one institution. However, from the leaders it was argued that this was a way to emphasise the academic quality. Thus, academic quality and market relevance were juxtaposed to some extent. However, also here the experience was that the introduction of HELOs was challenging the academic autonomy, interpreted as the right for each to design his or hers own course. Also, a tension between academic quality and teaching was emphasised, with the argument that it was hard to get top researchers, often assumed to be top teachers as well, to engage in teaching, as their research took so much time. The balance between two core duties of the academic institution, teaching and research, seemed even harder to find when the teaching had to be reorganized and the importance of teaching was increased through the implementation of HELOs. One of the engineering program leaders interviewed argued that his task was more complex than before, they had to seize new opportunities and "complete loops of quality", assure the quality in outcome descriptions and follow up on subject teachers in a new way. This required, according to the program leader, strong leadership, lots of follow-up, and more attention to consequences and results. These kind of changes cannot be done without having everybody on board, engagement and enthusiasm have to be generated among the teachers: "A stick won't do, you need a carrot", one leader said, and added: "at least it should look like a carrot".

In the humanities, the leaders we interviewed argued in general that HELOs were administrative and academic tools, as well as political symbols. It was also added that HELOs provided a special opportunity for connecting with the labour market and employers' expectations, and providing graduates with easily accessible descriptions of what they can after finishing a higher education degree in the humanities. The introduction of HELOs also made way for administrative changes, where the responsibility for courses was delegated downwards. The change was backed with the allocation of resources as well. By the program leaders it was also argued that besides all good intentions, the introduction of HELOs was hard to administrate, because of an "unruly" academic staff. Too little administrative power was delegated to leaders, meaning that the administrative staff did not perceive program leaders as authorities. This meant that the implementation was probably more of an administrative change, and not the profound change it could have been. The role as a program leader was compared to "shepherding wild cats".

Within the humanities, the teacher education program was a story of its own. The symbolic dimension was heavily emphasised, and it was argued that the process was all about aligning the outcome descriptions with the bureaucratic intention: "The implementation was part of a bureaucratic educational policy, an EU-perspective, although that part of the process has been toned down a bit". The rhetoric behind the implementation was perceived as provocative, implying that the focus on learning was something brand new, while the leaders always had felt that they had student learning and development as the ultimate goal in their teaching.

WHAT DOES USE OF HELOS TELL US ABOUT ACADEMIC LEADERSHIP?

The analysis of the data indicates that all the leaders we interviewed saw HELOs as both a tool to improve academic quality, an administrative tool and as a mere symbol. They reflect upon crucial dilemmas and contradictions that the introduction of HELOs entails, and conceive of HELOs as managerial tools in all three directions. The findings are summed up in Table 1.

We note that even leaders in the "pure" university disciplines like the humanities and natural sciences underline that HELOs can be used as tools to improve the relevance of their subject. We find also a number of other dilemmas incorporated in HELOs in addition to the pressure for improved relevance. The leaders reflect upon how HELOs push the attention towards teaching and learning, while research activities and academic ambitions still have to be catered for. HELOs also entail a pressure in the direction of "de-privatisation" of teaching in the sense that study programs as collective structures gain more attention, while still teaching in higher

Table 1. Summary of findings in different groups

	For what purposes are HELOs introduced?	How are HELOs used?
Medicine	Minor shift in language and descriptions	Gives information overload; replaces curriculum; reorganisation of courses ---> constructive alignment tool,
Nursing	Opportunity for change – "revolution"	Redesign courses, see everything from a new perspective
Linguistics	Minor shift, but also opportunity	Connecting with labour market, but hard to use as tool with "unruly" staff. Administrative change
Teaching	Threat, part of "reform package"	Symbolic alignment with bureaucratic intentions
Technology (BA)	Opportunity for change	Inclusion of employers in panels, provides leaders a tool for follow-up
Technology (MA)	Opportunity for change	De-privatisation of courses; new possibilities for creating core-modules. Tension between research and teaching.

education is related to the individual researcher and his classes. Finally, the leaders experience a pressure towards policy implementation and educational authorities.

As we argued in the analytical section of the paper, we expected that the different leadership roles would relate differently to HELOs as managerial tool. We reasoned that leadership legitimized by the academic authority role would emphasise HELOs as tools for improving learning activities and outcomes as well as the quality of learning processes. The collegial coordinator would perceive of HELOs as tools for political-symbolist activities while also catering for their potential for improving teaching and learning. We saw the business executive as focusing mainly on HELOs as tools for administrative management. Finally the social responsible leader, whom we reasoned would perceive of HELOs as multifaceted managerial tools that can be used as political symbols, to improve management and administration and also as a tool to improve academic quality and relevance, has a clearer presence in out material than perhaps could be expected. Can this presence be related to changes in modes of governance in higher education?

OLD MODES OF NEW GOVERNANCE

Due to increased professionalization of leadership and the introduction of managerialism, higher education has changed. However, our suggestion is that new managerialism is no longer new – but has been around for at least three decades, as stated in the introduction. Over time, leadership in higher education has shifted as from the collegial coordinator to the business executive, while at the same time different constituencies and stakeholders in higher education still direct diverging sets of claims towards universities (Olsen, 1987). What we might be experiencing at the time can possibly be described as a turn in which the business executive leadership transforms slightly back to the old academic ideals. Also over the last three decades, higher education has changed in the sense that the higher education institutions have gained more autonomy and the national state has withdrawn from detailed steering and control. Since this has been the main way of managing higher education for a considerable long time, the way leadership is conducted might have encapsulated this state of affairs of increased autonomy out of which the social responsible leadership is legitimized. We would also see this development as a modernization of academic leadership. The social responsible leader has to balance requirements and claims from a multi-institutional setting and be able to handle a range of managerial tools to fulfil this task.

In this light, potentially, all leadership templates can be argued to use HELOs as managerial tools in different ways. Leaders, irrespective of leadership ideals, will seek to improve the content of higher education, and to do this they also need to use available administrative and governance tools, and in some instances also invoke HELOs as a symbol. In our understanding, however, we understand the different usages of HELOs as more of a continuum, from a more content-and-quality orientation, to an orientation towards the external relations of higher education with society.

The interpretation above fits well with our data, although teacher education is the odd one out. Leaders in teacher education see HELOs only as an attempt at more and increased top-down steering of higher education. Introduction of HELOs is perceived as yet another reform of higher education pushing and pressing higher education in line with the perspectives of national authorities.

However, relating back to teacher education and the reception of HELOs, it could be argued that, at least in Norway, teacher education has had a different relationship with governance than other groups, being constantly subjected to reforms and changes in order to solve problems in the entire system of education. Thus, the withdrawal from detailed steering and control can be argued to not have taken place to the same extent in teacher education as in other programs. Therefore, the use of HELOs as a leadership tool can be expected to be different in the Norwegian teacher education than in other groups, which is also what we have found.

SHIFTING TEMPLATES OF LEADERSHIP

As shown, leadership means adapting to different policies, and maximising opportunities within given boundaries. Nevertheless, there is still a need for discussing the actual meanings and implications of the different leadership templates. What does the notion of leaders as "business executive" actually imply?

In Bleiklie's account (2005) it is closely linked to New Public Management and managerialism, emphasising efficiency in the guise of quality, and bottom line outcomes. Attention is given to the instrumental aspects of leadership, and leadership is seen as a profession in itself, not dependent on academic subject knowledge in the field one is leading.

However, as Bleiklie also argues, this description should not be taken for given without empirical scrutiny, which is what has been attempted in this paper. And, as discussed, we argue that the business executive-template is less prominent than the social responsible leader. It should also be added that in "real business", in trade and industry, leadership ideals are also rapidly changing. Today's business executive must give more and more attention to all aspects of the organisation: bottom line outcomes come hand in hand with corporate social responsibility and lobbying and interacting with government administration. Strategic leadership, or any other phrase used to coin leadership, implies balancing and handling demands and tensions within and outside the organisation (Kraatz & Block, 2008). Thus, being a business executive might just mean being a socially responsible leader. In this light, leadership in higher education might have seen a similar development. Although the development in leadership in higher education has started from varieties of academic authority, and leaders as collegial coordinators might be idiosyncratic for higher education, the more recent development from "simple" efficiency to social and political responsibility corresponds with larger shifts in leadership ideals. Thus, although the internal development in higher education might be a turn from one extreme to another, followed by settlement in the middle, this is not necessarily only driven by internal developments, but also connected to larger shifts in leadership ideals.

TEMPLATES OF LEADERSHIP CR TEMPLATES OF REFORMS

In a similar line of argument, it can be asked how well the leadership templates actually describe leadership roles, or if they are better understood as presentations of different kinds of reforms and governance. Frølich and Sahlin (2013) argue that much research on institutional change is based on empirical studies of organizational reforms. From such research one can learn that reforms emerge from and carry new institutions, while institutions mix and blend in the idiosyncratic organizational setting. The general discussion on new managerialism implies such a logic. However, institutional mix is as much a feature of university reforms as it is featuring in organizational responses to such reforms. Reforms are not a linear shift from one logic of governance to another, but are themselves carriers of mixed and blended logics and institutions. Thus, reforms carry ambiguous templates, also of leadership. The history and reforms of universities can be described in terms of shifting and distinguishing institutional ideal types of governing and organization, but also in terms of a more profound way of mixing and translating organizations. This perspective implies that new understandings and templates of academic leadership should be developed. Empirical investigations of leadership, such as in this paper, is one first step on the way in this process.

CONCLUSIONS

We started the paper with two overall questions, to which we now return. Our first question was: how do academic leaders conceive HELOs as a tool? Second, we asked: how are different modes of leadership played out in relation to the introduction of HELOs?

We have found that the leaders we interviewed draw on a complex set of leadership templates in their daily practices in relation to the introduction of learning outcomes. HELOs are seen as a device to improve the quality of teaching and learning. They are also seen as political symbols to which the leaders has to negotiate between these and the academic quality they potentially enhance. In addition, HELOs are clearly seen as measures on which leaders can manage their business of higher education. However, most notably the leaders draw substantially on all these configurations of the introduction of learning outcomes in a way that resonates with the social responsible leadership template.

Our analysis indicates that HELOs as managerial tools are not just a simple question of whether policies are effectively implemented, but of whether LOs primarily serve as a managerial symbol, an administrative ritual activity or work as a tool in academic leadership potentially linked to learning activities and affect the outcome of learning processes. We find that academic leaders cannot chose one approach or the other, but have to manage all of these different aspects of leadership.

Based on our findings we have discussed different suggestions to explain this state of affairs. It could be that we are witnessing a situation where the (previously) new modes of governance are no longer new. Hence, what we see is old modes of new governance, played out in relation to new policy initiatives such as HELOs. Secondly, that over time business administration both in the private and the public sector may have changed into a situation where the business executive template actually resembles more the social responsible manager. And thirdly, that policy reforms are not pure in any sense. They carry mixed and blended versions of the templates themselves, to such an extent that the present leadership templates might be understood as templates of reforms, rather than templates of leadership practices.

REFERENCES

Abbott, A. (1988). *The system of professions: An essay on the division of expert labor.* Chicago, IL: University of Chicago Press.

Amaral, A., Meek, V. L., & Larsen, I. M. (Eds.). (2003). *The higher education managerial revolution.* Dordrecht, The Netherlands: Kluwer Academic Publisher.

Blackmore, P. (2007). Disciplinary differences in academic leadership and management and its development: A significant factor. *Research in Post-Compulsory Education, 12*(2), 225–239.

Bleiklie, I. (2005). Academic leadership and emerging knowledge regimes. In I. Bleiklie & M. Henkel (Eds.), *Governing knowledge: A study of continuity and change in higher education.* Dordrecht, The Netherlands: Springer.

Bleiklie, I., & Frølich, V. N. (2014). Styring, organisering og ledelse i høyere utdanningspolitikk. In N. Frølich, E. Hovdhaugen, & L. I. Terum (Eds.), *Kval.tet, kapasitet og relevans: Utviklingstrekk i norsk høyere utdanning.* Oslo, Norway: Cappelen Damm Akademisk.

Bleiklie, I., Høstaker, R., & Vabø, A. (2000). *Policy and practice in higher education: Reforming Norwegian universities.* London, UK and Philadelfia, PA: Jessica Kingsley Publishers.

Bleiklie, I., Ringkjøb, H.-E., & Østergren, K. (2006). Nytt regime i variert landskap: Ledelse og styring av universiteter og høyskoler etter Kvalitetsreformen. *Delrapport, 9.*

Bleiklie, I., Enders, J., Lepori, B., & Musselin, C. (2011). New public management, network governance and the university as a changing professional organization. In T. Christensen & P. Lægreid (Eds.), *The ashgate research companion to new public management.* Farnham, England: Ashgate Publishing Limited.

Bolden, R., Petrov, G., & Gosling, J. (2008). Tensions in higher education leadership: Towards a multi-level model of leadership practice. *Higher Education Quarterly, 62*(4), 358–376. doi: 10.1111/j.1468-2273.2008.00398.x

Bryman, A. (2007). Effective leadership in higher education: A literature review. *Studies in Higher Education, 32*(6), 693–710. doi:10.1080/03075070701685114

Burrage, M. (1993). From practice to school-based professional education: Patterns of conflict accommodation in England, France, and the United States. In S. Rothblatt & B. Wittrock (Eds.), *The European and American university since 1800.* Cambridge, England: Cambridge University Press.

Caspersen, J., & Frølich, N. (2014, forthcoming). Læringsutbytte som styringsredskap for ledelsen i høyere utdanning. In N. Frølich, E. Hovdhaugen, & L. I. Terum (Eds.), *Kvalitet, kapasitet og relevans.* Oslo, Norway: Cappelen Damm Akademisk.

Caspersen, J., Frølich, N., Karlsen, H., & Aamodt, P. O. (2014). Learning outcomes across disciplines and professions: Measurement and interpretation. *Quality in Higher Education, 20*(2), 195–215. doi:10.1080/13538322.2014.904587

Clark, B. R. (1983). The higher education system: Academic organization in cross-national perspective. Los Angeles, CA: University of California Press.

DiMaggio, P. J., & Powell, W. W. (1983). The iron cage revisited: Institutional isomorphism and collective rationality in organizational fields. *American Sociological Review, 48*(2), 147–160.

Durand, J., & Pujadas, C. (2004). Self-assessment of governance teams in an argentine private university: Adapting to difficult times. *Tertiary Education and Management, 10*(1), 27–44. doi:10.1080/13583883.2004.9967115

Frølich, N. (2005). Implementation of new public management in Norwegian universities. *European Journal of Education, 40*(2), 223–234.

Frølich, N. (2011). Multi-layered accountability: Performance funding of universities. *Public Administration, 89*(3), 840–859.

Frølich, N., & Sahlin, K. (2013). *University organization as bridging: Ambigous, competing and mediated institutions.* Paper presented at the EGOS, Montreal.

Heggen, K. (2010). *Kvalifisering for profesjonsutøving : sjukepleiar - lærar - sosialarbeidar.* Oslo, Norway: Abstrakt forl.

Jameson, J. (2012). Leadership values, trust and negative capability: Managing the uncertainties of future English higher education. *Higher Education Quarterly, 66*(4), 391–414.

Johnson, R. (2002). Learning to manage the university: Tales of training and experience. *Higher Education Quarterly, 56*(1), 33–51.

Juntrasook, A. (2014). You do not have to the boss to be the leader: Contested meanings of leadership in higher education. *Higher Education Research & Development, 33*(1), 19–31.

Kingston, P. W., & Lewis, L. S. (1990). *The high status track: Studies of elite schools and stratification.* Albany, NY: SUNY Press.

Kraatz, M. S., & Block, E. S. (2008). Organizational implications of institutional pluralism. In R. Greenwood, C. Oliver, K. Sahlin, & R. Suddaby (Eds.), *The sage handbook of organizational institutionalism.* London, UK: Sage Publications.

Krücken, G., Kosmütsky, A., & Torka, M. (Eds.). (2007). *Towards a multiversity? Universities between global trends and national traditions.* Bielefeld, Germany: Transcript Verlag.

Meyer, J. W., & Rowan, B. (1977). Institutional organizations: Formal structures as myth and ceremony. *American Journal of Sociology, 83*(2), 340–363.

Muller, J. (2009). Forms of knowledge and curriculum coherence. *Journal of Education and Work, 22*(3), 205–226.

Nussbaum, M. C. (2012). *Not for profit: Why democracy needs the humanities.* Princeton, NJ and Oxford, England: Princeton University Press.

Olsen, J. P. (1987). Universitetet: Sentralisering, autonomi og markedsstyring. *Nytt Norsk Tidsskrift, 4,* 16–26.

Rosenhaupt, H. W. (1940). Modern foreign language study and the needs of our times. *Monatshefte für deutschen Unterricht, 32*(5), 205–216.

Sahlin, K., & Wedlin, L. (2008). Circulating ideas: Imitation, translation and editing. In R. Greenwood, C. Oliver, K. Sahlin, & R. Suddaby (Eds.), *Handbook of organizational institutionalism.* Los Angeles, CA: Sage.

Selznick, P. (1957). *Leadership in administration.* New York, NY: Harper & Row.

Shattock, M. (2002). Re-balancing modern concepts of university governance. *Higher Education Quarterly, 56*(3), 235–244.

Stensaker, B., & Vabø, A. (2013). Re-inventing shared governance: Implications for organisational culture and institutional leadership. *Higher Education Quarterly, 67*(3), 256–274. doi:10.1111/hequ.12019

Stensaker, B., Vabø, A., Frølich, N., Bleiklie, I., Kvam, E., & Waagene, E. (2013). *Styring og strategi. Betydningen av ulike styringsmodeller for lærestedenes strategiarbeid, NIFU Report 43/2013.* Oslo, Norway: NIFU Nordic Institute for Studies in Innovation, Research and Education.

Uusiautti, S., Syväjärvi, A., Stenvall, J., Perttula, J., & Määttä, K. (2012). It's more like a growth process than a bunch of answers: University leaders describe themselves as leaders. *Procedia – Social and Behavioral Sciences, 69,* 828–837.

Joakim Caspersen
NIFU – Nordic Institute for Studies in Innovation
Research and Education
Oslo
Norway

Research Professor Nicoline Frølich (Dr.)
NIFU – Nordic Institute for Studies in Innovation
Research and Education
Oslo
Norway

MAREK KWIEK

8. INEQUALITY IN ACADEMIC KNOWLEDGE PRODUCTION

The Role of Research Top Performers across Europe

INTRODUCTION

This paper focuses on the inequality in academic knowledge production and finds the productivity distribution patterns across European systems to be strikingly similar, despite starkly different national academic traditions. The upper echelons of highly productive academics (the upper 10 percent of academics who are ranked highest in terms of their publishing performance in 11 European countries) provide, on average, almost half of all academic knowledge production.

The primary data analyzed comes from the large-scale global CAP and European EUROAC research projects on the academic profession ("Changing Academic Profession" and "Academic Profession in Europe"), with 13,908 usable cases of research-involved academics. In particular, the data studied in this paper refer to a subpopulation of highly productive academics (N = 1,583), contrasted with a subpopulation of 90 percent of the remaining academics (N = 12,325). If a research question can be "the theoretical or empirical puzzle that motivates a given study" (Brady & Collier, 2010: 347), then our study was motivated by the puzzle of the impact of highly productive academics on overall European publishing output.

In short, the inequality in academic knowledge production in Europe is as follows: about 10 percent of academics – termed research top performers here – produce on average almost half (45.9 percent) of all articles, and 20 percent produce two-thirds of them (65.4 percent). The remaining 80 percent of academics produce on average only about one third of all articles (34.6 percent). If the research-active segment of the European academic profession is divided into two halves, the upper most productive half produces almost all the articles (94.1 percent), and the lower most productive half produces less than 6 percent. From a gender perspective, the proportion of male academics among research top performers is higher (three out of four) than that of female academics but "productivity concentration indexes" for both genders (linking the percentages of male and female top performers to the percentages of all male and all female academics in national systems) clearly show that the role of highly productive female academics is much higher than traditionally assumed in the literature on social stratification in science.

E. Reale & E. Primeri (Eds.), The Transformation of University Institutional and Organizational Boundaries, 203–230.

This paper provides another, this time large-scale and cross-national, corroboration of the systematic inequality in knowledge production, for the first time argued for by Alfred Lotka (1929) and Derek de Solla Price (1963). We show here that the traditional stratification of the academic profession based on different publishing patterns still holds across Europe. While it is important to "measure science" (Irvine & Martin, 1984), following the advent of a new "metric of science" (Elkana et al.,1978) through sophisticated bibliometric tools (Leydesdorff, 2001), we argue that it is still useful to refer to traditional survey-based individual productivity analyses to explore both the "what" of academic knowledge production and the "why" of it (individual and institutional predictors of high research performance).

The corroboration for systematic social stratification and academic inequality in science is one line of research, pursued here. Through a combination of descriptive and inferential analyses, in an accompanying paper (Kwiek, 2015b) we explore highly productive academics as a distinctive segment of the European academic profession. European research top performers, as discussed there, are a highly homogeneous group of academics whose high research performance is driven by structurally similar factors. They work according to similar patterns, they share similar academic attitudes, and the general research productivity literature applies to them only to a limited extent. Highly productive academics are similar from a cross-national perspective and likewise substantially differ intra-nationally from their lower-performing colleagues. They are more highly cosmopolitan, more fundamentally hard-working, and more substantially research-oriented than the remaining academics, despite differentiated national contexts.

This paper is organized as follows: the next section is "Analytical Framework" (with subsections on "research productivity", "the quality-quantity dilemma in productivity studies" and "gender and research performance"). Section 3 is focused on "Data and Methods" and includes two subsections on "the dataset used" and on "research top performers vs. the rest of academics". The core of the paper is in section 4, "Research Findings", divided into four subsections: "research top performers and the national research output", "a brief statistical profile", and two subsections on the gender distribution of research top performers. Finally, section 5 presents "Discussion" and Section 6 "Conclusions".

ANALYTICAL FRAMEWORK

Research Productivity

Faculty research productivity and its predictors have been thoroughly explored in the academic literature, mostly in single-nation contexts (especially the USA, the United Kingdom, and Australia: see Cole & Cole, 1973; Allison & Stewart, 1974; Fox, 1983; Ramsden, 1994; Shin & Cummings, 2010), and rarely in cross-national contexts (see Teodorescu, 1994; Drennan et al., 2013). While most studies did not use national samples and focused on faculty from selected academic fields, especially from the natural sciences, our study used national samples and refers to all academic fields grouped in five large clusters.

So far, international higher education comparative studies have not explored highly productive scientists; and though they have been mentioned in passing in various single-nation academic profession studies (for instance, Crane, 1965; Cole & Cole, 1973; Allison, 1980), they were not researched in any detail either quantitatively or qualitatively in these studies (exceptions include a discussion of "big-output writers" or "big producers" in *Little Science, Big Science* by Derek J. de Solla Price (1963), a foundational book for scientometrics; a study of "star scientists" in the context of sex differences in research productivity in Italy in Abramo, D'Angelo and Caprasecca 2009; and studies of productivity of nationally-listed "eminent scientists" in Croatia in Prpić, 1996).

Thus highly productive academics as a separate segment of the academic profession are a very rare scholarly theme. We assume that because about one tenth of European academics produce about half of all research output (and one in twenty produces about a third of it), this distinct academic population deserves more scholarly attention.

We do not explore in this paper the larger issue of "academic productivity" which would combine both "research productivity" and "teaching effectiveness", as in John A. Centra (1983) and in Herbert W. Marsh and John Hattie (2002), which would allow us to study what James S. Fairweather (1999) termed "the complete faculty member" through faculty teaching and faculty research productivity combined. We explore *research* productivity only, defined here, following Daniel Teodorescu (2000: 206) in his influential comparative study of ten countries based on the Carnegie dataset (a predecessor of the CAP/EUROAC dataset), as the "self-reported number of journal articles and chapters in academic books that the respondent had published in the three years prior to the survey". Our study thus explores both intra-national and cross-national differences in academic productivity between the research top performers and "average" (Stephan & Levine, 1992: 57–58) academics within and across national systems. It explores research top performers working across a long continuum of national systems, from the lowest-performing (Poland) to the highest-performing (Italy and the Netherlands, followed by Switzerland and Germany, see Kwiek, 2015a) in terms of average publishing output.

The Quality-Quantity Dilemma in Productivity Studies

We do not argue in this paper that the number of publications (here: journal articles and book chapters, excluding books) is the best way to measure academic research productivity for cross-national comparative purposes; also no link is made between publications and their value, current or future (as normally no link is made between citations and their value, now or in the future), or between publications and the prestige of publication journals. Consistently with prior research on publication productivity, we assume, following Mary Frank Fox (1983: 285), that the principal means of communication in science is the publication process, "it is through publication that scientists receive professional recognition and esteem, as well as promotion, advancement, and funding for future research". "Recognition" in science comes from "scientific output" (Cole & Cole, 1967) and the reward system in science is designed to give recognition and esteem to those scientists who have best fulfilled their roles: in Robert K. Merton's (1973: 297) formulation, "the institution of science has developed an elaborate system for allocating rewards to those who variously lived up to its norms". Publications and citations increasingly matter and, in general, as Jerry Gaston (1978: ix) put it in his book on reward systems, the question is "whether or not people get what they deserve". Academics publish their work in exchange for scientific recognition: as Warren O. Hagstrom (1965: 168) formulated the idea in his theory of social control in science, "recognition is given for information, and the scientist who contributes much information to his colleagues is rewarded by them with high prestige". Consequently, research productivity studies are at the heart of studies on the academic profession.

On the basis of the CAP/EUROAC dataset used in this paper, only the self-reported number of publications for the past three academic years prior to the survey date could be used. There were no technical opportunities to combine the number of publications with the number of citations for either the total sample of 13,908 European research-involved academics, or for the 1,583 subsample of research top performers. The anonymization of all eleven national datasets prior to their merger into a single European dataset precludes any study of correlations based on both academic production and its impact measured through citations (as can be done separately for some national systems with specific datasets, usually resulting from various national research assessment exercises: see e.g., a study by Abramo, D'Angelo, & Caprasecca, 2009; Abramo, D'Angelo, & Di Costa, 2011 for an entire population of Italian academics).

The quality-quantity dilemma in academic productivity studies based on publication numbers is not easy to solve. This paper follows the explicit assumption that more productive academics produce more articles and less productive academics produce fewer articles – but no link is made here to either the originality of journal articles or their current or future impact in academic disciplines or beyond them, in science or beyond it, in the wider society. Consequently, from among the four ideal types of academic research production (based on both quantity and quality of published research) suggested by Jonathan R. Cole and Stephen Cole (1973: 91–93) for physicists in their study of social stratification in science – "prolific", "perfectionists", "mass producers" and "silent" – our study tends to focus on the "prolific" segment in which academics are defined by both the high quantity and high quality of their publications. As Cole and Cole (1973: 111) argued, "since quality and quantity of research output are fairly highly correlated, the high producers *tend* to publish the more consequential research. ... engaging in a lot of research is in one sense a 'necessary' condition for the production of high-quality work". Also Paula E. Stephan and Sharon G. Levin argue (1991: 364) that the prolific scientists they studied have not "traded quality for quantity by publishing in journals which have lower impact". Or, finally, as Price (1963: 41) argued along similar lines, "although there is no guarantee that the small producer is a nonentity and the big producer a distinguished scientist, there is a strong correlation". Our study uses the most comprehensive cross-national academic profession dataset currently available, with all its inherent limitations (widely reported in the last two decades, following 1994 when a benchmark for such datasets was produced in a global Carnegie study of the academic profession. For a discussion on the limitations of this type of dataset and the limitations of the resulting comparative research, see Teichler, Arimoto, & Cummings, 2013: 35).

Gender and Research Performance

This study also explores gender differences in research productivity and the gender distribution of research top performers. From a gender perspective, early differences in motivation between male and female academics can have far-reaching consequences for their productivity rates in the future: as Cole and Cole argued (1973: 150–151), even receiving the doctorate may have a qualitatively different meaning for male and female academics. Historically, until a few decades ago, while for male academics, PhD degrees may have been just entry cards to the academic profession, for female academics to have earned the degree was "in some measure, a triumph". In some countries, and Poland is the best example, only a minority of women entering the academic profession (as studied through the category of "new entrants", or those holding the degree for no more than 10 years) show a preference for research, compared with the majority of men entering the profession. Polish women academics in the "new entrants" category show the lowest research interest across all the systems studied (Kwiek, 2014a). Consistent with the accumulative advantage theory (Allison et al., 1982; Allison & Stewart, 1974), and even more so, consistent with what the Coles referred to as the reinforcement of research activity by the reward system, an early lack of success leads to smaller chances of later scientific success. This is the darker side of the accumulation of rewards in science – it is "the accumulation of failures – the process of 'accumulative disadvantage'" (Cole & Cole, 1973: 146). Productivity is heavily influenced by the recognition of early work and consequently, as the Coles argue:

> if women fail to be as productive in the years immediately following their degree, the social process of accumulative disadvantage may take over and contribute to their falling further behind in the race to produce new scientific discoveries. (Cole & Cole, 1973: 151)

In other words, as Jonathan R. Cole (1979: 8) argued in *Fair Science. Women in the Scientific Community*, the skewed distribution of scientific productivity and of subsequent rewards also results from "the poor getting poorer": "the growing inequality between the 'haves' and 'have-nots' of science results in part from a decline in productivity among those scientists who started their careers as moderately productive researchers, while the elite remain moderately or highly prolific researchers. Potentially, this process can influence the careers of women scientists".

While the "glass ceiling" for women in science appears to have already been broken (Cummings & Finkelstein, 2012: 76 in a US context), globally, "academic men have better academic networks and use them more often" and "the traditional gender differences in academic work seem to be reproduced through international academic activities" (Vabø et al., 2014: 191, 202). As there is a strong correlation between internationalization in research and individual research productivity (as we have shown for the same 11 European systems, Kwiek, 2015a; see Abramo et al., 2011 for Italy), the research productivity of female academics – who are generally more "internationalized at home" but less "internationalized abroad" than male academics – is more affected by the mounting pressures of internationalization than that of male academics. Not surprisingly, based on the CAP data, Michel Rostan, Flavio A. Ceravolo, and Amy Scott Metcalfe (2014: 130) conclude that "the prototypical academic figure in international research collaboration is a man, in his mid-50s or younger, working as a professor in a field of the natural sciences at a university in a small, non-Asian and non-English speaking country with a mature economy". The gender gap in research productivity continues (Padilla-Gonzáles et al., 2012: 275) and gender differences and inequalities still remain, with "the permanence of some barriers to women's careers" (Goastellec & Pekari, 2013: 76). In general, though, sex differences in productivity are "not immune to social change": while women academics used to publish at "50–60 percent" of the male academic rate, now they do so at around "70–80 percent" rate, as Yu Xie and Kimberlee A. Shauman conclude in their *Women in Science. Career Processes and Outcomes* (2003: 182–183) in a US context. The reasons for what Cole and Zuckerman (1984: 218) termed "the productivity puzzle", as explored through a systematic multivariate approach, are as follows:

> Women scientists publish fewer papers than men because women are less likely than men to have the personal characteristics, structural positions, and facilitating resources that are conductive to publication. There is very little *direct* effect of sex on research productivity. ... Women and men scientist are located in different academic structures with different access to valuable resources. ... Once sex differences in such positions are taken into account ... net differences between men and women in research productivity are nil or negligible. (Xie & Shauman, 2013: 191–193)

The implications for the scientific productivity of both male and female academics in the Coles' cumulative advantage and reinforcement theories are clear, as Stephan and Levin (1992: 29) emphasize:

Success breeds success. Consequently, those who enjoy success continue to be productive throughout their lives; those who have less success become discouraged and eventually look to other pursuits for satisfaction.

DATA AND METHODS

The Dataset Used

The data used in this study are drawn from eleven European countries involved in both the CAP and EUROAC projects (Austria, Finland, Germany, Ireland, Italy, the Netherlands, Norway, Poland, Portugal, Switzerland, and the United Kingdom), subsequently cleaned and weighted in a single European dataset by a University of Kassel team.[1] The combined CAP/EUROAC dataset is the most comprehensive source of cross-national data on European academics (see the wide panorama of research themes explored using this dataset in the last three years: Shin, Arimoto, & Cummings, 2014 on "teaching and research"; Locke, Cummings, & Fisher 2011 on "governance and management"; Huang, Finkelstein, & Rostan, 2014 on "internationalization"; Teichler & Höhle, 2013 on "work situation"; Bentley et al., on "job satisfaction"; Teichler, Arimoto, & Cummings, 2013 on "the changing academic profession", from the long list of cross-national and single-nation studies available). The quality of the data is high (Teichler, Arimoto, & Cummings, 2013: 35; Teichler & Höhle, 2013: 9).

A survey questionnaire was sent out to the CAP countries in 2007 and to the EUROAC countries in 2010. The total number of returned surveys was 17,211 and included between 1,000 and 1,700 returned surveys from all the countries studied except for Poland where it was higher, as shown in Table 1 in the Appendices. Overall, the response rate differed from over 30 percent (in Norway, Italy, and Germany), to 20–30 percent (in the Netherlands, Finland, and Ireland), to about 15 percent in the United Kingdom, 11 percent in Poland and 10 percent or less in Austria, Switzerland and Portugal. The relatively low response rates may be caused by the increasing number of surveys to which the academic profession is routinely exposed (Mesch, 2012: 316 ff.). There are no indications that the pool of respondents differs from the pool of non-respondents, though, and consequently the "non-response bias" (Stoop, 2012: 122) does not seem to occur. The Polish subsample of 3,704 academics is a special case: it is highly representative of the population of about 79,000 Polish academics, even though the response rate for Poland was 11.22 percent. Overall, simple random sampling, systematic sampling, and stratified random sampling methods were used, depending on the country. In Poland, the sampling method of an "equal probability of selection method" (Hibberts et al., 2012: 55) was used: every element in a sample (every Polish academic) having an equal chance of being selected for the study. In contrast, in Germany, Switzerland and Austria, cluster sampling methods were used, with the pre-selection of some institutions.

Individual data files were produced by all participating countries but all specifically national categories (faculty rank structures, institutional type structures etc.) were reduced to internationally comparable categories. An international codebook was created and a number of coding modifications were introduced into national data files, in particular the dichotomization of all faculty into "senior" and "junior" faculty and into faculty employed in "universities" and those employed in "other higher education institutions". The data cleaning process included the use of "survey audits" prepared by national teams. In the process of international data coordination, sample values were weighted so that national samples in the countries studied were broadly representative of national academic populations for most independent variables, especially gender, academic field, institutional type and institutional rank (national-level sampling techniques are described for the CAP European countries in RIHE, 2008: 89–178; Teichler, Arimoto, & Cummings, 2013: 30–35; Huang, Finkelstein, & Rostan, 2014: 23–36; and for the EUROAC countries in Teichler & Höhle, 2013: 6–9). The distribution of faculty by academic field cluster is shown in Table 2 in the Appendices.

Research Top Performers vs. the Rest of Academics

The sample of European academics studied here has been divided into two complementary subsamples: academics reporting research involvement and academics reporting *not* being involved in research. Then the first subsample was divided into two subgroups: the first being "research top performers" identified as academics ranked among the top 10 percent of academics with the highest research performance in each of the 11 national systems (separately) and in all five major research field clusters (also separately).[2] The second subgroup being that of the remaining 90 percent of academics involved in research.

The distribution of the sample population by country is shown in Table 3 below; and includes the number of surveys usable in the current research (i.e., with all relevant data), surveys of the academics involved in research activities (N), the share of academics involved in research activities, surveys of research top performers, and the share of research top performers in the sample population of academics involved in research (assumed to be about 10 percent, data cut-off points permitting). What is especially important is the cross-national differences in the share of academics involved in research activities across national systems: at one extreme, in some countries (e.g., Poland and Italy) almost all academics surveyed reported being involved in research (about 98–99 percent, and in Norway about 90 percent); at the other extreme, in other countries (e.g., the Netherlands and the UK), only about half of the academics surveyed reported being involved in research. The remaining seven countries are somewhere in the middle, with the mean for all eleven countries being about 80 percent. The survey instrument was used to study the academic profession in general rather than merely its research-involved subgroup. No research involvement being reported both in the university and non-university ("other higher education institution") sectors. In more diversified systems, academics from the non-university sector constituted a higher proportion of respondents, with the Netherlands and the UK as prime examples. The non-university sector involves for instance *hogescholen* in the Netherlands, *Fachhochschulen* in Germany, and *statlige høgskoler* in Norway; only in Italy and Austria were no other institutional types other than universities represented in the sample.

Table 3. The distribution of the sample population, by country

	All Academics	Research-involved Academics (N)	% Research-involved Academics	Research top performers	% Research top performers
Austria	1,492	1,297	86.9	146	11.3
Finland	1,374	1,063	77.4	126	11.9
Germany	1,215	1,007	82.9	110	10.9
Ireland	1,126	865	76.8	101	11.7
Italy	1,711	1,674	97.8	191	11.4
Netherlands	1,209	536	44.3	61	11.4
Norway	986	876	88.8	106	12.1
Poland	3,704	3,659	98.8	411	11.2
Portugal	1,513	944	62.4	104	11.0
Switzerland	1,414	1,210	85.6	138	11.4
UK	1,467	777	53.0	89	11.5
Total	17,211	13,908	80.8	1,583	11.4

RESEARCH FINDINGS

Research top performers give substance to European research production: in a word, without them, it would be halved. Because, consistently across all the European systems studied, on average, slightly less than half (46 percent) of all academic research production as measured by journal articles comes from about 10 percent of the most highly productive academics. And in four systems, the share is near or exceeds 50 percent (Austria, Finland, Poland, and Portugal), see Table 4 below.

Specifically, in a representative European sample of 17,211 academics from 11 systems, a subsample of about 1,583 highly productive academics (Derek J. de Solla Price's "big-output writers of scientific literature" and "large producers", and the Coles' "scientific frontiersmen") produced 32,706 out of 71,248 journal articles

Table 4. Journal articles (and book chapters) produced in the three-year reference period, by research top performers and the remaining academics, by country

	By top performers	By the rest	Total	% by top performers
Austria	3,330	1,206	4,536	73.4
Finland	2,445	2,435	4,880	50.1
Germany	2,702	3,506	6,208	43.5
Ireland	2,419	2,684	5,103	47.4
Italy	5,096	10,162	15,259	33.4
Netherlands	1,513	1,647	3,160	47.9
Norway	1,902	2,340	4,243	44.8
Poland	6,767	6,831	13,599	49.8
Portugal	1,992	1,952	3,945	50.5
Switzerland	2,798	3,304	6,102	45.9
UK	1,740	2,475	4,215	41.3
Total	32,706	38,543	71,248	45.9

(or 45.9 percent) in the three-year period studied (and the upper 5 percent of highly productive academics produced on average 33 percent of all journal articles).

Research Top Performers and the National Research Output

There are powerful linkages between academic cultures (the "tribes") and disciplinary knowledge (their "territories"), and an individual's powerful sense of belonging to his or her academic tribe (Becher, 1987; Becher & Trowler, 2001). Not surprisingly, there are substantial cross-disciplinary differences in the share of the research output among top performers in the total research output of the systems studied (Table 5 below): the highest level of concentration is discernible in engineering as well as in the physical sciences and mathematics; and the lowest for the humanities and social sciences as well as for life sciences and medical sciences (see "field means"). For instance, in Finland and Germany, about 60 percent of all articles in engineering are produced by top performers. In general, our findings for Norway – a system with the lowest cross-disciplinary variation in the share of output produced by top performers – are consistent with Svein Kyvik's (1989: 210) study of Norwegian academics in which no essential differences in publishing inequality across academic fields were reported. The only country that does not fit the general European pattern is Italy: the share of output by its top performers in total output is markedly smaller than in other countries (at about one third), and it is highly differentiated by academic fields. This deviation can be explained by Italy having the highest academic productivity index and the highest productivity index for articles (Kwiek, 2015b) so that the difference between top performers and the rest of academics is lower than elsewhere (Abramo et al., 2009: 143 have shown that 12 percent of highly-performing Italian academics produce about 35 percent of total academic production as seen through the Science Citation Index, compared to 33.4 percent produced by 11.4 percent of academics derived from the dataset we use; also the male and female concentration indexes for Italy are exactly the same. Italy is the only European system for which comprehensive data on top performers are available, and the convergence of research results for this country tends to support high levels of reliability for the research results found in this paper).

Table 5. Average research output (= total number of articles in 3 years) of research top performers as a share of national research output, by disciplines, for all countries (in percent).

Fields / Countries	FI	DE	IE	IT	NL	NO	PL	PT	CH	UK	Field mean
Life sciences and medical sciences	50.9	39.2	45.8	31.5	51.0	44.7	48.5	49.2	41.4	36.6	43.9
Physical sciences, mathematics	44.1	53.3	46.1	29.4	45.7	42.5	61.2	54.3	47.6	54.2	47.8
Engineering	61.5	58.5	49.7	38.8	52.5	47.2	55.8	52.2	49.5	49.1	51.5
Humanities and social sciences	43.3	38.5	49.6	41.4	40.8	41.8	43.3	45.4	48.1	34.0	42.6
Professions	47.5	48.0	44.7	32.9	52.7	45.1	45.8	57.4	50.3	41.0	46.5
Country mean	50.1	43.5	47.4	33.4	47.9	44.8	49.8	50.5	45.9	41.3	

In short, from among all research-active academics in Europe (from both university and non-university sectors, employed both full-time and part-time), about 10 percent are the most productive academics who produce almost half (45.9 percent) of all articles, with 20 percent producing two-thirds of all articles (65.4 percent). The remaining 80 percent produce only about one third of all articles (34.6 percent). If the research-active European academic profession is divided into two halves, the upper most productive half produces almost all published articles (94.1 percent), with the lower most productive half producing less than 6 percent.

If we focus on a specific subsample of European academics; those who are research-active and employed full-time in universities only; the emergent picture is only slightly different. The upper most productive 10 percent produce about four in every ten articles (41.5 percent) and the upper 20 percent produce about six in every ten articles (61.2 percent). The remaining 80 percent produce less than four in every ten articles (39.8 percent). And if the research-active European academic profession employed full-time in universities is divided into two halves, the upper most productive half produces more than 90 percent of all articles (91.5 percent), and the lower most productive half produces less than 9 percent.

RESEARCH TOP PERFORMERS: A BRIEF STATISTICAL PROFILE

We have explored the differences between research top performers and the remaining 90 percent of academics through eight dimensional groupings. Some of them were linked in the research literature as factors influencing individual research productivity, others were not. In general, they are either individual or institutional. The dimensional groupings are as follows: demographics, socialization, internationalization, academic behaviors, academic attitudes and role orientation, overall research engagement, institutional policies, and institutional support.

An analysis of the descriptive statistics for the two subsamples demonstrates that there are a number of universal characteristic patterns that hold for research top performers in all eleven systems studied (we studied multi-dimensional relationships which require a model approach, using a regression analysis, see Kwiek, 2015b). There are also very strong patterns holding in all systems but one.

The universal patterns regarding European research top performers are the following:

- being a male academic (that is, in all systems, the share of male academics is higher among research top performers than the share of female academics) (*demographics*),
- higher mean age (in all systems, the mean age of research top performers is higher than the mean age of the rest of academics),
- being employed full-time (in all systems, the share of full-time employed academics is higher among research top performers than among the rest of academics) (*demographics*),
- being a professor (*demographics*),
- collaborating internationally, collaborating domestically, publishing in a foreign language, and conducting research that is international in scope or orientation (*internationalization*),
- viewing research as reinforcing teaching (*academic attitudes and role orientation*),
- being research-orientated, viewing scholarship as original research, and viewing scholarship as basic/theoretical research (*academic attitudes and role orientation*),
- sitting in national/international committees/boards/bodies, being a peer reviewer, and being an editor of journals/book series (*overall research engagement*), and, finally,
- writing research grant proposals.

In terms of the major groupings of characteristics, the strongest universal patterns are discernible in four of them: demographics, internationalization, academic attitudes and role orientation, and overall research engagement (4 characteristics in each). In contrast, there are no universal patterns discernible in the other four remaining clusters: socialization, academic behaviors, institutional policies, and institutional support. In view of previous research on academic productivity, it is especially surprising in the case of the socialization and academic behaviors groupings, as the institutional characteristics from the two institutional groupings are commonly believed to be less relevant to academic productivity than individual characteristics (Teodorescu, 2000; Drennan et al., 2013).

In most systems research top performers are on average more research-oriented than the remaining academics by about 30 percentage points; they collaborate internationally more often by about 20 p.p. (and domestically by about 30 p.p.), publish in a foreign country more often by about 20 p.p., sit on national and international boards and committees more often by about 30 p.p., are peer reviewers more often by about 40 p.p., are editors of journals/book series by about 20–30 p.p., and write research grant proposals more often by about 20–30 p.p. (Table 6 below).

RESEARCH TOP PERFORMERS: A GENDER DISTRIBUTION

The gender differential in academic productivity rates and the gender stratification in science are highly important issues from the perspectives of public policy (Leathwood & Read, 2009; Fitzgerald, 2014) and equity as well as women's status in higher education (Allan, 2011). They are also, undoubtedly, hot political issues. Our research shows that, consistently across Europe, the distribution of research top performers by gender is skewed towards male academics: their share is on average 2–5 times higher than the share of female academics (there are only three exceptions to this rule: in the UK, their share is much lower, in Germany it is lower, and in Portugal the gender difference is marginal). However, is there a consistent gender distribution among research top performers across Europe?

The mere *share* of women among top performers is not a fair measure. To explore the inequality in academic knowledge production along gender lines, a more sophisticated measuring instrument is needed. Following Abramo et al. (2009: 143) who focused on "star scientists" in Italy, we have constructed a similar "productivity concentration index" for all European countries, for both genders.

The concentration index is a "measure of association between two variables" based on frequencies data and varying around the neutral value of 1: the percentage of male top performers divided by the percentage of all male academics in a given system, or the share of male academics among top performers divided by the share of male academics among all academics. "The index of concentration, equaling 1.60, indicates that the relative frequency of this profile among star scientists is over 60% greater than the frequency of the same profile in the entire population" (Abramo et al., 2009: 143–144). That is, in the case of male academics from the

Table 6. Various personal and institutional characteristics linked to individual research productivity; all countries: research top performers (T) vs. the remaining academics (R); universal characteristics only (and those for all countries with one exception (+). In some cases, in percent "agreement", we refer to percentages of answers 4 and 5 (or 3 and 4) combined, on a five-point (four-point) Likert scale, depending on the question.

Items / Countries (%)	AT		FI		DE		IE		IT		NL		NO		PL		PT		CH		UK	
	T	R	T	R	T	R	T	R	T	R	T	R	T	R	T	R	T	R	T	R	T	R
Female (yes)	33.8	38.7	30.8	43.0	16.2	34.1	30.5	48.9	17.8	33.9	21.5	50.1	20.8	32.7	23.9	41.2	35.9	46.0	25.7	44.0	21.4	38.4
Mean age (years)	46.9	40.8	48.7	43.0	50.6	47.0	44.2	52.5	52.0	50.1	46.2	47.2	46.3	47.9	54.2	46.3	48.3	47.9	47.4	42.3	46.3	37.6
+Job satisfaction (4 & 5)	64.8	63.7	78.0	66.0	56.4	61.0	56.7	69.7	63.8	57.2	44.2	80.0	76.5	66.3	68.7	71.7	61.3	57.7	50.5	83.6	83.6	70.9
Full-time	82.8	66.6	91.4	81.9	91.6	71.5	95.0	92.1	96.3	96.9	97.1	85.4	85.7	63.5	95.2	89.7	98.6	97.8	95.1	90.0	77.1	57.7
Professor	8.5	4.8	44.8	8.3	34.0	5.2	32.7	6.7	43.8	29.2	40.1	8.2	41.9	8.1	69.5	18.3	16.5	6.3	9.4	1.8	31.6	6.3
Collaborating internationally	68.2	61.7	88.4	67.8	82.9	57.5	82.2	59.4	89.4	75.5	85.2	66.0	88.6	57.9	80.4	54.0	75.8	61.1	77.1	63.8	83.1	65.9
Collaborating domestically	91.7	74.4	98.7	67.8	72.4	42.8	99.0	69.7	81.2	56.6	90.8	58.0	85.7	49.4	86.8	57.4	64.4	45.0	74.9	49.1	91.0	63.3
Publishing in a foreign country	92.8	81.5	92.0	69.1	80.3	62.7	93.0	73.7	81.4	65.9	73.5	53.6	0.0	0.0	92.4	73.5	78.2	51.8	96.8	65.8	92.0	66.1
Research international in scope	80.7	62.0	80.9	57.0	63.5	49.9	77.8	66.2	72.7	88.3	84.5	60.5	83.0	59.9	77.8	65.1	53.6	36.9	82.2	48.1	75.0	55.7
Research-oriented (3 & 4)	82.0	78.6	93.9	76.1	81.4	67.5	92.0	54.4	91.4	74.6	97.0	69.8	93.5	67.3	94.6	82.6	81.9	55.7	78.0	46.8	84.5	77.6

(Continued)

Table 6. (Continued)

Items / Countries (%)	AT		FI		DE		IE		IT		NL		NO		PL		PT		CH		UK	
	T	R	T	R	T	R	T	R	T	R	T	R	T	R	T	R	T	R	T	R	T	R
Research reinforces teaching	85.3	80.4	87.3	77.7	83.7	63.4	87.4	87.2	88.6	81.7	88.7	77.6	82.4	83.2	89.6	81.2	60.1	47.9	90.4	72.2	83.3	64.6
Scholarship is original research	81.2	71.7	76.3	60.6	80.0	68.8	73.3	71.1	78.1	72.5	79.9	68.1	83.6	75.3	95.4	87.4	74.5	67.8	84.6	69.1	0.0	0.0
Basic/theoretical research	72.1	70.2	72.4	55.1	57.0	64.6	48.6	61.4	56.6	69.8	52.0	54.2	51.7	69.7	67.5	62.0	57.8	50.1	41.5	46.5	43.7	
National/international committees	64.8	33.7	53.1	19.1	32.5	11.3	75.0	48.9	70.2	49.9	58.2	23.3	73.0	26.7	73.2	30.3	33.8	15.4	44.5	26.1	84.7	42.0
A peer reviewer	82.0	57.3	86.3	35.1	50.1	21.0	99.0	69.1	77.7	53.2	92.9	64.6	94.3	45.4	89.4	43.9	68.5	39.5	69.2	30.5	88.3	41.7
Editor of journals/book series	62.2	30.6	38.7	10.7	43.7	12.2	34.0	20.0	19.0	8.6	47.5	17.7	42.3	16.8	33.6	8.3	9.8	6.4	27.0	9.6	51.6	12.8
+ Involved in technology transfer	15.3	11.0	37.8	30.4	31.7	14.2	9.9	11.0	22.9	13.1	26.6	15.8	32.1	12.1	19.4	10.0	9.9	8.9	24.1	13.4	31.9	21.5
Writing research grant proposals	81.9	59.0	82.7	59.2	89.3	54.0	49.5	45.3	86.0	69.2	83.2	62.8	81.8	55.3	97.2	74.0	69.0	56.3	55.2	19.1	83.8	48.0
+ Research equipment (4 & 5)	52.1	45.1	59.6	53.5	54.6	52.9	64.7	54.6	36.9	29.7	44.4	38.4	58.9	38.6	39.5	52.3	36.4	34.1	36.4	30.8	72.5	70.8

Note: In three cases; Italy; "full-time" and "mean age", and the Netherlands; "research reinforces teaching"; the difference of less than 1 percent was disregarded.

UK (Table 7 below), the productivity concentration index of 1.5 for male academics shows that the relative frequency of male research top performers among all research top performers is 50 percent higher than the frequency of male academics among all academics. Similarly, in the case of female academics from the UK, the productivity concentration index of 0.5 for female academics shows that the relative frequency of female research top performers in all research top performers is 50 percent lower than the share of female academics in all academics.

Universally, across all systems, male productivity concentration indexes are higher than 1 (from 1.1 in Austria to 1.5 in the UK) and female productivity concentration indexes are lower than 1 (from 0.5 in Germany and the UK to 0.9 in Austria). Male academics are over-represented among top performers, and female academics are under-represented. In other words, what matters is not only the gender distribution of top performers, as shown in the "frequency" line in Table 7 below (and the *share* of male top performers, ranging from two-thirds to four-fifths) but also the *relative* presence of male and female academics in the subpopulation of research top performers as measured by a productivity concentration index by genders, as shown in the "concentration" line in the same table. The concentration of men among top performers is precisely twice that of the concentration of women among top performers in Italy, Norway, Switzerland (1.2 vs. 0.6) and it is slightly lower in Finland, Ireland, the Netherlands, and Poland. It is the lowest in Austria, and the highest in the UK, with a male concentration three times higher.

In the context of the traditional sociology of science and social stratification literature (Wilson, 1995; Hagstrom, 1965; Merton, 1973; Cole & Cole, 1973; Zuckerman, 1996), these research results strongly support the argument of the historically growing role of female academics in academic knowledge production: in almost all countries studied, the difference between the *relative* presence of male and female academics in the subpopulation of research top performers is by a factor of only two. In the emerging, consistent patterns of inequality in knowledge production, the high role of women academics among the upper echelons of highly productive academics is undeniable. The gender productivity gap among research top performers (and the under-representation of female academics in this group) is clearly lower than expected.

There is a long list of caveats here, though, leading to reservations of various natures. We will focus on two. First, the research production data in this paper is self-reported and male academics in some systems may tend to overestimate the number of articles they produce, while female academics may tend to underestimate the number. In other words, different national academic cultures may lead to different levels of overestimation and underestimation of research production contingent on the gender factor. Second, the various systems studied here are differently populated by female academics in general (20–50 percent), and by female academics in the university sector in particular (15–55 percent). Also, there are gender-based choices of research problems, of academic disciplines, and of research styles; including publication patterns, and matters relating to research productivity. Robert Leslie

Table 7. Gender distribution of top performers by country (numbers and percentages), for all countries. The productivity concentration index is the percentage of male top performers/divided by the percentage of male researchers in a given country; the same applies to female top performers.

Items / Countries	AT		FI		DE		IE		IT		NL		NO		PL		PT		CH		UK	
	M	F	M	F	M	F	M	F	M	F	M	F	M	F	M	F	M	F	M	F	M	F
Number	87	44	87	39	89	17	66	29	156	34	45	12	80	25	257	144	74	26	107	29	58	16
Frequency	66.2	33.8	69.2	30.8	83.8	16.2	69.5	30.5	82.2	17.8	79.2	20.8	76.1	23.9	64.1	35.9	74.3	25.7	78.6	21.4	78.5	21.5
Concentration	1.1	0.9	1.2	0.7	1.2	0.5	1.3	0.7	1.2	0.6	1.2	0.7	1.2	0.6	1.2	0.8	1.3	0.6	1.2	0.6	1.5	0.5

Fisher argues (2005: 275) that differences in research styles (for instance, publishing less frequently) between men and women scientists may be linked to the issue of women being "latecomers to the academic world":

> women scientists are keenly aware that their work is regarded more skeptically than men's research. Women scientists understand that not only men in their discipline may be looking more critically at research by women scientists. Women colleagues will also be quick to condemn the low quality work of women scientists. This is because these colleagues are afraid that poor quality work by women will provide ammunition to those hostile to women in the discipline.

Not surprisingly, our research shows that female academics already in the top academic ranks are often on average more productive than men in the same ranks, work longer total weekly hours, longer weekly research hours, and are more research-oriented: to reach the highest levels of recognition, they had to survive in often hostile academic environments. But female academics in lower ranks often work on average shorter weekly research hours and show lower research engagement than male academics (for Poland, see Kwiek, 2014a).

"SUPER" RESEARCH TOP PERFORMERS: A FURTHER GENDER DISTRIBUTION

Giovanni Abramo and colleagues (2009: 145) in their study on the whole population of Italian academics show that "female star scientists are primarily concentrated in the lesser levels of productivity. ... From lowest to highest frequency of production ... there is an evident reversal of the sexes". To test this Italian conclusion on European academics, we have briefly explored a smaller group, a subsample of highly productive academics from its upper layer (termed here "super research top performers"). The group has been defined here arbitrarily as those who had published at least 28 journal articles in the three years prior to the execution of the survey. Super research top performers are a group of between 1.2–1.5 percent of academics in such countries as Poland, Portugal, and Finland; and between 3.3–4.6 percent in such countries as Germany, the Netherlands, and Italy, as shown below in Table 8.

Our research results clearly demonstrate that indeed the gender distribution among the upper layer of research top performers is heavily skewed towards male academics, as in the Italian case. Consequently, the productivity concentration indexes by gender for these two groups would be different from those shown in Table 7 above: they would be still higher for male academics and still lower for female academics belonging to the super research top performers. So the gender productivity gap increases in the upper layers of top performers (see Table 9 below): while the mean share of female academics among top performers in Europe is 25.3 percent, their mean share among super top performers decreases to 18 percent. Also, cross-national differences in gender distribution increase heavily. While for top performers, in only two countries is the share of female academics lower than 20

Table 8. Super top performers (those who published at least 28 papers within 3 years); by country, by gender, in %

	Super top performers		
	Percent of all academics	Gender	
		Male	Female
Austria	2.6	90.9	9.1
Finland	1.5	80.0	20.0
Germany	3.3	79.3	20.7
Ireland	2.3	78.9	21.1
Italy	4.6	83.4	16.6
Netherlands	3.5	91.1	8.9
Norway	2.0	83.7	16.3
Poland	1.2	82.3	17.7
Portugal	1.6	69.5	30.5
Switzerland	2.4	94.4	5.6
UK	1.7	68.8	31.2

percent (Germany and Italy), for super top performers it is lower than 20 percent in the majority of countries, and in three of them (Austria, the Netherlands and Switzerland), the share does not exceed 10 percent. In contrast, in three countries, the share of female academics actually *increases* among super top performers: these are Germany, Portugal, and the UK (in the last two reaching the highest levels in Europe and slightly exceeding 30 percent). In the majority of countries, the share of male academics increases by about 10–15 percentage points.

A more detailed cross-national analysis could be performed in selected academic disciplines, for instance life sciences and medical sciences on the one hand, and humanities and social sciences on the other (to see to what extent European universities might be disciplinarily-divided institutions, as explored at Polish universities in Kwiek, 2012; see Wanner et al., 1981), a path not followed here because of space limitations. The context for such an analysis could be the paths of academic careers across Europe becoming more volatile (Kwiek & Antonowicz, 2015) and the generally deteriorating working conditions in European higher education (Kwiek & Antonowicz, 2013).

DISCUSSION AND CONCLUSION

Our research clearly shows the validity across Europe of traditional generalizations according to which "only a small proportion of scientists produce the bulk of

Table 9. Top performers and super top performers; by gender (in percent)

	Top performers		Super top performers	
	Male	Female	Male	Female
Austria	66.2	33.8	90.9	9.1
Finland	69.2	30.8	80.0	20.0
Germany	83.8	16.2	79.3	20.7
Ireland	69.5	30.5	78.9	21.1
Italy	82.2	17.8	83.4	16.6
Netherlands	79.2	20.8	91.1	8.9
Norway	76.1	23.9	83.7	16.3
Poland	64.1	35.9	82.3	17.7
Portugal	74.3	25.7	69.5	30.5
Switzerland	78.6	21.4	94.4	5.6
UK	78.5	21.5	68.8	31.2
Mean	74.7	25.3	82.0	18.0

science which emerges from the scientific community" (Cole & Cole, 1973: 59). Academic knowledge production, in Europe as elsewhere, has always been highly stratified, "no matter how it is measured, there is enormous inequality in scientists' research productivity" (Allison, 1980: 163) because research productivity "varies enormously" (Fox, 1983: 286). Our study provides large-scale empirical support from 11 European systems to the conclusions from previous, usually single-nation and smaller-scale, research studies.

Based on the Carnegie dataset of the academic profession, Philip G. Altbach and Lionel S. Lewis (1996: 24) argued, without much further details, that "actual productivity is in fact limited to a minority of the profession". Paul Ramsden's (1994: 223) conclusions in his study of research productivity based on surveys of 890 academics from 18 Australian institutions were similar: "most publications are produced by a small proportion of the total number of staff". Also, Mary Frank Fox (1992: 296), based on surveys of 3,968 American social science academics, argued that "few people produce many articles and many publish few or none". Therefore our guiding research puzzle was as follows: is this the case across European systems too? Our findings consistently show that such productivity distribution patterns strongly hold for almost all European higher education systems and for all five major academic fields.

From a more historical perspective, our findings are consistent with the productivity patterns based on the estimations provided by Derek Price in the 1960s (in *Little Science, Big Science*, 1963) and Alfred J. Lotka's "The Frequency

Distribution of Scientific Productivity" (1926). The so-called "Lotka's law" (an inverse-square law of productivity) states that "the number of people producing n papers is proportional to $1/n2$. For every 100 authors who produce a single paper in a certain period, there are 25 with two, 11 with three, and so on" (Price, 1963: 43). Or, as Cole and Cole argued in their study of American physicists (1973: 218), "using Price's model, we can estimate that roughly 50 percent of all scientific papers are produced by approximately 10 percent of the scientists". And this is exactly the case in Europe today: we certainly expected it but there has been no large-scale, cross-European empirical evidence to support the claim so far.

Consequently, our empirical findings show that there are different "academic professions" in European universities, with a small share of highly productive researchers and a large share of relatively middle to low productive academics. Cross-national similarities among highly productive academics are as strong as the intra-national differences between them and the remaining research-involved academics in their national systems; as we show in a parallel paper focused on academic behaviors, academic attitudes, and predictors of high research productivity (Kwiek, 2015b).

The academic profession in Europe is highly stratified: the upper 10 percent of highly productive academics are responsible for about a half of all academic production; and the upper 50 percent – for more than 90 percent. Among highly productive academics the concentration of women is stable across Europe, and relatively high when compared with a few decades ago. This paper revisits Alfred Lotka's "law" of the skewed frequency distribution of journal publications, revived by Derek Price, and confirms its unfading validity across Europe today. With the increasing role of individualized competitive research funding in most European higher education funding architectures (and at the European level, European Research Council grants), the role of research top performers in national systems is bound to increase in the future.

The distribution of academic knowledge production in Europe is highly skewed towards highly productive academics. The policy implications for this historically consistent pattern of research productivity are more important in systems in which research funding is increasingly based on individual research grants (such as Poland following the 2008–2012 wave of reforms, Kwiek, 2014b) than in systems with primarily institutionally-based research funding (such as Italy, Abramo et al., 2011), and are different for competitive and non-competitive systems in Europe (or with strong "up or out" vs. "once in – forever in" employment policies). A major emergent policy dilemma is whether to support more high-performing academics (wherever they are located) or highly-ranked institutions, with the option of concentrating high-performing academics in highly ranked-institutions, leading to a growing national research concentration in selected institutions only. Additionally, the tension between teaching and research is likely to increase in systems in which more competitive research funding systems are introduced (which some call "social Darwinism at its baldest", Thornton, 2012: 191).

Policy conclusions regarding knowledge production as viewed through the proxy of publishing articles and book chapters are perplexing: if European systems dismissed its top performers (the upper 10 percent of their research-active academics), they would lose on average about half of their national academic production. And if European systems dismissed the bottom half of their research-active academics in terms of research productivity, they would lose less than 6 percent of their national knowledge production (in the case of research active academics employed full-time in the university sector, the loss would be 8.5 percent).

Consequently, a new typology of the European academic profession emerges, based on the measurable contribution to knowledge production: in the research-active segment of the academic profession, there are research top performers, research middle performers (high-middle and low-middle), and research non-performers, or no-publishers. (These are the Coles' "silent scientists", whose share among full-time academics employed in the university sector ranges from less than 10 percent in Ireland, Italy, the UK and the Netherlands to more than 40 percent in Poland, see Table 10 in the Appendices). On top of that, both higher education institutions in general and universities in particular are populated by non research-active faculty, an additional segment of research non-performers. The academic behaviors and academic attitudes of research top performers are worlds apart from those of both middle performers and non-performers. And in terms of research productivity, there is no single "academic profession" (as has always been the case in the last half a century), only "professions" in the plural. "Academic professions" in the plural appear in a similar vein in Enders and Musselin (2008: 127) when they refer to the growing internal differentiation of the academic profession; in Marginson (2009: 110) when he summarizes the impact of globalization on the stratification "between those with global freedoms and those bound to the soil within nations or localities"; and in Teichler (2014: 84) when he explores the validity of the traditional Humboldtian teaching-research nexus in Germany and restricts it solely to a group of German "university professors". The growing stratification of academics across Europe is the name of the game in town, and the persistent inequality in academic knowledge production is one of its major dimensions.

We have explored in this paper a distinctive subgroup of highly productive academics from a cross-European comparative perspective to show the complexities inherent in the "academic profession" concept. The disaggregated picture of faculty research performance in Europe highlights a powerful divide between research top performers and the rest of academics which does not seem to have been studied so far from a European comparative perspective.

ACKNOWLEDGMENTS

The author gratefully acknowledges the support of the National Research Council (NCN) through its MAESTRO grant DEC-2011/02/A/HS6/00183 (2012–2017). The work on this paper would not be possible without the invaluable support given by Dr.

Wojciech Roszka as part of the MAESTRO team. The author also wishes to thank Ulrich Teichler, the coordinator of the EUROAC project, "Academic Profession in Europe: Responses to Societal Challenges" (2009–2012), part of the European Science Foundation, EUROCORES EuroHESC scheme. The Polish research team also included Dr. Dominik Antonowicz, responsible for the in-depth interviews.

NOTES

[1] We worked on the final data set dated June 17, 2011 created by René Kooij and Florian Löwenstein from the International Centre of Higher Education and Research, INCHER-Kassel. The Polish research team also included Dr. Dominik Antonowicz who was chiefly responsible for the in-depth interviews with Polish academics.

[2] We studied five major academic field clusters: "life sciences and medical sciences" (termed "life sciences" and "medical sciences, health-related sciences, social services" in the survey questionnaire), "physical sciences and mathematics" ("physical sciences, mathematics, computer sciences"), "engineering" ("engineering, manufacturing and construction, architecture"), "humanities and social sciences" ("humanities and arts" and "social and behavioral sciences"), and "professions" ("teacher training and education science", "business and administration, economics", and "law").

REFERENCES

Abramo, G., D'Angelo, C. A., & Caprasecca, A. (2009). The contribution of star scientists to overall sex differences in research productivity. *Scientometrics*, *81*(1), 137–156.

Abramo, G., D'Angelo, C. A., & Solazzi, M. (2011). The relationship between scientists' research performance and the degree of internationalization of their research. *Scientometrics*, *86*, 629–643.

Allan, E. J. (2011). Women's status in higher education: Equity matters. *ASHE Higher Education Report*, *37*(1).

Allison, P. D. (1980). Inequality and scientific productivity. *Social Studies of Science*, *10*, 163–179.

Allison, P. D., & Stewart, J. A. (1974). Productivity differences among scientists: Evidence for accumulative advantage. *American Sociological Review*, *39*, 596–606.

Allison, P. D., Long, J. S., & Krauze, T. K. (1982). Cumulative advantage and inequality in science. *American Sociological Review*, *47*, 615–625.

Altbach, P. G., & Lewis, L. S. (1996). The academic profession in international perspective. In P. G. Altbach (Ed.), *The international academic profession: Portraits of fourteen countries* (pp. 3–48). Princeton, NJ: Carnegie.

Becher, T. (1987). The disciplinary shaping of the profession. In B. R. Clark (Ed.), *The academic profession: National, disciplinary, and institutional settings*. Berkeley, CA: University of California Press.

Becher, T., & Trowler, P. R. (2001). *Academic tribes and territories* (2nd ed.). Berkshire, Shire county and New York, NY: Open University Press.

Bentley, P. J., Coates, H., Dobson, I. R., Goedegebuure, L., & Meek, V. L. (Eds.), (2013). *Job satisfaction around the academic world*. Dordrecht, The Netherlands: Springer.

Blackburn, R. T., & Lawrence, J. H. (1995). *Faculty at work: Motivation, expectation, satisfaction*. Baltimore, MD: The Johns Hopkins University Press.

Brady, H. E., & Collier, D. (Eds.). (2010). *Rethinking social inquiry: Diverse tools, shared standards* (2nd ed.). Lanham, MD: Rowman & Littlefield.

Brew, A., & Lucas, L. (2009). *Academic research and researchers*. Maidenhead, England: Open University Press.

Centra, J. A. (1983). Research productivity and teaching effectiveness. *Research in Higher Education*, *18*(2).

Cole, J. R., & Cole, S. (1967). Scientific output and recognition: A study in the operation of the reward system in science. *American Sociological Review, 32*(3), 377–390.

Cole, J. R., & Cole, S. (1973). *Social stratification in science*. Chicago, IL: The University of Chicago Press.

Cole, J. R., & Zuckerman, H. (1984). The productivity puzzle: Persistence and change in patterns of publication of men and women scientists. *Advances in Motivation and Achievement, 2*, 217–258.

Crane, D. (1965). Scientists at major and minor universities: A study of productivity and recognition. *American Sociological Review, 30*, 699–714.

Cummings, W. K., & Finkelstein, M. J. (2012). *Scholars in the changing American academy: New contexts, new rules and new roles*. Dordrecht, The Netherlands: Springer.

de Solla Price, D. (1963). *Little science, big science*. New York, NY: Columbia University Press.

Dey, E. L., Milem, J. F., & Berger, J. B. (1997). Changing patterns of publication productivity: Accumulative advantage or institutional isomorphism? *Sociology of Education, 70*, 308–323.

Drennan, J., Clarke, M., Hyde, A., & Politis, Y. (2013). The research function of the academic profession in Europe. In U. Teichler & E. A. Höhle (Eds.), *The work situation of the academic profession in Europe: Findings of a survey in twelve countries* (pp. 79–108). Dordrecht, The Netherlands: Springer.

Elkana, Y., Lederberg, J., Merton, R. K., Thackray, A., & Zuckerman, H. (Eds.). (1978). *Toward a metric of science: The advent of science indicators*. New York, NY: John Wiley & Sons.

Enders, J., & Musselin, C. (2008). Back to the future? The academic professions in the 21st century. *Higher Education to 2030: Demography* (Vol. 1). Paris, France: OECD.

Enders, J., & Teichler, U. (1997, October). A victim of their own success? Employment and working conditions of academic staff in comparative perspective. *Higher Education, 34*(3), 347–372.

Finkelstein, M. J. (1984). *The American academic profession: A synthesis of social scientific inquiry since world war II*. Columbus, OH: Ohio State University Press.

Finkelstein, M. J., Seal, R. K., & Schuster, J. H. (1998). *The new academic generation: A profession in transformation*. Baltimore, MD: The Johns Hopkins University Press.

Fisher, R. L. (2005). *The research productivity of scientists*. Lanham, MD: UP of America.

Fitzgerald, T. (2014). *Women leaders in higher education: Shattering the myths*. London, UK: Routledge

Fox, M. F. (1983). Publication productivity among scientists: A critical review. *Social Studies of Science, 13*, 285–305.

Fox, M. F. (1992, October). Research, teaching, and publication productivity: Mutuality versus competition in academia. *Sociology of Education, 65*(4), 293–305.

Gaston, J. (1978). *The reward system in British and American science*. New York, NY: Wiley & Sons.

Goastellec, G., & Pekari, N. (2013). Gender differences and inequalities in academia: Findings in Europe. In U. Teichler & E. A. Höhle (Eds.), *The work situation of the academic profession in Europe: Findings of a survey in twelve countries* (pp. 55–78). Dordrecht, The Netherlands: Springer.

Hagstrom, W. O. (1965). *The scientific community*. New York, NY: Basic Books.

Hattie, J., & Marsh, H. W. (1996). The relationship between research and teaching: A meta-analysis. *Review of Educational Research, 66*(4), 507–542.

Hattie, J., & Marsh, H. W. (2002). The relation between research productivity and teaching effectiveness. *The Journal of Higher Education, 73*(5), 603–641.

Hibberts, M., Burke Johnson, R., & Hudson, K. (2012). Common survey sampling techniques. In L. Gideon (Ed.), *Handbook of survey methodology for the social sciences* (pp. 53–74). Dordrecht, The Netherlands: Springer.

Huang, F., Finkelstein, M., & Rostan, M. (2014). *The internationalization of the academy: Changes, realities and prospects*. Dordrecht, The Netherlands: Springer.

Irvine, J., & Martin, B. R. (1984). *Foresight in science: Picking the winners*. London, UK: Frances Pinter.

Kehm, B. M., & Teichler, U. (Eds.). (2013). *The academic profession in Europe: New tasks and new challenges*. Dordrecht, The Netherlands: Springer.

Kwiek, M. (2009). The changing attractiveness of European higher education: Current developments, future challenges, and major policy issues. In B. Kehm, J. Huisman, B. Stensaker (Eds.), *The European higher education area: Perspectives on a moving target* (pp. 107–124). Rotterdam, The Netherlands: Sense Publishers.

Kwiek, M. (2012). Changing higher education policies: From the deinstitutionalization to the reinstitutionalization of the research mission in Polish universities. *Science and Public Policy, 39*(5) 641–654.

Kwiek, M. (2013). *Knowledge production in European universities: States, markets, and academic entrepreneurialism.* Frankfurt, Germany and New York, NY: Peter Lang.

Kwiek, M. (2014a). The internationalization of the Polish academic profession: A European comparative approach. *Zeitschrift für Pädagogik, 60*(5), 681–695.

Kwiek, M. (2014b). Structural changes in the Polish higher education system (1990–2010): A synthetic view. *European Journal of Higher Education, 4*(3). 266–280.

Kwiek, M. (2015a). The internationalization of research in Europe: A quantitative study of 11 national systems from a micro-level perspective. *Journal of Studies in International Education, 19*(2).

Kwiek, M. (2015b). The European research elite: A cross-national study of highly productive academics in 11 countries. *Higher Education* (OnlineFirst, June 14). doi:10.1007/s10734-015-9910-x

Kwiek, M., & Antonowicz, D. (2013). Academic work, working conditions and job satisfaction. In U. Teichler & E. E. Höhle (Eds.), *The work situation of the academic profession in Europe: Findings of a survey in twelve countries* (pp. 37–54). Dordrecht, The Netherlands: Springer.

Kwiek, M., & Antonowicz, D. (2014). The changing paths in academic careers in European universities: Minor steps and major milestones. In T. Fumasoli, G. Goastellec, & B. M. Kehm (Eds.), *Academic careers in Europe – Trends, challenges, perspectives* (pp. 41–68). Dordrecht, The Netherlands: Springer.

Kyvik, S. (1989). Productivity differences, fields of learning, and Lotka's law. *Scientometrics, 15*(3–4), 205–214.

Leathwood, C., & Read, B. (2009). *Gender and the changing face of higher education: A feminized future?* Maidenhead, England: Open University Press.

Leydesdorff, L. (2001). *The challenge of scientometrics?: The development, measurement, and self-organization of scientific communications.* Leiden, The Netherlands: DSWO Press.

Locke, W., Cummings, W. K., & Fischer, D. (Eds.). (2011). *Changing governance and management in higher education.* Dordrecht, The Netherlands: Springer

Lotka, A. (1926). The frequency distribution of scientific productivity. *Journal of Washington Academy of Sciences, 16*(12), 317–323.

Marsh, H. W., & Hattie, J. (2002). The relation between research productivity and teaching effectiveness. *The Journal of Higher Education, 73*(5), 603–641.

Merton, R. K. (1973). *The sociology of science: Theoretical and empirical investigations.* Chicago, IL: The University of Chicago Press.

Mesch, G. (2012). E-mail surveys. In L. Gideon (Ed.), *Handbook of survey methodology for the social sciences* (pp. 313–326). Dordrecht, The Netherlands: Springer.

Padilla-González, L. E., Metcalfe, A. S., Galaz-Fontes, J. F., Fisher, D., & Snee, I. S. (2012). Gender gaps in North American research productivity: Examining faculty publication rates in Mexico, Canada, and the U.S. In M. Vukasović, P. Maassen, M. Nerland, R. Pinheiro, B. Stensaker, & A. Vabø (Eds.), *Effects of higher education reforms: Change dynamics* (pp. 259–278). Rotterdam, The Netherlands: Sense Publishers.

Prpić, K. (1996). Characteristics and determinants of eminent scientists' productivity. *Scientometrics, 36*(2), 185–206.

Ramsden, P. (1994). Describing and explaining research productivity. *Higher Education, 28,* 207–226.

RIHE. (2008). *The changing academic profession over 1992–2007: International, comparative, and quantitative perspective.* Hiroshima, Japan: RIHE

Rostan, M., Ceravolo, F. A., & Metcalfe, A. S. (2014). The internationalization of research. In F. Huang, M. Finkelstein, & M. Rostan (Eds.), *The internationalization of the academy. Changes, realities and prospects* (pp. 119–144). Dordrecht, The Netherlands: Springer.

Schuster, J. H., & Finkelstein, M. J. (2006). *The American faculty: The restructuring of academic work and careers.* Baltimore, MD: Johns Hopkins University Press.

Shin, J. C., & Cummings, W. K. (2010). Multilevel analysis of academic publishing across disciplines: Research preference, collaboration, and time on research. *Scientometrics, 85,* 581–594.

Shin, J. C., Arimoto, A., & Cummings, W. K. (2014). *Teaching and research in contemporary higher education: Systems, activities and rewards*. Dordrecht, The Netherlands: Springer.

Stephan, P. E., & Levin, S. G. (1992). *Striking the mother lode in science: The importance of age, place, and time*. Oxford, England: Oxford University Press.

Stoop, I. (2012). Unit non-response due to refusal. In L. Gideon (Ed.), *Handbook of survey methodology for the social sciences* (pp. 121–147). Dordrecht, The Netherlands: Springer.

Teichler, U., & Höhle, E. A. (Eds.). (2013). *The work situation of the academic profession in Europe: Findings of a survey in twelve countries*. Dordrecht, The Netherlands: Springer.

Teichler, U., Arimoto, A., & Cummings, W. K. (2013). *The changing academic profession: Major findings of a comparative survey*. Dordrecht, The Netherlands: Springer.

Teodorescu, D. (2000). Correlates of faculty publication productivity: A cross-national analysis. *Higher Education, 39*, 201–222.

Thornton, M. (2012). *Privatising the public university. The case of law*. New York, NY: Routledge.

Vabø, A., Padilla-González, L. E., Waagene, E., & Næss, T. (2014). Gender and faculty internationalization. In F. Huang, M. Finkelstein, & M. Rostan (Eds.), *The internationalization of the academy: Changes, realities and prospects* (pp. 183–206). Dordrecht, The Netherlands: Springer.

Wanner, R. A., Lewis, L. S., & Gregorio, D. I. (1981). Research productivity in academia: A comparative study of the sciences, social sciences and humanities. *Sociology of Education, 54*, 238–253.

Wilson, L. (1995). *The academic man: A study in the sociology of a profession*. New Brunswick, NJ: Transaction Publishers.

Xie, Y., & Shauman, K. A. (2003). *Women in science: Career progresses and outcomes*. Cambridge, MA: Harvard University Press.

Zuckerman, H. (1996). *Scientific elite: Nobel laureates in the United States*. New Brunswick, NJ: Transaction Publishers.

Marek Kwiek
Professor and Director
Center for Public Policy Studies, and Chair holder
UNESCO Chair in Institutional Research and Higher Education Policy
University of Poznan, Poland

APPENDICES

Table 1. Characteristics of the samples, by country

	Grand N	Universities %	Other HE institutions %	Full-time %	Part-time %
Austria	1,492	100.0	0.0	65.8	34.2
Finland	1,374	76.5	23.5	82.4	17.6
Germany	1,215	86.1	13.9	70.7	29.3
Ireland	1,126	73.3	26.7	91.2	8.8
Italy	1,711	100.0	0.0	96.9	3.1
Netherlands	1,209	34.4	65.6	56.0	44.0
Norway	986	93.3	6.7	89.7	10.3
Poland	3,704	48.3	51.7	98.0	2.0
Portugal	1,513	40.0	60.0	90.3	9.7
Switzerland	1,414	45.6	54.4	58.5	41.5
UK	1,467	40.8	59.2	86.5	13.5

* *In Austria and Italy there was no distinction between "universities" and "other higher education institutions".*

Table 2. Proportion of faculty, by academic field cluster and by country (in percent)

	Life sciences, med. Sciences	Physical sciences, mathematics	Engineering	Humanities and social sciences	Professions	Other Fields	Total
Austria	20.2	9.8	11.9	41.3	8.7	8.2	1,492
Finland	15.7	9.7	21.5	18.6	12.1	22.4	1,374
Germany	29.3	15.2	14.8	15.6	11.1	13.9	1,215
Ireland	23.0	11.5	8.8	23.8	20.5	12.4	1,126
Italy	28.6	23.3	11.1	17.5	13.6	5.9	1,711
Netherlands	12.6	10.9	10.7	22.3	34.7	8.8	1,209
Norway	29.0	14.1	7.4	27.5	8.9	13.1	986
Poland	24.6	8.4	21.5	23.0	12.5	10.0	3,704
Portugal	16.9	7.9	20.4	10.5	20.6	23.7	1,513
Switzerland	30.8	10.2	12.7	16.9	23.9	5.5	1,414
UK	21.9	11.6	6.3	18.6	11.0	30.7	1,467

Table 10. The percentage of non-performers (= non-publishers) regarding full-time academics, universities only, by country (in percent)

	FI	DE	IE	IT	NL	NO	PL	PT	CH	UK	Mean
Non performers	20.2	15.4	9.1	5.4	2.7	15.9	43.2	18.3	12.4	5.7	14.8

EMILIA PRIMERI AND EMANUELA REALE

CONCLUSIONS

The main topic of the CHER 27th annual Conference in Rome was embedded in its title: "*Universities in transition: shifting institutional and organizational boundaries*". Studies on boundaries crossing represent a new and increasing strand of literature in different disciplines such as social and political sciences, economics, educational studies, psychology (Kaufmann & Tödtling, 2001; Ravinet, 2008). The term boundary crossing refers to the "negotiation and combination of ingredients from different contexts to achieve hybrid situations" and it might concern, among the other, the work of scientists, policy makers' activities and institutions' collaborations patterns (Engestrom et al., 1995). Talking about changes investing universities, the discussion about shifting boundaries should be a cause for reflection. Talking about academic institutions, different types of boundaries should be evaluated: organizational and institutional boundaries, disciplinary and sectoral boundaries, geographical and collaboration boundaries. Then the complexity of the discussion about boundaries crossing and universities transformation clearly emerges.

The 27th CHER conference, by bringing together researchers with different perspectives and disciplinary backgrounds stimulated the methodological and theoretical debates about shifting boundaries, including historical, comparative, societal, organisational, institutional, quantitative and qualitative approaches.

The conference, in fact, took advantage from contributions of scientists from about twenty countries from different scientific fields and who joined the conference with the aim to discuss changes in the Higher Education by sharing common ideas, mutual understanding, and related problems. Conference invited speakers set the tone for the main themes of the conference, bringing different perspectives and approaches to deepen the issue of changes of academic institutional and organizational boundaries.

The wide interest demonstrated towards the conference and its specific topic by more than 200 applicants confirm the centrality of this theme for the Higher Education scientific community which reflects upon boundaries crossing and the transformation of academic institutional and organizational environment.

This book entitled "*The transformation of University institutional and organizational boundaries*" collects the efforts of some of the speakers at the conference and the contributions of the two keynote speakers. The book sets the point for starting a wide discussion about the shift of boundaries in higher education which represents an emerging and relevant issue.

E. Reale & E. Primeri (Eds.), The Transformation of University Institutional and Organizational Boundaries, 231–236.

Through its contributions the book discusses the shift of academic institutional and organizational boundaries from different angles: the change in functions, objective and scope of HEIs, the move beyond sectoral and disciplinary boundaries and the modification of academic professions. The main contribution it should be acknowledged is in its capacity to tackle the issue of boundaries crossing in HE at least according to three major perspectives. Firstly it fosters a discussion over institutional and organizational changes for HEIs following the emergence of new actors and new organizational forms in the HE landscape (Chapters 1, 3 and 6). Secondly, the book focuses on changes of universities boundaries when new missions have to be accomplished or different competitive objectives are set (Chapters 2 and 8). Finally, shifts in doctoral training and in the production of science at large are addressed highlighting their impact on academic institutions internal organization and equilibria as well as on academic profession (Chapters 4, 5 and 7).

According to Beerkens, Krezt and Sá, and Bruckmann new actors and new organizational forms are modifying the HE sector. Beerkens (Chapter 1) reflects over the "agencification fever" which have characterized public sector reforms in Europe since 1990s onwards and the effect this had on the HE sector characterized by the increasing emphasis on quality assurance systems and the setting up of agencies devoted to its measure in education. Quality assurance agencies, becoming new regulatory actors in the HE landscape and new intermediaries between the state and academic institutions, represent interesting elements to think upon when reflecting over universities organizational boundaries shifts. Her main assumption is that the quality assurance systems developed in the four countries analysed followed different paths, but they rise some common problems too. Firstly, a problem is represented by the increasing fragmentation and the need for universities to accommodate different requests from different actors (i.e., evaluation agencies, policy makers, stakeholder groups). Secondly, the weakening of the political core, that is the steering capacities of policy makers over newly established agencies, which generates accountability problems. Kretz and Sá (Chapter 3) reflect over the introduction of entrepreneurship education and the way this drives into HE new external actors, introduces changes in academic curricula design and fosters new organizational forms in HE letting emerge an overlapping of boundaries between higher education and the entrepreneurship community. Such enlargement has widened the scope of universities and it represents a move beyond disciplinary boundaries in academic institutions. This, beyond witnessing a change in the HE landscape, figures out an adaptation process of universities to new and emerging societal needs. Through an analysis of changes occurred in six Portuguese universities after 2007 and the introduction of the RJIES, a new law introducing HE reform and new institutional framework for academic institutions, Bruckmann (Chapter 6) focuses on the impact of reforms on the HEIs and society relationships looking at the increasing presence of external stakeholders in main academic boards. The impact of this change on Universities governance and the way academics seem to respond to that is questioned: academics still maintain their role but changes are moving forward modifying the boundaries of university governance.

These contributions highlight the high degree of diversity which characterizes universities, their internal governance arrangements and the relationships with external actors (industries, stakeholders, State). This would suggest to study universities as collective systems incorporating different actors and disciplines and merging together highly diversified actions, goals and objectives (Engestrom & Sannino, 2010; Dimitrova, 2010). The discussion about boundaries crossing in public-private relationships seems to go beyond the analysis of different forms of collaborations between universities and industries to focus on emerging scientific and societal problem, more and more intertwined (Nowotny, 2007).

Moreover, reflecting on organizational and institutional boundaries crossing drives a discussion on the relationship between the State and academic institutions and between science and society, questioning the nature of public science as a whole (Lascoumes & Le Gales, 2009).

Focusing on new missions Universities have to accomplish and on new competitive objectives they are more and more likely to pursue (see the engagement in scientific productivity competition and the struggle for rankings positioning) also allow to depict a shift in HEIs boundaries. Koryakina et al. (Chapter 2) focuses the attention on the third role beyond teaching and research of universities and observe, with respect to two Portuguese universities, as they represent a relevant sources for income differentiation. The engagement in third mission activities and the way these might represent new and differentiated income sources become a way for analyzing and measuring the universities engagement and relationships with their external environments. The question their analysis might arise relate to the increasing financial constraints universities have to face and the extent to which these impact on universities missions, namely teaching, research and third mission, leading to an overlap among them or to the predominance of one upon the others, letting relevant and urgent policy questions to emerge. Both the shifts in academic missions and the emergence of new competitive imperatives seem to be related to the emergence of inequality in academic landscape. This is the core question addressed by Kwiek (Chapter 8) who observes as the distribution of academic knowledge production in Europe is highly skewed towards highly productive academics. The questions that this observation let arise are related to major policy concerns. Do different funding and incentive systems are likely to create the pave for highly diversified universities scientific production capacities? Are these differences likely to drive a concentration of funding resources to support best performing universities? Does this drives a segmentation of academic professions? The answer provided by the author is summarized into two concepts: "growing stratification of academics across Europe" and "persistent inequality in academic knowledge production".

Reflecting on these differences would allow criticizing the increasing push towards a unique model of university fostered today by competitive internal and external pressures (e.g., international rankings and evaluation processes) and also allow questioning performance-based policies which aim at measuring academic quality and performance-enhancing mechanisms introduced by national legislators through national HE systems reforms (Engestrom & Sannino, 2010; Maassen, 2008). Also looking at these changes allows depicting how universities are facing different external challenges and the way these trigger universities transformation and changes in HEIs and society boundaries.

Finally looking at shifts in doctoral training and in the production of science at large are the main contents of the chapters by Gagliardi, Cox, and Li, by Deem et al. and by Caspersen and Froelich. Gagliardi, Cox, and Li (Chapter 4) reflect upon the introduction of new technologies and the movement of the Open science. Operational barriers and institutional inertia towards major changes are addressed. Driving forces for change are considered too but they mostly appear to be relegated in the *"realm of professional curiosity"* and thus mostly dependent to personal willingness. Although their analysis highlight as scientific production practices are definitely changing, institutions are still extremely slow in changing and inertia if often the rule. Moving the boundaries of knowledge production-the way knowledge is produced- seems than still a challenge for academic institutions. Differently Deem et al. (Chapter 5) consider the changes recently introduced with respect to doctoral training policies in UK for social sciences and how universities have responded to these focusing on positive and negative unintended consequences. Looking at the shift towards collaborative doctoral schemes they witness through their histories relevant *"twists and turns in UK social science doctoral training"* with important consequences on the possibility for students to access doctoral training. Changes are then introduced but with the main effect of squeezing students capacity to engage in doctoral training. Beyond PhD changes these moves also highlight the weakness of universities to respond to such challenges and to changes coming from their external environment (i.e., national policies). Finally Caspersen and Froelich (Chapter 7) consider the relationship between the introduction of new assessment tools (HELO) and their effect on academic leadership. Their empirical investigation of changes to leadership models highlight as adaptive responses of academics to external pressures for changes in order to maximize opportunities within given boundaries are often the case. However evidences support that a unique response is not sufficient and that *"new understandings and templates of academic leadership should be developed."* So far, changes in the ways education is measured drive modification in the ways academics exercise leadership but neither linear nor unique changes and logics are likely to be observed.

The chapters detail then what Alice Lam and John Aubrey Douglass state in their initial chapters: on the one side the relationships between academic scientists and the marketplace are changing with consequences on academic work boundaries which become increasingly blurred. On the other side the "World Class University" is supposed to drive *"highly ranked research output, a culture of excellence, great facilities, a brand name that transcends national borders"* pushing universities toward a unique model. Should this be the future of universities or rather they could move towards a more holistic model, that of Flagship University?

These contributions allow observing shifts in disciplinary and sectoral boundaries, and the increasing interdisciplinarity which characterizes today research and education policies, which fosters the creation of new fields of science, bringing together traditional scientific field. The development of new research fields would allow reframing the "conventional hierarchies of knowledge" (Nowotny, 2003; Gibbons et al.,1994) fostering the development of new tools and environments for knowledge diffusion. Nonetheless this often drives the transformation of traditional research units (departments, laboratories) into new larger research structures, with effects on their internal organization and governance arrangements and on academic professions and academics working boundaries (Enders, 2005).

To conclude, several signals of shifting boundaries can be then envisaged in higher education and research institutions, such as the involvement of firms with research groups and university boards, new alliances, collaborations and networking with non-academic organizations (e.g., public or private research organizations, firms), the change in the internal academic organization and leadership models, the challenge to academic professions stemming from the introduction of new evaluation criteria and the replacement of permanent positions for researchers by temporary contracts.

Contributions in this book underline as changes of boundaries in institutional and organizational settings of HEIs mirror the transformations universities are undergoing and the complexity and heterogeneity which characterize scientific knowledge today.

With the analysis presented here of the different perspectives that can be adopted when looking at universities transformations and shifts in institutional and organizational boundaries the books allow arguing that changing boundaries concern how academic institutions relate to their environment, how do they deal with external elements and challenges (workers, technologies, technical and organizational expertise) and whether scientific knowledge should be re-conceptualized as a dynamic action and interactions across institutions, domains and sites. In so far, reflecting on boundaries shifts become a potential learning tool, a resource to frame and to capture multiple HEIs changes (Akkerman & Bakker, 2011; Lamont & Molnar, 2002).

REFERENCES

Akkerman, S. F., & Bakker, A. (2011, June). Boundary crossing and boundary objects. *Review of Educational Research, 81*(2), 132–169. doi:10.3102/0034654311404435

Dimitrova, A. L. (2010). The new member states of the EU in the aftermath of enlargement: Do new European rules remain empty shells? *Journal of European Public Policy, 17*(1), 137–148.

Enders, J. (2005). Border crossings: Research training, knowledge dissemination and the transformation of academic work. *Higher Education, 49*, 119–133.

Engestrom, Y., & Sannino, A. (2010). Studies of expansive learning: Foundations, findings and future challenges. *Educational Research Review, 5,* 1–24.

Engestrom, Y., Engestrom, R., & Karkkainen, M. (1995). Polycontextuality and boundary crossing in expert cognition: Learning and problem solving in complex work activities. *Learning and Instruction, 5,* 319–336.

Gibbons, M., Limoges, H., Nowotny, H., Schwartzman, S., Scott, P., & Trow, M. (1994). *The new production of knowledge: The dynamics of science and research in contemporary societies.* London, UK: Sage.

Kaufmann, A., & Tödtling, F. (2001, May). Science–industry interaction in the process of innovation: The importance of boundary-crossing between systems. *Research Policy, 30*(5), 791–804.

Lamont, M., & Molnàr, V. (2002). The study of boundaries in the social sciences. *Annual Review of Sociology, 28,* 167–195. doi:10.1146/annurev.soc.28.110601.141107

Lascoumes, P., & Le Galès, P. (2009). *Gli Strumenti per Governare.* Milano, Italy: Bruno Mondadori.

Maassen, P. (2008). The modernisation of European higher education: National policy dynamics. In A. Amaral, I. Bleiklie, & C. Musselin (Eds.), *From governance to identity.* Dordrecht, The Netherlands: Springer Science and Business Media.

Nowotny, H. (2007, July). How many policy rooms are there? Evidence-based and other kinds of science policies. *Science, Technology, & Human Values, 32*(4), 479–490.

Nowotny, H., Scott, P., & Gibbons, M. (2003). 'Mode 2' revisited: The new production of knowledge. *Minerva, 41,* 179–194.

Ravinet, P. (2008). From voluntary participation to monitored coordination: Why European countries feel increasingly bound by their commitment to the bologna process. *European Journal of Education, 43*(3), 353–367.

236

ABOUT THE AUTHORS

Sally Barnes is Director of the UK Economic and Social Research Council funded Southwest Doctoral Training Centre and Graduate Dean of the Social Sciences and Law Faculty at the University of Bristol, UK. She has long experience of working with doctoral students and developing programmes to enhance opportunities for them to extend their learning.

Maarja Beerkens is Assistant Professor of Public Administration at Leiden University, the Netherlands. Her research focuses on regulation and governance issues in higher education and science policy, with a special focus on market-based and other non-hierarchical policy instruments in this field. Her recent work has appeared in journals such as Research Policy, Higher Education, Educational Researcher, and Science and Public Policy. She received her PhD in public policy from the University of North Carolina at Chapel Hill, USA.

Sofia Bruckmann is a PhD student at the University of Aveiro and CIPES (Centre for Research in Higher Education Policies) in Portugal. She is currently enrolled in the Doctoral Programme on Higher Education Studies and holds a scholarship from FCT – Fundação para a Ciência e a Tecnologia (Foundation for Science and Technology). Her doctoral thesis focuses on "Changes in Government and Management in Portuguese Higher Education Institutions". She has recently published an article in Tertiary Education and Management and a book chapter in "Reforming Higher Education. Public Policy Design and Implementation".

Joakim Caspersen is senior researcher at NIFU- Nordic Institute for Studies in Innovation, Research and Education in Oslo, Norway (www.nifu.no/eng), and at NTNU Social Sciences in Trondheim, Norway (www.samforsk.no). His main research interests are sociological analyses of the relationship between quality in higher education and labour market qualification, particularly within the professions. His latest publications examines the introduction of learning outcomes in higher education, and how learning outcomes are introduced in Norwegian higher education as part of international reform movements such as the Bologna process and the development of qualifications frameworks. He has also examined empirically the statistical relationship between different measurements of learning outcomes and how these are related to disciplinary profiles.

Gill Clarke is an educational consultant, Vice-Chair of the UK Council for Graduate Education and also a doctoral student at the University of Oxford, UK. She was formerly Director of the Educational Support Unit at the University of Bristol and a one-time assistant director of the Quality Assurance Agency for England. Her knowledge of graduate education has been acquired through cross-disciplinary work with practitioners at university level and secondment to a UK HE-sector policy organization; both roles included policy development and implementation and some international experience.

Deborah Cox is a Research Fellow at the Manchester Institute of Innovation Research, Manchester Business School in The University of Manchester, UK. Her academic qualifications are in social sciences and information management. She has published, with colleagues, in a range of academic journals including Science and Public Policy, Research Evaluation, R&D Management, Foresight, Technology Analysis and Strategic Management, Accounting, Auditing & Accountability Journal, Journal of Documentation, is a co-author on the monograph Scrutinising Science: The Changing UK Government of Science published by Palgrave MacMillan and more recently with Dr John Rigby has edited a book entitled Innovation Policy Challenges for the 21st Century 2013 Routledge. Her current research is in the field of STI policy research and has recently been concerned with public sector research systems, open science and research evaluation.

Rosemary Deem is Professor of Higher Education Management, Vice Principal (Education) and Dean of the Doctoral School at Royal Holloway University of London, UK and has previously worked at the Universities of Bristol and Lancaster and the Open University. She is the first woman to Chair the UK Council for Graduate Education (from summer 2015 onwards) and is on the management group of the SouthEast UK Economic and Social Research Council funded Doctoral Training Centre. She is also a co-editor of the Springer journal *Higher Education.*

John Aubrey Douglass is Senior Research Fellow – Public Policy and Higher Education at the Center for Studies in Higher Education (CSHE) at the University of California – Berkeley. He is the author of *The New Flagship University: Changing the Paradigm from Global Ranking to National Relevancy* (forthcoming, Palgrave Macmillan), co-editor of *Globalization's Muse: Universities and Higher Education Systems in a Changing World* (Public Policy Press, 2009), and the author of *The Conditions for Admissions* (Stanford Press 2007) and *The California Idea and American Higher Education* (Stanford University Press, 2000 and 2007; published in Chinese in 2008). Among the research projects he co-founded and remains the Berkeley Principle Investigator is the Student Experience in the Research University (SERU) Consortium. He is also the editor of the Center's Research and Occasional Paper Series (ROPS), sits on the editorial board of international higher education journals in the UK, China, and Russia, and serves on the international advisory boards of a number of higher education institutes.

238

Nicoline Frølich is Research Professor and Head of Research at NIFU- Nordic Institute for Studies in Innovation, Research and Education in Oslo, Norway (www.nifu.no/eng). Her main research interests are organization, strategy, management and leadership in higher education. Her latest publications examines the introduction of learning outcomes in higher education, and how learning outcomes are introduced in Norwegian higher education as part of international reform movements such as the Bologna process and the development of qualifications frameworks.

Dimitri Gagliardi is a Research Fellow at the Manchester Institute of Innovation Research, The University of Manchester, UK. He received his PhD in Economics and Institutions from the University of Bologna in 2003. His interests are in innovation and dynamics in sectors such as Science, ICT, Pharmaceutical and high tech/knowledge intensive sectors; economics of innovation; science, technology and innovation management and policy.

Alice Lam is Professor of Organisation Studies at the School of Management, Royal Holloway University of London. Her recent research has focused on careers in the knowledge economy, and the relationship between organizational learning, innovation and societal institutions. She also has a long-standing interest in the work and careers of scientists and engineers and of other creative knowledge workers. Her current work examines the changing nature of academic scientific work and knowledge flows between university and industry. Her research has been published in *Organisation Studies, Journal of Management Studies, Research Policy and Human Relations*.
Address: School of Management, Royal Holloway University of London, Egham, Surrey, TW20 0EX, U.K.; E-mail: alice.lam@rhul.ac.uk

Yanchao Li is Research Associate at Manchester Institute of Innovation Research (MIoIR), The University of Manchester, UK. Her research interests lie in science and innovation studies, especially the design and evaluation of innovation policies. She obtained her PhD in 'Innovation, Management and Policy' in 2013 from The University of Manchester. Prior to this, she obtained her Master's and Bachelor's degrees at Tsinghua University and Shanghai Jiao Tong University, China.

Tatyana Koryakina is a junior researcher at the Centre for Research in Higher Education Policies (CIPES). She holds a Master's degree in Educational Administration from SUNY Buffalo, USA and a PhD in Social Sciences from the University of Aveiro, Portugal. Her research interests focus on topics related to higher education funding policies and mechanisms, funding diversification, third stream activities and entrepreneurial governance.

Andrew Kretz is a graduate of the Higher Education doctoral program in the Department of Leadership, Adult, and Higher Education at the Ontario Institute for Studies in Education of the University of Toronto. His research has focused on entrepreneurship education, technology transfer, and research policy.

Marek Kwiek, Professor and Director, Center for Public Policy Studies, and Chairholder, UNESCO Chair in Institutional Research and Higher Education Policy, University of Poznan, Poland. His research interests include university governance, welfare state, the academic profession, and academic entrepreneurialism. He has published 150 papers and 8 monographs, most recently Knowledge Production in European Universities. States, Markets, and Academic Entrepreneurialism (2013) and The University and the State: A Study into Global Transformations (2006). A higher education policy expert to the European Commission, USAID, OECD, the World Bank, UNESCO, OSCE, and the Council of Europe. Apart from about 30 international higher education policy projects, he has participated in about 20 international (global and European) research projects. The editor of HERP: Higher Education Research and Policy book series (Peter Lang). E-mail: kwiekm@amu.edu.pl

Emilia Primeri, Political scientist, has a PhD in evaluation of the internationalization of the University. Since February 2008 she is research fellow at IRCRES CNR (Research Institute on Sustainable Economic Growth- former CERIS- of the National Research Council) participating in several European and national research projects. Her main research interests concern policies for higher education and governance systems, evaluation of public research, the study of features and impact of joint programming at the EU level and of opening of national R&D programmes. Recent works include papers on indicators for the opening of national R&D programs (Research Evaluation, 2014), a book chapter on early careers researchers training and academic prestige (Sense publisher, 2014) and on Italian University system reform (Springer, 2014).

Emanuela Reale is senior researcher at IRCRES (former CERIS) of CNR the Italian National Research Council and Director of the IRCRES unit in Rome. Political scientist, she has a long experience in international and European collaborations in research policy, research evaluation, higher education policy and STI indicators areas. She was Vice President of the Italian Evaluation Association-AIV in 2009-2013 and cooperates at present as an Expert with the ANVUR-Italian Agency for the evaluation of university and research. She is Vice President of the European Forum for Studies on Policies for Research and Innovation-EU-SPRI, and Member of the executive board of the ENID European STI Indicators Conference Series. She publishes and serves as referee in several international journals and books.

Creso M. Sá is Associate Professor of Higher Education at the Ontario Institute for Studies in Education of the University of Toronto.

Cláudia S. Sarrico is an Associate Professor of Management at ISEG Lisbon School of Economics & Management, Universidade de Lisboa, and a researcher at CIPES – Centre for Research on Higher Education Policies. Her research interests focus on performance management in professional services, with an emphasis on education, higher education and science.

Pedro N. Teixeira is a Vice Rector for Academic Affairs and an Associate professor of economics at the University of Porto, Portugal. He is also a director of the Centre for Research on Higher Education Policies (CIPES) at the University of Porto. His research interests focus on the economics of higher education, in particular on the role of markets and privatization, and on the development and influence of human capital theory.

Lightning Source UK Ltd.
Milton Keynes UK
UKOW01f1038160815

256932UK00002B/114/P